DD210

Living Psychology: From the Everyday to the Extraordinary

Edited by Jim Turner and Meg John Barker

This publication forms part of the Open University module DD210 Living psychology: from the everyday to the extraordinary. Details of this and other Open University modules can be obtained from the Student Registration and Enquiry Service, The Open University, PO Box 197, Milton Keynes MK7 6BJ, United Kingdom (tel. +44 (0)845 300 60 90; email general-enquiries@open.ac.uk).

Alternatively, you may visit the Open University website at www.open.ac.uk where you can learn more about the wide range of modules and packs offered at all levels by The Open University. To purchase a selection of Open University materials visit www.ouw.co.uk, or contact Open University Worldwide, Walton Hall, Milton Keynes MK7 6AA, United Kingdom for a brochure (tel. +44 (0)1908 858793; fax +44 (0)1908 858787; email ouw-customer-services@open.ac.uk).

The Open University, Walton Hall, Milton Keynes MK7 6AA

First published 2015

Edited, designed and typeset by The Open University

Printed and bound in the UK by Bell & Bain Ltd, Glasgow

ISBN 978 1 7800 7859 5

1.1

Contents

Block 4: Making sense of the world, and sometimes failing

Chapter 10

Making sense of the world

Jim Turner

Contents

1   Introduction

In previous chapters of *Living psychology* you have learned how people make sense of themselves (in Chapters 4 and 7), of other people (in Chapter 1), of their relationships with both specific individuals and with wider society (in Chapters 5 and 6), and with the natural environment (in Chapters 8 and 9). The focus of this chapter is also on making sense of things, but in a very different way. This chapter is about how people make sense of the world around them ('world' in the sense of 'everything', not just the natural environment): how do people know what is 'out there' and come to an understanding of it?

This, as you can imagine, is a potentially vast topic. It is one that has interested philosophers for millennia and psychologists since the birth of psychology as an academic discipline. One chapter cannot hope to fully answer the question of how people make sense of the world, not least because psychology does not yet have a full answer. What this chapter will explore is the *cognitive* psychology of how people make sense of the world (i.e. the mental processes that are involved), focusing on the psychology of sensation, perception, pattern identification, logical inferences and story building.

The chapter is divided into four main parts. Section 2 briefly outlines how humans receive information from the world through the senses, and the limits of that sensed information. Section 3 shifts the focus to perception, the extraction of a representation of the world from sensory information, outlining the theories of perception put forward by two key cognitive psychologists, James Gibson and Richard Gregory. You will also learn how human perceptual abilities leave people prone to making errors, using examples of visual illusions, but how they also allow people to make a lot of sense of the world based on only very little sensory information. In Section 4 you will learn how people identify sequences and patterns in the world, and use logic to make accurate predictions and conclusions about the world. Finally, in Section 5 you will learn why stories are important in making sense of the world, and how psychologists have applied this knowledge to decision making by jurors.

After reading this chapter you should be able to:

- describe the psychological principles of sensation and perception, focusing on vision and visual perception

- understand how people can extract large amounts of meaning from small amounts of information, and usually do so accurately

- outline the evolutionary theory underlying psychological explanations of human perceptual and sense-making processes

- understand how people make connections between things in the world and use those connections to build and make sense of stories, including in the forensic context of the courtroom.

2   Getting information on what is 'out there'

The process of getting information from the world is called **sensation**, and it involves the senses. You are probably familiar with the idea that people generally have five of these senses: sight (vision), hearing (audition), taste (gustation), smell (olfaction) and touch (the tactile sense). You may also already be aware that the last of these, touch, involves a number of distinct senses that can be considered separately, such as feeling temperature (thermoception), feeling pain (nociception) and feeling pressure (mechanoception). In addition, there are senses that provide an individual with information about the internal world of their own body, some of which you touched on in Chapter 7. These include senses such as proprioception, which gives information about where different parts of the body are in relation to each other (e.g. you can tell whether your hands are in the air or by your side without actually seeing them), and hunger and thirst, which provide information about the need for food and water, respectively. However, this chapter is only concerned with those senses that provide information about what is 'out there', external to the individual self, and how that information is used by the individual to make sense of the world.

Sensation
The process of detecting information about the physical world (e.g. sight, hearing, touch).

2.1   Boundaries of sensation

Sensation is something that is easy to take for granted, and most people probably do not give it much thought unless they experience a temporary or permanent loss of one or more senses. The aim of this section is to get you thinking about the boundaries of human sensation.

Activity 10.1   Thinking about the boundaries of sensation

Pause for a moment to think about what you can sense about the world around you right now. What information are you sensing? Do you think you know what is 'out there' in the world?

Comment

Exactly what you can sense at the moment will, of course, depend on who you are and where you are. However, you probably feel that you have a pretty good idea of what is 'out there' in the world around you. For example, you may have a good sense of the room (or other location) in which you are reading this, be aware of other people around you (or be aware that there are no other people present), know whether what you are sitting on (assuming you are seated) is hard or soft, and so on. The remainder of Section 2.1 considers the boundaries and limitations of human sensation.

Some of the information that people get from the world is sensed fairly directly. For example, in the senses of touch, taste and smell the person is in direct contact with the substance being sensed. In the case of touch their skin is in contact with the substance, whereas in taste and smell the substance (or something given off by it) enters their body through the mouth or nose, respectively. However, in the sense of smell, although the molecules that the nose detects are in direct contact with the body, the source of those molecules may be some distance away. Obviously, each individual person is only ever in direct contact with a very small part of the world at any given time, so most of the information they receive from the world is indirect. For example, in Activity 10.1, if you could hear the sound of traffic outside, what your ears actually detected were pressure waves in the air molecules that were in contact with your eardrums. Those air molecules were not themselves in contact with the source of the sound: billions of other air molecules (and the molecules making up any walls, doors or windows that were between you and the traffic) passed the sound along. Similarly, if you saw a passing car, you did not really see the car itself: your eyes detected light (from another source, such as the sun or a street lamp) that had reflected off the surface of the car. Some things do not reflect (or emit) light, of course, and are therefore invisible (air, for instance).

In addition to this, human senses do not detect all of the information that is potentially available. This can be illustrated most clearly in the senses of vision and audition. The human eye detects light wavelengths between approximately 390 and 750 **nanometres**, that is, from violet to red, but cannot detect wavelengths outside this range. Figure 10.1 illustrates just how little of the potentially available information from electromagnetic radiation is available to human senses, even for someone with 'perfect' 20/20 vision.

Nanometre
A billionth of a metre, used as the standard unit of light frequency.

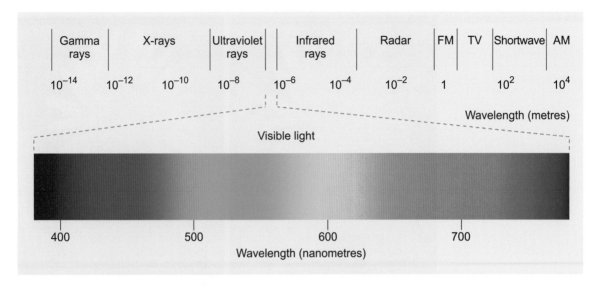

Figure 10.1 The electromagnetic spectrum showing the range of 'visible light' detectable by the human eye

All humans are therefore blind to most of the electromagnetic spectrum, detecting only the tiny part of it that is commonly referred to as 'visible light'. Some other species, however, can see outside this range. For example, Christopher Hogg and colleagues (2011) found that arctic reindeer can see ultraviolet wavelengths that humans cannot, and many insects are known to be able to see ultraviolet light – indeed, many plants look quite different to an insect from how they do to a human (see Figure 10.2). Similarly, the human ear can only detect sound frequencies from approximately 20 **hertz** to 20 kilohertz, while elephants can detect sounds lower in frequency than this range (infrasound) and many bats can detect sounds higher in frequency than this range (ultrasound) (Heffner and Heffner, 1983; Heffner et al., 2006).

The problem that everyone faces is having a world out there, only some of which can be detected, within which they need to survive and operate. What people need to do is build as accurate an internal representation of the world as they can based on the information they have about it. The processes by which the brain does that are collectively known as **perception**, which is explored in Section 3.

Hertz
The standard unit of sound frequency. One hertz (Hz) is one cycle per second; one kilohertz (kHz) is one thousand cycles per second.

Perception
The processes by which sensory information is interpreted by the brain to form a representation of that which is sensed.

(a)   (b)

Figure 10.2   A dandelion: (a) how a human sees it in 'visible' light; (b) how a honeybee sees it in ultraviolet light

3 Perception: turning information into a world

While what people interact with is the world 'out there' – sources of food, predators to avoid, and so on are all 'out there' – what people experience is a world 'in here', in the brain. Section 2 noted that when someone hears or sees a car they do not really hear or see a car itself, but detect changes in air pressure or the presence of reflected light. In fact, people's experience of the world is even further removed from reality than that: the brain does not directly detect air pressure or light, only nerve signals from the sensory apparatus (e.g. nerve signals from vibration-detecting cells in the ears that respond to the pressure changes, or from light-detecting cells in the retinas of the eyes). Specialised areas of the brain process these signals (Figure 10.3 illustrates these). For example, an area called the visual cortex in the occipital lobe at the back of the brain processes signals from the retinas, and areas of the temporal lobes (called the primary auditory cortex) on each side of the brain process signals from the ears. The sum of all the processing of sensory information that your brain does is the 'world' that you experience.

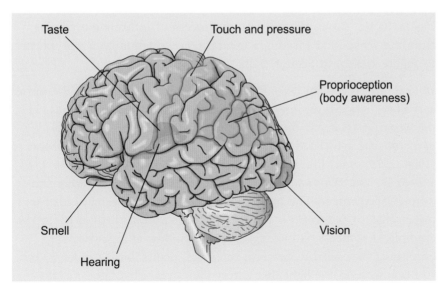

Figure 10.3 Brain areas involved in processing sensory information

There are two basic models for how the information from the senses is processed. The first is called **bottom-up processing**, and focuses on

Bottom-up processing
Within the field of perception, this view emphasises the role of information from the environment and its influence on perceptual experience.

Top-down processing
Within the field of perception, this view emphasises the role of existing knowledge and expectations on perceptual experience.

how the information that comes in from the senses is used in itself. The second is called **top-down processing**, and focuses on how incoming sensory information is incorporated with existing knowledge, experience and expectations. These two models are explored separately in Sections 3.1 and 3.2, but it is important to note that these are not 'either/or' models: human perception makes use of both types of processing. You should note that much of the research in this area has focused on visual perception, so Sections 3.1, 3.2 and 3.3 focus heavily on visual examples. However, the general principles also apply to the perception of information gathered by the other senses as well.

3.1   Working with what is there: bottom-up processing

To understand the term 'bottom-up' processing (and 'top-down' processing, which you will learn about in Section 3.2), you need to think of perception as a hierarchical process (bear in mind that this is a metaphor, not a literal description of the process). In this metaphorical hierarchy, the sensory information coming in from the world is at the bottom, and existing knowledge, experience and expectations of the world are at the top. In the middle is the person's internal perceptual representation of the world. Figure 10.4 illustrates this hierarchy: Figure 10.4(a) shows the bottom-up process of information coming from the senses and forming a mental representation (you will return to Figure 10.4(b) in Section 3.2).

Bottom-up processing takes the information coming in from the senses and works towards an internal representation of what is out there in the world based solely on what has been sensed. One of the key psychologists associated with bottom-up processing is James Gibson (1904–1979), who first wrote about it in his book *The Perception of the Visual World* (1950) and developed his ideas throughout a long and distinguished career. The basic principle is that everything needed to make sense of the world is there in the sensory information itself. For example, if someone is looking out of a window at a garden, everything they need to perceive the grass, plants, birds, squirrels, and so on is there in the light that enters their eyes. That light contains information not only about colour (in its wavelength), brightness (in its intensity) and shape (in its arrangement), but also about other physical properties of objects such as texture and contour (e.g. Gibson, 1960). At its most extreme, Gibson's approach to perception is that there is no such thing as 'perception' as a cognitive process, but that the whole process from detecting light (in vision) through to knowing what is out there should be considered a 'perceptual system'. In such a system it 'is no longer a question of how the mind operates on [what is sensed] ... or even how the brain can process the inputs' (Gibson, 1966, p. 319). Instead, there is simply incoming information – which is complete – and the individual's understanding of the world comes directly from their senses. For the person looking out of the window at a garden, for example, the light striking their retinas contains all that is needed to identify that the green bit over there is grass whereas that other green bit is a leaf on a tree, and so on.

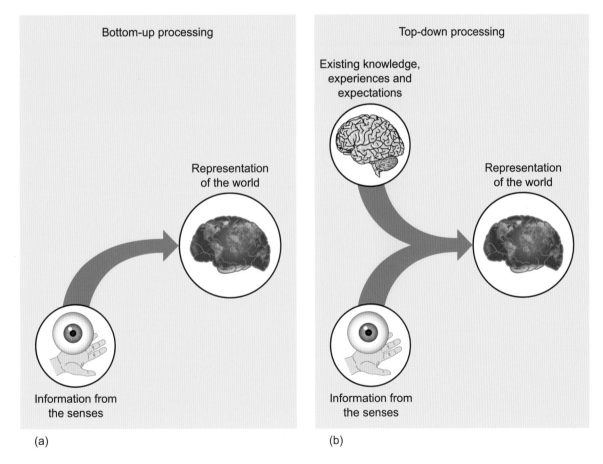

Figure 10.4   Perceptual hierarchy illustrating (a) bottom-up and (b) top-down processing

You might feel that the bottom-up model of processing seems intuitively correct. After all, where else would information about the world out there come from if not, well, the world out there? Gibson would have agreed with this view, and there is of course a lot of information in the light, sound, smells, and so on that people receive from the world. Nonetheless, it is often the case that human perception seems to go beyond the information received from the world. Figure 10.5 illustrates one example of this.

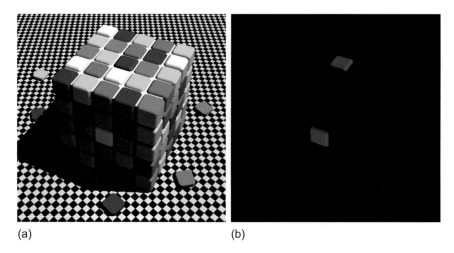

(a)   (b)

Figure 10.5 Cube colour illusion. The central squares on the front and top of the cube are exactly the same colour and brightness, but in (a) the top central square appears brown while the front central square appears yellow

In Figure 10.5 (adapted from Lotto and Purves, 2002) the central squares on the top and front of the cube are identical in terms of their colour (hue) and brightness (luminosity). They therefore have the same information in terms of the wavelength and intensity of light coming from them. This can be clearly seen in (b), where the surrounding information has been faded out. However, in (a) they appear to be different colours, showing that the brain interprets the same information differently.

While, as previously noted, psychologists researching perception have tended to concentrate on vision (and particularly optical illusions), the same principles apply to the other senses. For example, the work of a Foley artist (the person responsible for sound effects in radio, television and films) involves substituting one sound for another to give the listener the illusion of hearing something they have not really heard. Classic examples of Foley techniques are using coconut shells to simulate horses' hooves (used to great comic effect in the 1975 film *Monty Python and the Holy Grail*) or snapping a stick of crisp, fresh celery to simulate breaking bones. The sensory information contained in the sound of a stick of celery snapping is the same regardless of whether it is presented in the context of someone snapping celery or a violent fight scene, but it is perceived differently by the listener in the two different contexts.

If the same information is perceived differently in cases such as the above, something other than (or in addition to) bottom-up processing must be occurring. Psychologists refer to this as top-down processing, which you will explore in Section 3.2.

3.2   Going beyond what is there: top-down processing

At the beginning of Section 3.1, perception was described as a hierarchical process with incoming sensory information from the world at the bottom and existing knowledge, experience and expectations at the top. In top-down processing that knowledge, experience and expectation affects how people perceive the sensations coming in from the world (remember that this is a metaphorical description: information does not literally flow down from the brain into the sensory organs!). This is illustrated in Figure 10.4(b), which shows existing knowledge and so on influencing how the information from the senses is interpreted to form a representation of the world.

The top-down approach to perception assumes (unlike bottom-up processing) that the representation that someone has of the world out there is based on more than just the incoming sensory information. While the sensory information is still important, the individual's prior knowledge and experience of the world, including what they would expect to be there, are also part of the information that goes into the perceptual process.

Returning to the colour cube in Figure 10.5, image (a), as a whole, gives the impression that the cube is lit from above and behind. This would mean that the top surface was in the light whereas the front surface was in shadow. People's experience of seeing objects in the real world is invariably that if an object in shadow appears to be the same colour and brightness as another object in the light, the object in shadow is really lighter and of a brighter shade than the one in the light. This prior experience causes the viewer to perceive the two central squares in Figure 10.5 to be of different colours and brightness when they are in fact the same. An important point to note is that the viewer does not have to *consciously* work out how the figure is lit, and what effect that would have on the object being viewed, in order for the effect to occur. Top-down processing is still an *automatic* perceptual process, just like bottom-up processing.

The psychologist most closely associated with top-down processing is Richard Gregory (1923–2010), who derived much of his understanding of perception from his research into visual illusions. For example, Gregory (1968) described how several well-known visual illusions could be explained in terms of their relationship to visual features of the real world. These included the Ponzo figure illusion (Figure 10.6(a)), which is explained in terms of perspective cues that are seen in real-world features such as railway tracks (Figure 10.6(b)), and the Müller–Lyer illusion (Figure 10.6(c)), which is explained in terms of its visual similarity to the corners of walls pointing towards or away from the viewer (Figure 10.6(d)). In these two illusions, lines of the same length are perceived as being of different lengths because the cues (perspective, corners) give the impression that one line is further away than the other. If it is further away, but appears the same size, then it must be longer.

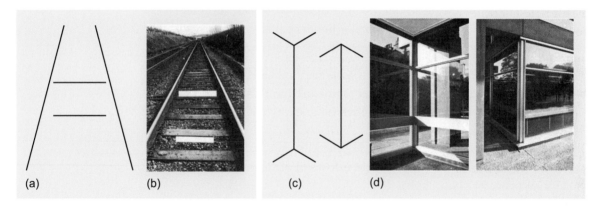

(a)   (b)   (c)   (d)

Figure 10.6   The Ponzo and Müller–Lyer illusions and their real-world counterparts

An excellent resource for learning more about Gregory and his work is the website of the Richard Gregory Foundation (www.richardgregory. org/), which includes freely downloadable copies of some of Gregory's key research papers and examples of some of the illusions that informed his theories.

While Gregory based much of his work on insights gained from studying visual illusions, which are essentially the perceptual system going 'wrong' and giving rise to an erroneous understanding, top-down processing is also important in obtaining a 'right' understanding of the world out there. The same processes that make human perception susceptible to visual illusions also allow people to extract a large amount of meaning from a small amount of information. Section 3.3 explores some examples of this.

3.3 Minimum information, maximum meaning

Before reading on, it is important to be aware of a key point about the research covered in this section. Much of the research discussed here used artificial stimuli, typically images or video clips viewed by participants in a laboratory experiment. Indeed, this was one of Gibson's critiques of a lot of perceptual research: Gibson argued that perception of images of the real world (e.g. a photograph of a scene) was not the same as perception of the real world itself (Gibson, 1979). The classic illustration of this is the René Magritte painting *The Treachery of Images* (colloquially known as *Ceci n'est pas une pipe*). The painting is of a pipe, labelled (in French) 'This is not a pipe'. The viewer arguing that it is, in fact, a pipe should ask themselves if it is possible to smoke it. Figure 10.7 makes a similar point: a picture of a motorcycle is not a motorcycle, and it is unlikely that you think you could use Figure 10.7 to go for a ride.

Figure 10.7 This is not a motorcycle

While Gibson had a valid point, and of course there are not many real-world situations in which people will confuse a picture with the scene or object it depicts, studying the perception of artificial stimuli does nonetheless provide useful information about perceptual processes. Partly this is because people use the same perceptual processes, and the same parts of the brain, to make sense of the incoming information regardless whether they are looking at a picture or a real scene, or hearing a real or a synthetic sound. There is not a separate visual cortex for photographs or paintings, nor a separate primary auditory cortex for music or voices played through speakers. In addition, of course, people are often faced with 'artificial' stimuli in the real world. For example, while a photograph or video recording of a face is not a real face, it is not uncommon to have to recognise a face from a photograph or video recording (e.g. border control staff matching passports to their bearers, or police officers identifying a suspect from CCTV footage). Similarly, a recorded voice is not a real voice, but people still listen to radio programmes, audiobooks, recorded music and the instructions given by satnav systems.

With that in mind, Activity 10.2 presents a number of (artificial) images. The task is to identify what is shown in each of them.

Activity 10.2   Making sense of images with minimal information

What do the images in Figure 10.8 show?

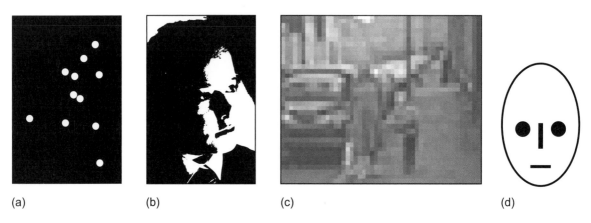

(a)   (b)   (c)   (d)

Figure 10.8   Images containing little visual information

Comment

The answers to this activity, explaining what the images in Figure 10.8 represent, can be found at the end of this chapter. The images actually contain very little information: the point-light image (a) is only a few white spots on a black background; image (b) contains only black and white splodges; image (c) contains far less information than would be seen in the real world or even a high-resolution photograph; and image (d) consists of two circles and two straight lines contained within an oval. Considering them from a bottom-up perspective, was there enough information in those images for them to be correctly perceived as what they represented? Arguably, there was if you did! However, strictly speaking, the information in image (a) was simply 'eleven small white circles on a black background' and their arrangement, not enough to identify a person. The same principle holds for the other images: if you correctly identified what they were images of then you extracted more meaning from the images than was present in them. This, along with the power of visual illusions, demonstrates that while bottom-up processing provides some of the understanding that people have of the world, a lot also depends on top-down processing.

In Sections 3.2 and 3.3 you have learned how people's existing sense of the world can make them prone to mistakes, for example in the case of visual illusions, but can also allow them to have accurate perceptions based on very little incoming sensory information (as shown in Activity 10.2). Why do these two phenomena occur? Section 3.4 explains the evolutionary basis of these processes.

3.4 Evolved cognition: how imaginary tigers shaped your perception

As you learned in Chapter 2, human cognitive abilities have a long evolutionary history behind them. Evolution tends to be a parsimonious process, with only features that provide an advantage being passed on to future generations. Why, then, would human cognition have evolved in such a way as to make basic mistakes, such as seeing things 'incorrectly' as in the visual illusions that you encountered in Section 3.2? You might also be wondering why humans would have evolved the ability to perceive large amounts of meaning in minimal amounts of information, as you learned in Section 3.3, when

Signal detection
The processes by which important information is distinguished from background 'noise', i.e. unimportant information.

the real world is rich in sensory information, as Gibson argued. An answer to these questions can be found by considering **signal detection** theory (Green and Swets, 1966). Signal detection theory describes processes whereby information that is important to the perceiver (known as the 'signal') is distinguished from other information that is unimportant and potentially distracting (known as the 'noise'). A simple everyday example would be having a conversation with someone in a loud environment such as a train: you need to be able to pick out their voice (the signal) from all the background sounds (the noise, in this case literally). A visual example would be spotting a friend in a crowd: their face would be the signal, and all the other people's faces would be the noise.

An important principle in signal detection theory is that responses are not simply 'right' or 'wrong', as there are different types of 'right' and 'wrong' responses depending on what is (or is not) really out there and what response is given. Being right that there *is* something there (i.e. identifying a signal) is not the same as being right that there is *not* something there (i.e. identifying that there is only noise), as you will shortly discover. The same is true for being wrong: being wrong that there is something there (i.e. perceiving a signal when there is only noise) is not the same as being wrong that there is nothing there (i.e. perceiving only noise when there is actually a signal). Figure 10.9 illustrates signal detection in a real-world context that might have been faced by your ancestors: the possible presence of a hungry, hunting tiger.

		What your ancestor perceives is out there	
		A tiger	Nothing, it was just the wind
What is really out there	A tiger	Your ancestor spots the tiger and runs away to safety	Your ancestor has been eaten by a tiger
	Nothing, it was just the wind	Your ancestor runs away from nothing at all and gets a bit tired for no reason	Your ancestor relaxes and nothing much happens

Figure 10.9 Signal detection outcomes for spotting a possible tiger

As Figure 10.9 illustrates, the four possible outcomes are not all equal, as they have different consequences. Importantly, whenever there was a tiger it was vital to spot it: doing so meant your ancestor survived, and not doing so meant they did not.

These are the four possible outcomes in a situation where two things are possible and the perceiver can come to two conclusions (it gets more complicated with more possibilities, such as where there might be more than one signal, but the principles are the same). Figure 10.10 illustrates these outcomes more generally, and gives the technical terms for the four possibilities.

		Perception	
		Something (signal)	Nothing (noise)
Reality	Something (signal)	Hit: you spotted what was there	Miss: you did not spot what was there
	Nothing (noise)	False alarm: you think something is there when it is not	Correct rejection: you spotted that there was nothing

Figure 10.10 Basic signal detection outcomes, for two possibilities

Going back to the example in Figure 10.9, only organisms that survive can pass on their genes to the next generation, so there is always a strong evolutionary pressure to make hits rather than misses when there really is a threat, such as a tiger. What about the situations where there is no real threat (as in the tiger example in Figure 10.9, when it was just the wind)? There is a cost to responding to a false alarm: it takes some energy, which a correct rejection would have saved, but it is a relatively small cost. In particular, it is a much smaller cost than being eaten by a tiger! There is therefore a definite advantage to being predisposed to perceiving that there is a tiger, or anything else that it is important to spot, such as food, water, a potential mate, and so on, even when there is very little information to go on (e.g. an unexpected rustle in the bushes).

This focus on the evolutionary costs and benefits of different cognitive judgements is the basis of **error management theory** (Haselton and Buss, 2000; for an overview see Haselton et al., 2005). The basic premise of error management theory is that, as it is not possible to be

Error management theory
The theory that organisms evolve to favour mistakes that have minimal costs over ones that have larger costs.

The evolutionary need to spot predators helped to shape human cognitive processes

right all the time when making perceptual judgements or other real-world inferences, there will be a tendency to manage errors so as to minimise the most costly ones (e.g. being eaten by a tiger). This will occur even if it increases the overall error rate, as long as the errors being made are low cost (e.g. wasting a small amount of energy running away from an imagined tiger). As Martie Haselton and colleagues (2005) put it: 'it is better to make *more* errors overall as long as they are of the relatively cheap kind' (p. 731).

While error management theory focuses, as the name says, on types of errors (misses versus false alarms, in signal detection terms), it also suggests that accurate perceptual judgements based on incomplete information (i.e. hits from minimal information) evolved from the same process. Put simply, error management theory says that evolution (and individual experience) favours the left-hand column of Figures 10.9 and 10.10: perceiving that there is something there. If someone walking through the jungle hears a rustle in the bushes and half-glimpses something stripy, it is better to swiftly reach the conclusion that there is a tiger than to wait for more information. Similarly, if something is seen that *might* be a human face, like in the

Mooney or Gestalt faces shown in Figure 10.8(b) and (d)
(Activity 10.2), it is advantageous to perceive it as *being* a human face,
as it is useful to identify other humans in the environment – and so on
for any potentially important stimuli.

So far in this chapter you have learned about taking in information
from the world (sensation) and processing it to understand what is 'out
there' (perception). However, that is only part of making sense of the
world. This chapter now moves from considering how the world is
represented in the mind by the processes of perception to considering
how people think about the world that they have perceived, in order to
make sense of it and decide how to act on it. In broad terms, this can
be referred to as 'reasoning', that is, making sense of the world
through (ideally) logical, rational thought processes (Chapter 11
explores the extent to which people's thought processes are *actually*
logical and rational). A particularly important aspect of reasoning about
the world is the ability to make connections between things, identifying
patterns and perceiving (or imposing) order, which is the focus of
Section 4.

4   Identifying order, connections and patterns in the world

It may seem an obvious point, but as people we do not live in a world of separate, unconnected objects that do not interact with each other (or us). Just as people need to be able to identify that the stripy growling thing over there is a tiger, something to run away from, they also need to be able to make meaningful connections between different objects in, and aspects of, the world around them. Trees bear fruit, clouds bring rain, day follows night, and so on. Making connections between things is the basis of learning in all animals, and understanding those connections is both an important part of what people mean by human 'intelligence' and an aspect of how some psychologists measure intelligence. In fact, many psychological **IQ tests**, which aim to measure specific cognitive skills associated with intelligence, such as logical or mathematical reasoning, include items designed to test people's ability to identify and extrapolate from patterns and sequences of various types. While IQ tests have been criticised on a number of grounds for quite some time, for example for being biased against people from particular sociocultural backgrounds (e.g. McLelland, 1973), such debates are beyond the scope of this chapter. This chapter is not concerned with individual differences between people in their IQ test scores but the general point that the ability to identify patterns and sequences is an aspect of human intelligence that is common to *all* people, not just those from particular sociocultural backgrounds. Section 4.1 outlines a basic type of sequence identification used in IQ testing.

IQ tests
Standardised tests of specific cognitive abilities associated with intelligence.

4.1   Identifying and extrapolating sequences

Naturally occurring patterns are typically very complex, and made up of large numbers of factors. For example, predicting the migratory patterns of herds of animals might involve factors such as the time of year, temperature, rainfall, number of animals in the herd, and so on. Psychologists tend to use much simpler types of pattern when testing people's cognitive abilities. One of the most basic types of pattern is the number sequence. A series of numbers that are connected by some sort of rule which can be mathematically deduced is presented to the person being tested, and their task is to work out the rule and predict what comes next. You can try some of these out in Activity 10.3.

Activity 10.3   Identifying and extrapolating number sequences

Below are some number sequences. In each sequence the numbers given are connected in a specific way. Your task is to identify the connection between them and use that connection to predict the next two numbers in the sequence. Try to work out the answers (and the connection) before reading the comment to the activity.

Sequence A:	1	2	3	4	5	6	7	?	?
Sequence B:	1	3	5	7	9	11	13	?	?
Sequence C:	1	2	3	5	8	13	21	?	?

Comment

You probably found sequence A very easy: it is, of course, simply the numbers counting upwards one at a time so the next two numbers are 8 and 9. Sequence B is also very easy: it is simply the odd numbers counting up (or the even numbers being skipped) so the next two numbers are 15 and 17. Experimental data show that the sorts of 'counting series' that sequences A and B represent are processed very rapidly and accurately by most people who have learned to count (e.g. LeFevre and Bisanz, 1986). In fact, sequences A and B may have come so easily that you did not really feel as though you were identifying a pattern and extrapolating a sequence at all, but that is exactly what you were doing. You probably found sequence C harder than A and B. Sequence C is part of the Fibonacci sequence (it is the start of the sequence, omitting '0' and the first '1'), which is constructed by adding consecutive pairs of numbers to calculate the next one in the sequence. So, in sequence C, $1 + 2 = 3$, $2 + 3 = 5$, $3 + 5 = 8$ and so on, meaning the missing two numbers are 34 and 55. If you were already familiar with the Fibonacci sequence you may have recognised it. However, even if you were not previously familiar with the Fibonacci sequence you may have been able to work it out mathematically from the numbers given. Unsurprisingly, Jo-Anne LeFevre and Jeffrey Bisanz (1986) showed that sequences involving calculation, such as sequence C, take people longer to do than simpler counting sequences. Nonetheless, people are generally able to identify and extrapolate sequences like these to a greater or lesser degree, depending on their mathematical ability.

An interesting question to think about is: at what point in each sequence in Activity 10.3 did you think you had enough information to know what the sequence was? It cannot have been the first number, which was the same in all three sequences (and '1' appears as the first number in a lot of different sequences!). Was it the second or the third? Sequences A and C are identical for the first three numbers. In these particular sequences, the fourth number is the earliest point at which all three sequences are different, but of course that point differs for different sequences. You learned in Section 3.4 that humans have evolved to come to quick conclusions, even when presented with incomplete information. Did you find yourself doing that with the number sequences?

Other types of sequence involve more 'natural' items than abstract number sequences, such as putting images into a logical order. Not only are these more natural, in that they can represent real-world situations in a way that things like the Fibonacci sequence do not, but they also tap into how people make sense of *cause and effect*. This is the focus of Section 4.2.

4.2   Making sense of real-world connections, causes and effects

Although they are no longer used in all IQ tests, picture sequences have been used as part of IQ testing since at least the 1950s (e.g. Wechsler, 1955). A typical picture sequence consists of a number of images showing individual snapshot 'scenes' of an event. The task is to arrange the images into a logical sequence, with events occurring first at the start of the sequence and events occurring last at the end. You can try an example of one of these in Activity 10.4.

Activity 10.4   Making sense of a picture sequence

Figure 10.11 shows four scenes from a person's day. Your task is to put them into the most logical order from first to last.

(a)

(b)

(c)

(d)

Figure 10.11   Example of a picture arrangement IQ test item

Comment

The correct order is: (b) (leaving home to go fishing), (a) (heading out in the fishing boat), (d) (catching a fish), (c) (cooking the fish).

The use of real-world examples such as the one in Activity 10.4 allows the assessment of people's understanding of the connection between practical, real things rather than just abstract sequences (although the sequences need to be culturally appropriate to the person being tested: someone with no cultural knowledge of boats or fishing would probably not understand the sequence in Activity 10.4). The examples also demonstrate an understanding of cause and effect: that some things happen before other things and cause them to happen. For example, a child knocks a cup off a table, which causes it to fall, which causes it to break, and these elements have to happen in that order. Understanding cause and effect is fundamental to making sense of the world (and important in sciences like psychology too), and humans seem to be predisposed to seek cause-and-effect relationships. In fact, psychologists have known for some time that, even from a young age, children seek to understand causality (e.g. Gelman and Kalish, 1993). The understanding of cause and effect has been described by Roberta Corrigan and Peggy Denton (1996) as a 'developmental primitive', that is, something that is either innate or develops very early in childhood. Parents, of course, do not need psychologists to tell them this ('But *why* ...?'). The human tendency to infer cause and effect is so strong, in fact, that people often assume causality even where there is actually none and events occur at random, an issue that is explored in Chapter 11.

Inductive reasoning
A type of logical reasoning that uses one or more specific observations to derive a general rule.

The understanding of cause and effect underpins much of the sense that people make of the world, particularly through **inductive reasoning**. Inductive reasoning is a form of logic that takes observations about the world and uses them to derive general rules, including about cause and effect. For example, after hearing a rustling noise in the bushes and then seeing a tiger coming out of the bushes (observations), a conclusion based on inductive reasoning would be that rustling bushes indicate the presence of a tiger (general rule, based on assuming a causal link between the tiger and the rustling). Children begin to apply causal inductive reasoning to their sense-making about the world from as young as 5 years old (e.g. Bright and Feeney, 2014), and it continues throughout adulthood.

Deductive reasoning
A form of logic in which conclusions are derived from premises (a syllogism is an example of deductive reasoning).

Once a general rule has been learned, either by direct observation or from other people, it can be applied in a logical process known as **deductive reasoning**, in which a conclusion is derived from two or more 'premises' (see, for example, Gauch, 2012, for a detailed overview of deductive logic). The general rule would constitute one premise (in formal logic referred to as the 'major premise') and a specific observation would constitute a second premise (referred to as the 'minor premise'). Arguments based on deductive reasoning are sometimes written in the form of **syllogisms**. A classic syllogism is 'all men are mortal' (major premise), 'Socrates is a man' (minor premise), 'therefore Socrates is mortal' (conclusion). Another example would be 'my cat is purring' (observation or minor premise), 'cats purr when they are happy' (general rule or major premise, based on the assumed

Syllogism
A type of logical argument in which a conclusion is made on the basis of two or more premises, such as an observation and a general rule.

causal link between purring and happiness), 'therefore my cat is happy' (conclusion).

Although this is a process of reasoning rather than perception, the same principles of signal detection theory and error management theory can be applied. Returning to the tiger example given earlier, your ancestor may have gone through a process of deductive reasoning along these lines: I just heard a rustling noise (observation or minor premise), a tiger in the bushes makes a rustling noise (knowledge of pattern or major premise), therefore there is a tiger nearby (conclusion). In signal detection terms, if there really was a tiger then that deductive reasoning process would have given a hit; if there was not then it would have given a false alarm. Just as with perception, error management theory, when applied to reasoning, argues that the less costly incorrect conclusion (a false alarm: thinking that there was a tiger when there was not) would be preferable to the potentially more costly incorrect conclusion (a miss: thinking that it was just the wind when there was really a tiger).

As with the models of perception, in practice people use both inductive and deductive reasoning to make sense of the world, using the former to arrive at general rules from their observations and the latter to apply those rules to new observations. Conclusions based on either type of reasoning can be right or wrong, and the tendency to be right or wrong will depend on the quality of the existing knowledge that the person has, the quality of their observations, and the reasonableness of any assumptions they make. For instance, in the 'tiger' inductive and deductive reasoning examples in the previous three paragraphs, there is an unstated assumption that a rustle in the grass could *only* be a tiger (you will learn more about factors affecting human reasoning and judgements in Chapter 11). While the processes of inductive and deductive reasoning may seem quite contrived, and indeed in most situations people do not work consciously through the processes (for instance, you probably know that a purring cat is a happy cat without having to think through any logical steps every time you hear a cat purr), they nonetheless underpin much of people's understanding of the world. The importance of logical reasoning in making sense of the world can particularly be seen in the way people construct and understand stories, or 'narratives', as discussed in Section 5.

5   Making sense of the world through stories

Stories, sometimes called 'narratives', are an important part of the way people make sense of the world. Corrigan and Denton (1996) argue that people understand the world, and particularly other people's behaviour within it, by 'constructing narratives where they relate the actions in an event by making causal inferences' (p. 189). People seem to be inherently predisposed to telling stories and using them to explain the world in general and each other's behaviour, and Stephen Read (1987) argues that humans are best understood as 'story understanders and storytellers' (p. 300). People are particularly sensitive to cause and effect in stories, from quite a young age, to the extent that inferences about causality are made even in written stories that do not explicitly mention cause-and-effect relationships. For example, Carole Beal (1990) found that children as young as 6 years of age made inferences from stories that had explicit cause-and-effect relationships, implicit cause-and-effect relationships, and even ambiguous cause-and-effect relationships. Table 10.1 illustrates some of the story types that Beal used in her research (note that the 'causes' were not italicised or emphasised in Beal's study, but are highlighted here for ease of reference). Each story takes place within a column, so should be read downwards rather than across the rows.

Table 10.1   Examples of story types used by Beal (1990) to explore children's sense-making (italics show the 'cause' in each example)

Explicit cause story	Implicit cause story	Ambiguous cause story
Cindy's family went to the beach	Cindy's family went to the beach	Cindy's family went to the beach
Cindy made a sandcastle	Cindy made a sandcastle	Cindy made a sandcastle
A big wave hit it	*The waves were big that day*	*Some kids were playing ball nearby*
Her sandcastle got smashed	Her sandcastle got smashed	*The waves were big that day*
		Her sandcastle got smashed

In the explicit cause story, children found it easy to draw the conclusion that the wave that hit Cindy's sandcastle was what smashed it. In the implicit cause story, children filled in the information that was not given in order to make the story make sense: they inferred that a big wave had smashed the sandcastle. Even in the ambiguous cause stories, children were able to fill in the gaps to make the story make sense, although younger children (US first-graders) tended to give only one explanation, while older children (US second- and third-graders) were more likely to identify both possible explanations (a wave smashed the sandcastle or the other children playing ball smashed the sandcastle). Interestingly, even when no cause (whether explicit, implicit or ambiguous) was given, children still added causal details to the story in order to make sense of it.

The need that people seem to have to create stories about the world is not limited to children, nor is it limited to identifying causal relationships between events. In addition to cause and effect, people often read in additional information to stories according to their own prior understanding of the world. Read (1987) provides a brief example to illustrate this, part of which is reproduced in Activity 10.5.

Activity 10.5   Making inferences in a story

Below is a short extract from Read (1987) recounting a brief interaction between two people. Read through the extract and then answer the questions following it.

> Anne walks in the front door and is greeted by her husband Dave.
>
> 'The doctor thinks the operation will be quite expensive,' says Anne.
>
> 'Oh well,' replies Dave, 'There's always Uncle Henry.'
>
> (Read, 1987, p. 288)

1   How are Anne and Dave related?

2   Who needs an operation?

3   Why did Dave suggest Uncle Henry?

Comment

The answer to question 1 is that Anne and Dave are married to each other: the information is in the first line of the extract ('her husband

Dave'). The answer to the other questions is 'I don't know', as the extract does not contain any information allowing you to answer either of those questions. However, just like the children in Beal's (1990) study, you may have found yourself making inferences to fill in the gaps. In response to question 2, you may have inferred that it is Anne who needs the operation, as it was Anne who mentioned it to Dave. However, perhaps Dave needs the operation and Anne merely took a phone call from the doctor while Dave was out. It may even be that someone not mentioned in the extract needs an operation, perhaps one of their children or parents. In response to question 3, Read suggests that a reasonable interpretation of the story would be that Anne and Dave cannot afford the operation, that they therefore need to find a source of money, and that Uncle Henry is a rich uncle who might help them out financially. If you came to a similar understanding of the story then you made quite a lot of inferences – probably more than the number of details in the story itself! One thing to note here, though, is that the inferences you made were very probably reasonable and logical and, if this was a real story, likely to be right.

As Beal's and Read's research demonstrates, making sense of the world through stories often goes beyond the information that is actually contained in the stories themselves. This is because a story which went 'A happened then B happened then C happened' would not provide an *explanation* for any of the events A, B and C. As Beal (1990) shows, when causal information is lacking in a story even young children will make inferences and add details so that the story makes sense. This is especially the case when the stories are about explaining people's behaviour, as Section 5.1 discusses.

5.1   Stories, event scripts and theory of mind

In Chapter 1 you learned about human theory of mind, the ability and tendency to ascribe knowledge, thoughts and intentions to others. Chapter 1 focused on theory of mind in terms of other people's cognitions, such as understanding what another person senses, perceives or knows. Theory of mind can also be related to the way people make sense of each other through stories. Daniel Hutto (2007) argues that people habitually engage in what he calls 'narrative practices', that is, constructing and sharing narratives or stories. These narrative practices not only reflect but also influence the way people, starting in childhood, learn to make sense of other people's actions and intentions. Hutto argues that stories about people and what they do (which is, after all, what many stories are) are not just descriptions but *explanations* of people's behaviour, that typically involve an indication that the people the story is about behave as they do for specific *reasons*. Hutto (2007, p. 43) gives two simple examples that illustrate this: 'He left the party because he believed the host had insulted him' and 'She will head for the cabin in the woods because she wants peace and quiet'. Almost all stories about people have an element of explanation along these lines, a 'because' of some kind, and it is this that makes them narratives rather than just statements of unconnected facts or opinions. The explanation in a narrative can be explicit or implicit (as in the examples from Beal's study given in Table 10.1), but it is always there, either in the narrative itself or inferred by the person hearing or reading it.

Not every situation requires an explanatory narrative, of course. For example, after visiting a shop you have probably never felt the need to work out a story about why the shop assistant said 'Thank you' at the end of the transaction. It is part of the normal social interaction that takes place between a customer and a shop assistant, so does not need explaining through a narrative. Social psychologists refer to people's understanding of the typical way in which a common social interaction happens as a **script** or an event schema (Abelson, 1981, provides a fairly straightforward overview of script theory). If an event happens according to the script or schema then it does not need an explanatory narrative: effectively, the script has already provided one. However, if a social interaction does not go according to the expected script then the person or people involved will wonder why, and attempt to create an explanatory narrative to identify a 'because'. Activity 10.6 illustrates the distinction between a situation where a script or an event schema is followed and one that might require a narrative explanation.

Script
A common understanding of how a particular social interaction is supposed to go (also known as an event schema).

Activity 10.6 Following or not following a script

Imagine yourself in each of the following two scenarios. Consider what you would think about each scenario afterwards, and whether or not you would be likely to construct a narrative explanation for what happened.

1   You go into a shop to buy some groceries, for which you pay in cash. When the shop assistant hands you your change they say 'Thank you'.

2   You go into a shop to buy some groceries, for which you pay in cash. When the shop assistant hands you your change they blow a party hooter and shout 'Hurrah!'

Comment

You probably did not think there was anything unusual about scenario 1, as it conforms to your script for how a visit to a shop goes. You are therefore unlikely to have felt the need to come up with a narrative explanation for what happened. Scenario 2, however, probably does not conform to your script for visiting a shop (unless you shop in some quite peculiar places). You are therefore likely to have felt that some kind of explanation would be needed: a narrative explaining that the shop assistant behaved in the way they did *because* of something.

Hutto describes the sort of situation in scenario 2 in Activity 10.6 as needing explanation because of the violation of social norms 'in ways that we can only make sense of by understanding them in a wider context; by acquiring the narrative that fills in or fleshes out the particular details of that person's story' (2007, p. 45). Hutto also argues, more broadly, that people learn, right from early childhood, that stories *should* have explanatory power, and that the explanations should be ones that infer mental states in others (you will recall from Chapter 1 that making inferences about others' mental states is a key element of theory of mind). Hutto uses the example of the fairy tale *Red Riding Hood* to illustrate how it employs mental state explanations such as Red having the false belief that the Big Bad Wolf in disguise is Red's grandmother. By constructing explanations that rely on inferring mental states in others, narrative practices draw heavily on human theory of mind abilities.

You now have an appreciation of the power of stories as part of everyday life in a wide variety of social contexts, which includes making sense of cause-and-effect relationships and other people's states of mind. The last section of this chapter considers an arena where the sense people make of the world through the stories they construct about it can have extremely serious consequences: the courtroom.

5.2   Stories with consequences: juror decision making

In jurisdictions following the British model of criminal law, such as the UK, USA, Canada, Australia and New Zealand, the courtroom is a place where stories are played out with serious consequences (in some states of the USA, which have the death penalty, potentially lethal consequences). In a typical criminal trial in such jurisdictions, the prosecution tells a story (itself built from the individual stories of various witnesses), then the defence tells a story (again, built from various other stories). This is known as an 'adversarial' approach, as two opposing sides (adversary means opponent) face off against each other. The task of the jury is to piece together all the evidence and arguments from both sides, work out the 'truth' of what happened in the case (i.e. the 'real' story), and deliver a verdict accordingly. Note that, although researchers and theorists typically talk about 'jurors' and 'juries', the same principles also apply to other legal decision makers, such as magistrates and judges, who are faced with the same task of making sense of evidence to reach a conclusion.

Some psychologists have proposed that jurors should take an objective approach to considering the evidence and coming to a verdict, perhaps even using statistical principles to weigh up the different pieces of evidence (e.g. Smith et al., 1996). However, most researchers in the field agree that what jurors generally do in practice is construct their own subjective stories about what happened: this is known, simply, as the 'story model' of juror decision making (Pennington and Hastie, 1991). Figure 10.12 illustrates the main components of the story model as put forward by Nancy Pennington and Reid Hastie. Note that this model is descriptive, not prescriptive: it is an explanation of what jurors actually do, based on experimental studies of mock jurors, not what the law expects them to do (Pennington and Hastie, 1992). You should also note that this is a model of *juror* decision making, as it focuses on individual interpretations of case evidence. A *jury* decision is a collective verdict after deliberation between the individual jurors, which this model does not address.

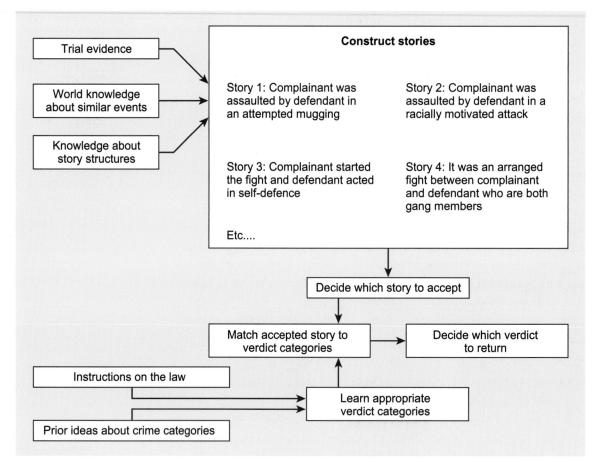

Figure 10.12 Story model of juror decision making (Source: based on Pennington and Hastie, 1991, Figure 1, p. 191)

The most obvious thing that you have probably noticed about the story model is that 'trial evidence' is only one component feeding into the construction of the stories. 'World knowledge about similar events' is also present, as is 'knowledge about story structures'. Both of these are things that allow jurors to make inferences that go beyond the case evidence.

Examples of 'knowledge about similar events' might be a juror knowing or believing that muggings typically happen after dark, that murderers typically know their victims, or that a particular pub where an assault is alleged to have taken place has a 'dodgy' reputation. An important point to note here is that such 'knowledge' may or may not be factually correct; it is just the pre-existing understanding of the world that the juror brings with them to the case. For example, there is a common stereotype that sex offences are usually committed by sinister strangers hiding in dark alleyways or lurking in public parks, whereas most sex offences actually occur in domestic settings and the offender knows their victim (Crown Prosecution Service, 2014). Note that the part of the story model dealing with 'prior ideas about crime categories' refers to a different concept, namely the ideas people have about legal definitions of different offences, for example, the technical difference between 'murder' and 'manslaughter'.

Examples of 'knowledge about story structures' might be that effects must have a cause, that stories have a beginning, a middle and an end, or that people usually have reasons for their actions (e.g. anger, jealousy, greed). If any of these elements is missing, for example, if there is no known motive for an offence, then that may undermine the plausibility of the story – unless one can be inferred (rightly or wrongly) by the juror. You may find it useful at this point to refer back to your notes on Activity 1.1 in Chapter 1, where you considered the inferences that jurors might make (and even be *required* to make) about a defendant's mental state, and think about the relationship between theory of mind explanations for people's behaviour and the explanatory narratives that a juror might construct.

Even the order in which evidence is presented can have an effect on legal decisions: if evidence is presented in chronological order (so that the story has a logical beginning, middle and end), then verdicts are more consistent with that evidence than if the evidence is presented non-chronologically (Asai and Karasawa, 2013). Nobuko Asai and Minoru Karasawa presented participants in an experiment with information about a fictional, but realistic, trial which pointed towards either a murder verdict or a verdict where there was an element of self-defence. In this study the participants' task was to indicate the appropriate sentence following a guilty verdict, rather than to indicate guilt or innocence (for reasons to do with the Japanese legal system that are beyond the scope of this chapter). If the trial evidence was presented in chronological order, that is, with the events that occurred first being described first and the events that occurred last being described last, jurors gave more severe sentences if the evidence suggested murder and shorter sentences if the evidence suggested an element of self-defence. The story-like presentation of the evidence enabled them to reach the 'right' verdict on the basis of the evidence, which was not the case if the evidence was presented in a non-chronological, disorganised order. This example illustrates that it is not only the content of stories that is important but also their narrative structure.

Section 5 has demonstrated the power and importance of stories in enabling people to make sense of the world. This is true of both everyday situations, such as going shopping, and extraordinary situations, such as serving on a jury, which can be, in some jurisdictions, literally a matter of life and death.

6 Summary

The world in which people live contains a vast amount of information, only some of which the human senses can detect and make meaningful. Human senses are fairly limited compared with those of some other animals, and yet most people are able to build up a detailed, complex and largely accurate internal model of the world around them. Some psychologists, such as Gibson, have argued that this is because human senses receive sufficient information directly from the world itself to form an accurate representation of what is out there (a bottom-up approach to perception). Other psychologists, such as Gregory, have argued that people's existing understanding of the world unconsciously affects their processing of sensory information (a top-down approach to perception). This can both help people to make sense of the world, for example by allowing the construction of a detailed internal model even with incomplete sensory information, and cause people to make mistakes, such as misperceiving colours or shapes in visual illusions. Nonetheless, most of the time the sense that people make of the world is fairly accurate, and the errors that are made tend to be relatively low cost, due to the way that human cognitive processes developed under the evolutionary pressures faced by the ancestors of modern humans.

However, making sense of the world involves much more than simply interpreting sensory information and arriving at a perceptual representation of what is 'out there'. The same evolutionary pressures that drove the development of human sensory and perceptual abilities also shaped the ability to identify patterns and connections in the world, something at which people seem to be very efficient and often quite accurate. Most people are able quite easily to identify abstract patterns, such as number sequences, as well as meaningful ones, such as picture sequences illustrating a story. The ability to do this is considered by cognitive psychologists to be a key part of human intelligence, and IQ tests often include items designed to measure aspects of pattern recognition. People also have a well-developed ability to use logic to theorise and come to conclusions about the world, using both inductive and deductive reasoning. Often these conclusions are accurate, although Chapter 11 will explore situations where people tend to be somewhat error prone.

The human tendency to make inferences and conclusions is perhaps seen most strongly in the way people build stories to make sense of the world. Just like in the processes of perception and pattern identification, constructing stories may require people to make sense of incomplete information. The evidence from psychological studies suggests that this is something that children develop the ability to do from a very young age, filling in gaps in incomplete stories based on what else they know about the world. One context where the power of stories has particular application is the courtroom, where jurors use their knowledge of the world – and of stories themselves – to structure, make sense of, and even fill in gaps in the evidence that is presented in criminal cases. Making sense of the world is both an everyday and an extraordinary part of human psychology.

References

Abelson, R. P. (1981) 'Psychological status of the script concept', *American Psychologist*, vol. 36, no. 7, pp. 715–29.

Asai, N. and Karasawa, M. (2013) 'Effects of the ease in story construction on judicial decisions concerning a criminal case', *Japanese Journal of Social Psychology*, vol. 28, no. 3, pp. 137–46.

Beal, C. R. (1990) 'Development of knowledge about the role of inference in text comprehension', *Child Development*, vol. 61, no. 4, pp. 1011–23.

Bright, A. K. and Feeney, A. (2014) 'Causal knowledge and the development of inductive reasoning', *Journal of Experimental Child Psychology*, vol. 122, pp. 48–61.

Corrigan, R. and Denton, P. (1996) 'Causal understanding as a developmental primitive', *Developmental Review*, vol. 16, pp. 162–202.

Crown Prosecution Service (2014) *Rape and Sexual Offences: 21: Societal Myths* [Online]. Available at www.cps.gov.uk/legal/p_to_r/ rape_and_sexual_offences/societal_myths/ (Accessed 28 October 2014).

Gauch, H. G. (2012) *Scientific Method in Brief*, Cambridge, Cambridge University Press.

Gelman, S. and Kalish, C. (1993) 'Categories and causality', in Pasnak, R. and Howe, M. (eds) *Emerging Themes in Cognitive Development, Vol. II: Competencies*, New York, Springer-Verlag, pp. 3–32.

Gibson, J. J. (1950) *The Perception of the Visual World*, Boston, MA, Houghton Mifflin.

Gibson, J. J. (1960) 'The information contained in light', *Acta Psychologica*, vol. 17, pp. 22–30.

Gibson, J. J. (1966) *The Senses Considered as Perceptual Systems*, Boston, MA, Houghton Mifflin.

Gibson, J. J. (1979) *The Ecological Approach to Visual Perception*, Hillsdale, NJ, Lawrence Erlbaum Associates.

Green, D. M. and Swets, J. A. (1966) *Signal Detection and Psychophysics*, New York, Wiley.

Gregory, R. L. (1968) 'Perceptual illusions and brain models', *Proceedings of the Royal Society B*, vol. 171, pp. 179–296.

Haselton, M. G. and Buss, D. M. (2000) 'Error management theory: a new perspective on biases in cross-sex mind reading', *Journal of Personality and Social Psychology*, vol. 78, pp. 81–91.

Haselton, M. G., Nettle, D. and Andrews, P. W. (2005) 'The evolution of cognitive bias', in Buss, D. M. (ed.) *The Handbook of Evolutionary Psychology*, Hoboken, NJ, John Wiley & Sons Inc., pp. 724–46.

Heffner, R. S. and Heffner, H. E. (1983) 'Hearing in the elephant (Elephas maximus): absolute sensitivity, frequency discrimination, and sound localization', *Journal of Comparative and Physiological Psychology*, vol. 96, no. 6, pp. 926–44.

Heffner, R. S., Koay, G. and Heffner, H. E. (2006) 'Hearing in large (Eidolon helvum) and small (Cynopterus brachyotis) non-echolocating fruit bats', *Hearing Research*, vol. 221, nos 1–2, pp. 17–25.

Hogg, C., Neveu, M., Stokkan, K., Folkow, L., Cottrill, P., Douglas, R., Hunt, D. M. and Jeffery, G. (2011) 'Arctic reindeer extend their visual range into the ultraviolet', *Journal of Experimental Biology*, vol. 214, pp. 2014–19.

Hutto, D. D. (2007) 'The narrative practice hypothesis: origins and applications of folk psychology', *Philosophy*, vol. 60, pp. 43–68.

LeFevre, J. and Bisanz, J. (1986) 'A cognitive analysis of number-series problems: sources of individual differences in performance', *Memory and Cognition*, vol. 14, no. 4, pp. 287–98.

Lotto, R. B. and Purves, D. (2002) 'The empirical basis of color perception', *Consciousness and Cognition*, vol. 11, no. 4, pp. 609–29.

McLelland, D. C. (1973) 'Testing for competence rather than for "intelligence"', *American Psychologist*, vol. 28, no. 1, pp. 1–14.

Pennington, N. and Hastie, R. (1991) 'A cognitive theory of juror decision making: the Story Model', *Cardozo Law Review*, vol. 13, pp. 5001–39.

Pennington, N. and Hastie, R. (1992) 'Explaining the evidence: tests of the Story Model for juror decision making', *Journal of Personality and Social Psychology*, vol. 6, no. 2, pp. 189–206.

Read, S. J. (1987) 'Constructing causal scenarios: a knowledge structure approach to causal reasoning', *Journal of Personality and Social Psychology*, vol. 52, no. 2, pp. 288–302.

Smith, B. C., Penrod, S. D., Otto, A. L. and Park, R. C. (1996) 'Jurors' use of probabilistic evidence', *Law and Human Behavior*, vol. 20, no. 1, pp. 49–82.

Wechsler, D. (1955) *Manual for the Wechsler Adult Intelligence Scale*, Oxford, Psychological Corp.

Answer to Activity 10.2

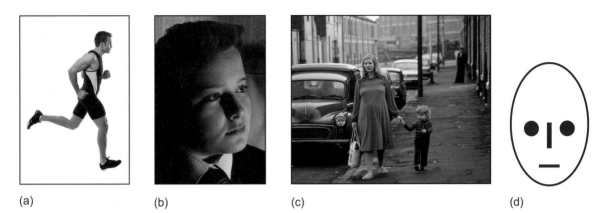

(a) (b) (c) (d)

Figure 10.13 Image (a) shows a running man, with the white dots corresponding to key points such as the head and major joints (e.g. knees, elbows). Image (b) shows the face of a young boy, lit from one side and reduced to pure black and white. Image (c) shows a street scene, of a woman and child walking past a row of parked cars, in which the resolution of the image is reduced as is often found in CCTV footage. Image (d) shows a schematic, or 'Gestalt', face, which despite having only minimal features is nonetheless perceived as a face by most people

Chapter 11

Everyday errors in making sense of the world

David Hardman

Contents

1 Introduction

As you learned in Chapter 10, humans have a highly evolved ability to make sense of the world, particularly when it comes to identifying patterns in information and connections between things. Often this allows quick and accurate judgements and decisions to be made, even on the basis of incomplete information. However, it can also lead to quick and *in*accurate judgements and decisions. These can occur because of incomplete information; because additional information is considered that should not be; or because the available information is interpreted inappropriately. In this chapter you will learn about some of the errors that people make when making sense of the world that occur not because of perceptual processes (such as the optical illusions you learned about in Chapter 10), but because of cognitive processes of thinking and reasoning. You will also discover that the errors arising from these processes can have quite serious real-world consequences.

The chapter will introduce you to some of the key literature on human judgement, examining the ways in which people try to make sense of the world and the mental short cuts ('heuristics') they apply when faced with complex information to process or difficult judgements to make. As you will learn, and as the chapter title suggests, many researchers have focused on the errors that can arise from such heuristics, and you will explore several real-world contexts in which such errors can occur. Other psychologists have argued that heuristics can lead to highly accurate judgements, at least in some circumstances, and you will also learn about these theories.

After reading this chapter you should be able to:

* identify some areas of human sense-making that are particularly prone to errors

* describe some of the main cognitive processes leading to errors in making sense of the world, focusing on representativeness, availability and anchoring heuristics

* outline the role of hindsight bias in affecting people's judgements, and the perceived accuracy of their previous judgements

* describe the concept of 'fast and frugal' heuristics as an alternative model of human sense-making.

2   Finding patterns in randomness

On 17 July 2014, the passengers and crew of Malaysian Airlines Flight MH17 were killed when the plane crashed over eastern Ukraine, apparently hit by a missile. Seven days later a plane crashed over Taiwan, and the day after that another airliner crashed en route from Burkina Faso to Algeria. While all these events were occurring, flight MH370, which went missing on 8 March 2014, remained unaccounted for. Quite reasonably, during this time many people wondered whether it was safe to fly (especially those who had already booked tickets to do so).

Because of the horrific nature of these events, it is of course understandable that many people were concerned, even frightened, about such a sudden spate of deadly incidents and may have felt that flying had suddenly become unsafe. However, it is not uncommon for major incidents to occur in clusters rather than being evenly spread over time, as the director of the Aviation Safety Network tried to reassure people at the time (e.g. the BBC reported on this in Gee, 2014). Contrary to intuition, such clustering is actually a feature of random distributions, as you will learn in Section 2.1. The BBC article featured the following explanation from Professor Arnold Barnett of the Massachusetts Institute of Technology.

'It is essentially a coincidence, except for the technicality that adverse weather involving thunderstorms and typhoons is more common in some seasons than others,' says Arnold Barnett, a Professor of Statistics at the Massachusetts Institute of Technology.

However, Barnett also draws attention to the theory of Poisson distribution, which implies that short intervals between crashes are actually more probable than long ones.

'Suppose that there is an average of one fatal accident per year, meaning that the chance of a crash on any given day is one in 365,' says Barnett. 'If there is a crash on 1 August, the chance that the next crash occurs one day later on 2 August is $1/365$. But the chance the next crash is on 3 August is $(364/365) \times (1/365)$, because the next crash occurs on 3 August only if there is no crash on 2 August.'

'It seems counterintuitive, but the conclusion follows relentlessly from the laws of probability,' Barnett says.

(Gee, 2014)

For the purposes of this chapter you do not need to know the mathematics behind the **Poisson distribution**, but the extract from the BBC article illustrates two important points. First, there is a statistical explanation for why random events often occur in clusters. Second, the statistical explanation is quite complicated and unlikely to make sense to people who do not have a fairly high level of mathematical knowledge and understanding. Indeed, as Professor Barnett says, it is counter-intuitive. For most people, then, the idea that 'flying has become more dangerous' is much easier to understand than the calculations needed to work out the Poisson distribution and conclude that the clustering is just something that has occurred randomly.

Poisson distribution
A method of calculating the probability of random events occurring over a particular period of time or in a particular place.

2.1 Clustering of random events: lessons from the Luftwaffe

One of the classic examples of the inferences that people make from observing a cluster of events comes from the Second World War, when it became apparent that some areas of London were receiving multiple hits from German bombs, while other areas remained relatively unscathed. For example, Figure 11.1 shows a map of bomb strikes in east London, in which there is a cluster of hits around Walthamstow and an area almost completely free of hits around Wanstead. After the war, the statistician R. D. Clarke (1946; see also Feller, 1950) showed that the pattern of hits during the Blitz was entirely consistent with a Poisson distribution, meaning that the areas struck were random rather than specifically targeted. However, when the war was actually happening a popular explanation for the uneven pattern of hits was that the Germans were avoiding targeting those areas inhabited by their own spies. Clearly, people had their own way of making sense of the random data, and were able to create a story that seemed to them to fit. There is a term for the human tendency to find patterns that are not really there in random information: **apophenia**. Apophenia is a consequence of the highly developed ability to identify patterns that you learned about in Chapter 10. The same cognitive processing that enables people to identify patterns based on very little information (see

Apophenia
The tendency to find illusory patterns in random information.

Section 4 of Chapter 10) also sometimes causes people to identify patterns based on unconnected information.

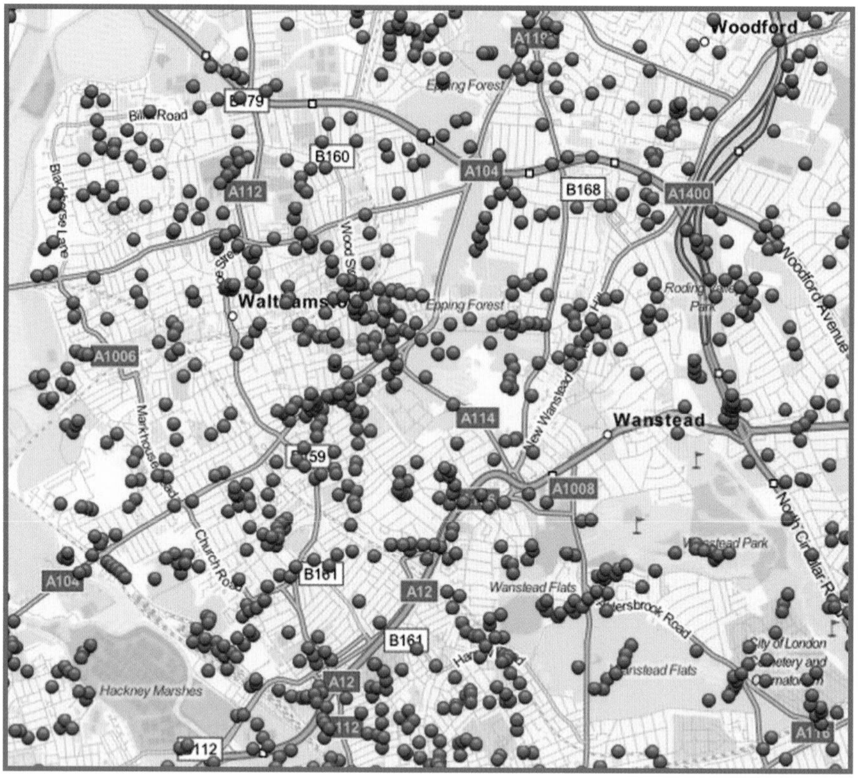

Figure 11.1 Was Walthamstow targeted during the Blitz while Wanstead was deliberately avoided? (Source: Bomb Sight, n.d.)

A more modern example of apophenia, less dramatic than the Second World War bombing of London but no less fascinating, comes from the Apple iPod shuffle (and similar devices with a random play function). This device can store large amounts of music and offers its users the facility for playing an unpredictable selection of music via its random shuffle function. However, many users of the iPod shuffle developed the distinct impression that their device preferred some artists over others (Levy, 2005, 2006). For example, someone might believe that their iPod shuffle had developed a distinct favouritism towards the Beatles, perhaps sometimes scheduling two or three of their tracks in sequence or close together, whereas the Rolling Stones were hardly ever played. Were users correct to perceive this iPod bias? Did the devices have sufficient artificial intelligence to have developed personal preferences? Was there a conspiracy by the device makers to favour some artists over others, perhaps to increase sales of those artists' work? No. Just as was the case with the Second World War bomb sites, random sequences of events tend to result in clustering rather than a neat, even spread, so it is actually quite likely that clusters of an artist's work will appear in randomly selected playlists.

This probably still seems hard to believe, but the phenomenon of 'clumpy' distribution is something that you can investigate for yourself quite simply, in Activity 11.1. If you keep a record of a large number of coin tosses (100 or more, say) you will almost always observe that within the overall sequence of outcomes there are long sequences where only 'heads' appear or where only 'tails' appear. As sequences get longer and longer the overall proportions of heads and tails get closer to 50 per cent each, but the distribution of heads and tails will be clustered rather than even.

Activity 11.1   Randomness and clustering in coin tosses

For this activity you will need a normal, everyday coin. Toss the coin repeatedly and keep a record each time of whether the coin comes up 'heads' or 'tails'. Once you have reached 30 coin tosses (more if you have the patience), stop and consider the 'pattern' of the random sequence that you have generated. Do you have an equal number of heads and tails? Do you have any particularly long runs of heads or of tails? Try also thinking of each head as a point for the Heads team and each tail as a point for the Tails team, as if they were goals in a football game, and count how often the lead changes. Are you surprised by the outcome?

Comment

It is, of course, not possible for me to comment on the exact random sequence of heads and tails that your coin tosses gave you, but here is mine:

T T T T T T T H H H H H T T T T T H T T H H H T H H T H H T T

Out of 30 tosses, I got 17 tails and 13 heads. Rounded to whole numbers, that is 57 per cent tails and 43 per cent heads – not quite 50:50 but not too far off (if only two of my tails had been heads instead, it would have been perfectly 50:50). However, I opened with a run of seven tails and, in all honesty, was beginning to wonder if my coin was actually fair or if it was biased in some way, perhaps being slightly heavier on one side. This was followed by a run of five heads, then another run of four tails – both fairly sizeable clusters in a total of only

30 tosses. This is quite a good illustration of how clusters can occur in a random sequence, and my concern at whether my coin was really fair shows how my judgement was influenced by what *seemed* to be a non-random sequence at the start (even though I was in the process of writing about clustering in random sequences – clearly I am not immune to apophenia!).

The question of how often the lead changed illustrates another counter-intuitive point. Because a coin toss is a 50:50 random event, you may have expected the lead to change quite frequently: sometimes heads will be in the lead and sometimes tails will be in the lead (you may even have expected each to be in the lead for about half the time). However, a change in the lead does not usually happen very often. As mentioned above, your sequence will differ but in mine the lead *never* changed: tails took an early lead and always stayed ahead. Whichever side, heads or tails, comes up first has a head start: the other side needs to come up next (a 50:50 chance) just to draw level, but has to come up twice to take the lead (requiring two 50:50 chances). Combined probabilities like this are calculated by multiplication, so the probability of the other side coming up twice in a row is $1/2 \times 1/2$ (or 0.5×0.5 in decimal notation), which is $1/4$ (0.25). Whichever side comes up first, the other side has only a 25 per cent chance of taking over within the next two tosses. It is actually a little more complicated than that, because if the second toss is the same as the first then the other side no longer has that 25 per cent chance of taking the lead: it is now two behind, and needs to come up three times in a row to take the lead ($0.5 \times 0.5 \times 0.5 = 0.125$, or 12.5 per cent, or 1 in 8). After a while the mathematics gets a little complicated, but the psychological point is that people's intuitions about random events are generally wrong.

The essential point to take from all this is that people expect random data to *seem* random, in a way that they usually are not. Random events often cluster, in ways that people do not expect them to, so sequences that are quite likely can seem unlikely and vice versa. In the case of some random events (e.g. Second World War bomb sites, random playlists in iPod shuffles), apophenia causes people to interpret clusters as meaningful when they are not. Even something as everyday, familiar and obviously random as tossing a coin can throw up counter-intuitive effects, such as the fact that the lead in a sequence of coin tosses changes much less frequently than most people intuitively expect.

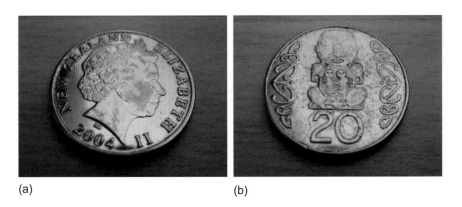

(a)   (b)

Figure 11.2 The coin that I used for Activity 11.1, which caused me to experience apophenia: (a) heads; (b) tails

However, errors in making sense of the world are not limited to people's understanding of probabilistic events which are mathematically difficult to understand, such as the distribution of random sequences. There are a large number of cognitive processes that can cause people to make erroneous judgements, even (perhaps especially) in common, everyday contexts. Many of these take the form of heuristics and biases, some of the most powerful of which are outlined in Section 3.

3   Heuristics and cognitive biases

Why do people struggle so much to accept the randomness of random patterns? Perhaps it is because so many of the events people encounter in the real world are genuinely connected and, as you learned in Chapter 10, the evolution of human cognition has made people very efficient at identifying such connections, making sense of information, and coming to decisions based on the sense they make. There seem to be particular mental short cuts that help make the human mind efficient at this, which are known as **heuristics**. These heuristics can be both beneficial, allowing quick and accurate judgements, and problematic, leading to errors. Some heuristics take the form of **cognitive biases**, which are tendencies to think in a particular way in a given situation, whether or not it is likely to be the most accurate – the implication being that biased thinking tends to be highly prone to errors. In this section you will learn about several examples of specific heuristics and biases, drawing particularly on the work of the Nobel Laureate Daniel Kahneman and his late colleague Amos Tversky (who only did not share the Nobel prize because it is not awarded posthumously).

As you will discover, many researchers have studied human judgements by setting real-world problems for their participants and seeing whether their responses accord with the rules of probability or logic. Often they do not, but perhaps this should not be surprising. The mathematics that allow an understanding of probabilistic concepts only began to be developed in the seventeenth century, with the works of people such as Blaise Pascal (1623–1662) and Pierre de Fermat (1601–1665), whereas human cognitive processes have been evolving for considerably longer. Even with a modern education, many people struggle to understand and consciously apply the rules of probability unless they have had a considerable degree of education in, and practice using, probability theory. For many domains of judgement, including those for which probabilistic reasoning would be helpful, researchers such as Kahneman, Tversky and others have proposed that people respond by applying the general 'rules of thumb', or in other words simplifying operations, that psychologists refer to as heuristics.

Heuristics
Mental 'short cuts' which help make sense of the world efficiently, but may give rise to errors.

Cognitive biases
Tendencies to think in a particular way, often causing errors in judgement.

Heuristics are generally supposed to be useful, and may often be so, but they do not guarantee a correct solution to a problem. Tversky and Kahneman (1974) described three such heuristics that have subsequently been the subject of much investigation: representativeness, availability, and anchoring (see also the influential collection of papers and original articles in Kahneman et al., 1982). In the following sections you will explore these heuristics, including trying out some of the problem-based tasks that Kahneman and colleagues used in their research which discovered them.

3.1   The representativeness heuristic

The representativeness heuristic incorporates several types of thinking. Before reading on, try the short problem-based task in Activity 11.2.

Activity 11.2   Evaluating Toyah

Consider the following problem (adapted from Tversky and Kahneman, 1983):

> Toyah is 31 years old, single, outspoken and very bright. She graduated with a degree in psychology from The Open University. As a student, she was deeply concerned with issues of discrimination and social justice, and also participated in anti-fracking demonstrations.

Which of the following statements do you think is more likely to describe Toyah now?

(a) Toyah works in a bank.

(b) Toyah works in a bank and is an environmental activist.

Comment

When thinking about Toyah, did you think that statement (b) was more likely than statement (a)? If so, you are in the majority: Tversky and Kahneman (1983) found that approximately 85 per cent of their participants rated (b) as more likely than (a) when given similar statements about 'Linda'. However, that is logically incorrect. Given the description of Toyah as a student, you may think it fairly unlikely that she works in a bank (statement (a)). However, statement (a) does not say anything about whether Toyah is an environmental activist or not, and therefore encompasses both the possibility that she is *and* that she is not. Because it encompasses both possibilities this statement must logically be more probable than the more specific statement (b), which only allows for one of these possibilities.

Conjunction fallacy
The mistaken belief that two (or more) events together are more likely than either event on its own.

Representativeness heuristic
A mental short cut where the likelihood of something is judged based on how representative or typical it seems.

The logical principle that most people (85 per cent in the original study) fail to take into account in examples like Activity 11.2 is that the conjunction of two events can never be more likely than the occurrence of either event by itself. Tversky and Kahneman (1983) referred to people's responses on this kind of task as a **conjunction fallacy**. They proposed that this fallacy occurs when people apply the **representativeness heuristic** to the problem (the original work on the representativeness heuristic is described in Kahneman and Tversky, 1972). This heuristic involves making a judgement of resemblance between the specific person or thing that is being judged and a stereotypical example of the category to which that person or thing belongs. In the case of Toyah, the description of her does not seem to bear much resemblance to the stereotype of the category 'bank worker'. However, add 'environmental activist' to 'bank worker' and the resemblance to Toyah seems to increase. Critically, a judgement of resemblance is logically not the same as a judgement of probability, but the combination of the representativeness heuristic and the conjunction fallacy makes people respond as though it is.

The conjunction fallacy is one way that judgements by representativeness can manifest themselves. Another way is lack of sensitivity to sample size, that is, how many of something are being considered. You may have some intuitive idea about sample size already; for example, you would probably trust the results of a survey which sampled 1000 people more than one which sampled 10 people. Activity 11.3 will test how accurate your intuitions about sample size are.

Activity 11.3   Sample size and hospital birth rates

Consider the following problem, adapted from Kahneman and Tversky (1972):

> Normville has two hospitals with maternity wards. In the larger hospital about 45 babies are born each day and in the smaller hospital about 15 babies are born each day. Overall, about 50 per cent of all the babies born in Normville are boys. The exact percentage of baby boys, however, varies from day to day. Sometimes it may be higher than 50 per cent, sometimes lower. For a period of one year, each hospital recorded the days on which more than 60 per cent of the babies born were boys.

Which hospital do you think recorded more such days? Was it (a) the larger hospital, (b) the smaller hospital, or (c) about the same for each (say, within 5 per cent of each other)?

Comment

Of 50 participants in the original study, 28 thought both hospitals would have recorded roughly the same number of days (answer (c)), 12 thought the larger hospital would have recorded more such days, and 10 thought the smaller hospital would have recorded more such days. In fact, it is the smaller hospital that is likely to have recorded more days on which over 60 per cent of the babies born were boys. The reason for this is that small samples are less reflective of the general population than large samples. Think about this in terms of the coin toss example in Activity 11.1: a longer sequence will tend towards the 50:50 result that you would expect overall, but a shorter sequence can easily be biased one way or the other. If I had stopped after my first five coin tosses, for example, I would have had a sample consisting of 100 per cent tails, but my whole sequence of 30 tosses was 57 per cent tails and 43 per cent heads, not far off 50:50. The same principle applies to the proportions of boys and girls born in larger and smaller hospitals, or any other set of data: small samples exhibit more variation than large samples and are therefore less representative.

Tversky and Kahneman (1971) refer to this principle as the 'law of small numbers', a corollary to the 'law of large numbers'. The law of large numbers states that a larger sample size will be more representative of what is being sampled than a smaller sample size. The law of small numbers extends this by pointing out that smaller sample sizes will therefore be less representative of what is being sampled, and are thus more likely to give extreme (i.e. not close to the average) results, than larger sample sizes. This point is important to remember, both academically and in the real world. When reading about scientific studies, always be cautious of those with very small sample sizes as they may not be representative. Similarly, when engaging with everyday data such as surveys and official statistics, always treat small sample sizes with caution.

Gambler's fallacy
The erroneous belief that past random events influence future random events to 'even things out'.

Another aspect of the representativeness heuristic is the **gambler's fallacy**. Someone who applies representative thinking to randomising devices (e.g. coins, dice, roulette wheels) will expect short sequences of outcomes to resemble the outcomes from longer sequences. For example, when thinking about a sequence of coin tosses, most people believe that the sequence HTHTTH is more likely than the sequence HHHTTT, which appears less reflective of a random process, and they believe it is more likely than HHHHTH, which does not appear to reflect a fair coin (Kahneman and Tversky, 1972). Think back to your and my coin toss sequences in Activity 11.1 and (unless you think one or both of us had a biased coin) the illogic of the gambler's fallacy should become clear.

Using representative thinking in the context of gambling means that the person is treating the randomising device as though it has a memory: for example, the coin is somehow keeping track of how many times it has landed heads and how many tails and is wilfully aiming to balance them out. Of course, this is not the case: a coin does not have a memory and each toss is independent of the one(s) that went before. Nonetheless, people do treat randomising devices as though they have a memory, sometimes with tragic consequences, as the news story in Extract 11.1 indicates.

Extract 11.1 Number 53 brings relief to Italy

The elusive number 53, blamed for several deaths and bankruptcies, has finally popped up in the Venice lottery after a two-year wait.

Italians had bet more than 3.5bn euros (£2.4bn), hoping that 53 would turn up, in what became a national obsession. Last month a woman drowned herself in the sea off Tuscany after she bet the family savings on 53, Reuters reports. And police said a man living near Florence shot his wife and son and then himself because of his number 53 debts.

[...]

A consumer group, Codacons, recently urged the government to ban the number 53 from the draw, to halt the country's 'collective psychosis'.

Source: BBC News, 2005

This story presents a case where people expected a specific random event to occur, namely the number '53' to come up on an Italian lottery, simply because it had not occurred for some time. Lottery players also do the converse: they avoid picking numbers that have recently appeared as part of a winning combination. For example, a study of Maryland's 'Pick 3' lottery found that it took three months before winning numbers regained their popularity (Clotfelter and Cook, 1993; see also Terrell, 1994). A more astute lottery player might deliberately choose numbers that have recently won, on the basis that this reduces the chance of sharing the jackpot, should he or she be lucky enough to win!

John Haigh (2003) observed that the first 282 draws of the British National Lottery included 132 occasions when the winning combination contained an adjacent pair of numbers, which lottery players seldom choose because consecutive numbers do not 'seem' random. Consequently, there were fewer winners (330) than would be expected on the basis of genuinely random selection (514, given the number of tickets sold), resulting in a larger prize for those who did pick the winning combination. Lottery organisers do nothing to combat errors in thinking such as the gambler's fallacy, and even actively encourage them as the lottery announcers typically give information on how often each number has come up before, how long it has been since a number last came up, and point out any clusters (e.g. 'number 42, that's the third week running').

Another phenomenon that can arise as a result of representative thinking is the neglect of base rates. The term 'base rate' refers to the frequency with which certain events occur in the population, and making a mistake about something due to misunderstanding or ignorance of its base rate is called the **base rate fallacy**.

Base rate fallacy
An error in judgement based on not knowing or understanding how often something usually occurs.

In one of their classic studies, Kahneman and Tversky (1973) presented university students with a description of 'Tom W'. Tom W was said to have been chosen at random from the whole population of students at the university, and was described as being:

> of high intelligence, although lacking in true creativity. He has a need for order and clarity, and for neat and tidy systems in which every detail finds its appropriate place. His writing is rather dull and mechanical, occasionally enlivened by somewhat corny puns and by flashes of imagination of the sci-fi type. He has a strong drive for competence. He seems to feel little sympathy for other people and does not enjoy interacting with others. Self-centered, he nonetheless has a deep moral sense.
>
> (Kahneman and Tversky, 1973, p. 238)

Some students were asked how similar Tom was to a typical student in various fields of specialisation, while others were asked how likely it was that Tom was actually enrolled in each of these fields. Overall, people tended to think that Tom was a student on one of the less popular courses, even though logically it is more likely that a randomly selected student would be on a more popular course than a less popular one, simply because there are more students on the popular courses. For example, a randomly chosen Open University student is more likely to be studying psychology than economics, because The Open University has more psychology students than economics students. Moreover, the judgements of how likely Tom was to be a student on any given course were almost perfectly correlated with the judgements of how similar people thought Tom was to a 'typical' student in that subject. Thus, people appeared to be neglecting base rates (how many students were on each course) and relying on representativeness (how well Tom represented their stereotype of particular courses' students).

3.2   The availability heuristic

The second major type of heuristic identified by Kahneman and colleagues is the availability heuristic. Before reading on, try Activity 11.4, which is based on some of the early research into this heuristic.

Activity 11.4   Remembering famous names

Read once through the following list of names, then cover it up and answer the question that follows it.

> Marilyn Monroe, Guy Doleman, Stephen Crabb, Beyoncé, Jane Austen, Paul Muni, Richard Dix, Rihanna, Margaret Thatcher, Adrien Brody, Scarlett Johansson, Bruce Welch, Kate Winslett, Maurice Gosfield, Felix Papparlardi, Halle Berry, Jules Munshin, Sharon Osborne, Kylie Minogue, Stanley Baker, Bette Davis, Steve Jordan, Leona Lewis, Jonas Armstrong, Noah Taylor.

Without referring back to that list of names, try to answer: did that list contain more men's names or more women's names, or were the numbers exactly the same?

Comment

There is a good chance that you will have estimated the list of people in Activity 11.4 to contain more women's names than men's names. In fact there were more men's names (13) than women's (12). In the study by Tversky and Kahneman (1973) from which this activity was adapted, approximately 80 per cent of the participants got it wrong. Why do you think that might be?

In the original study from which Activity 11.4 was adapted, the participants were presented with lists of 39 names, in which there were either (a) 19 famous women and 20 less famous men, or (b) 19 famous men and 20 less famous women. After reading the lists, 81 per cent of participants (80 out of 99) judged that the gender with the more famous names was the most numerous. A second group of 86 participants was asked to actually recall the names that had been presented, and recalled on average 12.3 of the 19 famous names (63 per cent) and 8.4 of the 20 less famous names (43 per cent). In other words, it seems that familiarity with names made them more easy to recall and this influenced people's assessments of which gender was more frequent. Assuming that you were familiar with more of the women on the list than the men, you too probably found the women's names easier to remember and therefore assumed that there were more of them.

Availability heuristic
The assumption that more easily remembered things occur more often than less easily remembered things.

When people make judgements of probability and frequency based on the ease with which they can think of relevant examples they are said to be using the **availability heuristic** (Kahneman and Tversky, 1973). In this heuristic, things that are more readily available to people's conscious minds (i.e. those that are more easily remembered) are judged to be more frequent, common or likely than things that are less readily available. Sometimes this heuristic can lead to a correct inference, such as when easily remembered things really are more common. For example, whether you are a fan of them or not, you can probably recall more Beatles hits than hits by most other bands, which would not be surprising as they are the biggest-selling pop group in history. However, although more frequent events do tend to be more easily brought to mind, other factors also have an influence. For example, things that happened recently tend to be more easily recalled than similar things that happened longer ago, and dramatic events that lend themselves to the construction of vivid mental images tend to be more easily recalled than bland or mundane events.

To return to the example used at the beginning of this chapter, aeroplane crashes are exceedingly rare but when they do occur they are widely reported (and, as noted earlier, rare events often happen in clusters, which may make them seem more frequent than they truly are). They are also easy to visualise, regardless of whether pictures appear in the media. Such factors may increase the availability of fatal crashes in the minds of the public, at least for a period of time following a crash, feeding into their fear of such events. Having a fear that is out of proportion to the risk can have serious consequences. For example, people who are afraid to fly may seek an alternative mode of transport that is actually more dangerous, such as driving. An analysis of US traffic fatalities between October 2001 and September 2002 (the 12 months following the 9/11 terror attacks) found that there were 1600 more road deaths than would be expected in a typical year. This figure is six times the number of passengers and crew who were killed in the aircraft on 11 September (Gigerenzer, 2006; see also Gaissmaier and Gigerenzer, 2012).

Figure 11.3 If you drive to an airport to catch a flight, once you get to the airport the most dangerous part of your journey is over (at least until you get into a car again at the other end)

As well as affecting the perception of events in the world, the availability heuristic can also affect people's perceptions of themselves. Activity 11.5 asks you to consider some aspects of your own past behaviour and how you see yourself in relation to those behaviours. Please try to answer the activity as honestly and accurately as you can.

Activity 11.5   Judging your assertiveness and kindness

For this activity you will need something to write on.

Number the left side of your page from 1 to 12, leaving enough space to write a sentence or two in each case. Then try to think of 12 occasions when you have behaved in an assertive fashion (i.e. you were bold or confident towards another person) and list these in your numbered sections.

Having done this, write down on a scale from 1 to 7 how assertive a person you are in general (1 = not at all assertive; 7 = extremely assertive).

The next part of the activity is to do a similar exercise for the quality of kindness. However, rather than list 12 occasions when you behaved kindly, you only need to list six occasions. Once you have done this, rate how kind a person you are in general, also on a scale from 1 to 7 (1 = not at all kind; 7 = extremely kind).

Which of the two tasks did you find the more difficult to perform?

Comment

This activity was based on research by Norbert Schwarz and colleagues (1991), in which participants were asked to do the same task that you just did. The only difference is that the study was counterbalanced, so that half the participants listed 12 'assertive' and six 'kind' acts, as you did, and the other half listed 12 'kind' and six 'assertive' acts. Clearly, it is harder to remember 12 examples of anything than six examples. Schwarz and colleagues predicted that people would rate themselves higher on the characteristic for which they gave six examples than the one for which they gave 12 examples, simply owing to finding it easier to think of examples for that characteristic. This is indeed what Schwarz and colleagues found: if participants found it harder to think of examples (because they were asked to list a lot of them), they interpreted that as meaning they were relatively low in that characteristic compared with the one for which they found it easy to think of examples. In the version of the task you did in this activity, you probably found it harder to answer the 'assertive' part and easier to answer the 'kind' part. This may have led you to conclude that you must be more kind than you are assertive. Schwarz and colleagues' study also shows that the availability heuristic does not just affect estimates of frequency or probability of events, because the outcome measure in this case was a rating of participants' own personality.

Tversky and Derek Koehler (1994) proposed that when people assess the likelihood of events, what they actually make a judgement about is a *description* of that event. These descriptions can be seen as analogous to a scientific hypothesis, and the estimated likelihood of the event depends on the *support* that a person can call on for that hypothesis (for that reason, this is sometimes referred to as 'support theory'). Differences in the way an event is described can therefore lead to different assessments of its probability. Tversky and Koehler asked one group of people to estimate the likelihood of dying from 'heart disease, cancer, or any other natural cause', while another group were simply asked to estimate the likelihood of dying from 'natural causes'. The two groups should have given similar estimates, because 'natural causes' includes heart disease and cancer. However, the participants who had to consider only the 'natural causes' category underestimated the likelihood relative to those who also had to consider some specific categories of natural causes. The reason for this is that naming heart disease and cancer in the question brought them to mind when the participants were considering their judgements, so they were available to support an estimate of higher likelihood.

3.3   Anchoring and adjustment

The third major heuristic considered in this section is the anchoring effect, sometimes known as the anchoring and adjustment heuristic. Once again, before reading on, try Activity 11.6.

Activity 11.6   Mortality trivial pursuit

This activity takes the form of some (slightly morbid) trivia questions. If you do not know the answers, give your best guess rather than looking them up.

1   Was the composer Johann Sebastian Bach 100 years old when he died? (Answer yes or no.)

2   How old was Johann Sebastian Bach when he died? (Give a number in years.)

3   Was the author Lewis Carroll 30 years old when he died? (Answer yes or no.)

4   How old was Lewis Carroll when he died? (Give a number in years.)

(a)   (b)

Figure 11.4   How old were (a) J. S. Bach and (b) Lewis Carroll when they died?

Comment

The answer to questions 1 and 3 is 'no', Bach did not die aged 100 and Carroll did not die aged 30. The interesting part is what answers you gave to questions 2 and 4. Did you give a higher estimate for Bach's age when he died than Carroll's? As it happens, they both died aged 65 – but the question about Bach dying aged 100 probably made you think of a high number, and the question about Carroll dying at 30 probably made you think of a low number. The first question about each person gave you an anchor for your answer to the second question.

Anchoring
The tendency to give an estimate that is close to a previously suggested value, even if that value is irrelevant.

Activity 11.6 illustrates the **anchoring** effect, first identified by Tversky and Kahneman (1974). In this effect, when someone is asked to estimate a quantity, date, probability or anything else that can be expressed numerically, presenting them with some other number before they do so will influence the estimate they give. Their estimates will tend to be closer to the anchor than estimates given by someone who was not presented with an anchoring value first. When an anchor provides no useful information (as was the case in Activity 11.6), being influenced by the anchor is a source of error.

Anchoring and *adjustment* occurs when someone arrives at a numerical estimation by making an adjustment away from an initial value that has been arrived at. Sometimes the anchor may be fairly logical and potentially useful, such as using the roughly nine-month human gestation period as a starting point to estimate the gestation period of an elephant (e.g. thinking 'elephants are bigger than humans, so their gestation period is probably more than nine months'; see Epley and Gilovich, 2001). Adjustments, however, are typically not sufficient, so that the final value is often unreasonably close to the original anchor. Furthermore, even random numbers can form an anchor. In one of the original demonstrations of anchoring and adjustment, Tversky and Kahneman (1974) spun a wheel of fortune, similar to a roulette wheel, in participants' presence and asked them to assess whether some quantity (e.g. the percentage of African countries in the United Nations) was more or less than the number given by the wheel of fortune. Having answered a comparative question, the participants then estimated the exact percentage, in a similar way to the task you did in Activity 11.6 with Bach's and Carroll's ages of death. Tversky and Kahneman reported that estimates tended to be close to the anchor provided by the wheel of fortune. For example, when the anchor was 10 the median estimate was 25, and when the anchor was 65 the median estimate was 45.

Subsequent research has identified anchoring effects in a wide range of domains, including many everyday contexts, indicating that it may be an even more general cognitive process than the representativeness or availability heuristics (Keren and Teigen, 2004). In one of the most worrying examples, several researchers have found evidence for anchoring effects in legal contexts. Section 3.4 outlines some of these studies.

3.4 Anchoring effects in the courtroom

In a study by Birte Englich and Thomas Mussweiler (2001), 19 professional German criminal court judges were asked to read materials relating to a fictional trial. The materials themselves had been developed by the researchers in close collaboration with another group of experienced trial judges to be as realistic as possible. After reading the information about the case, half the judges were told that the prosecutor had asked for the defendant to be given a jail sentence of 34 months and the other half were told that the prosecutor had asked for the defendant to be given a jail sentence of two months. The judges were asked to indicate whether the sentence asked for by the prosecutor was too high, too low, or about right, and then to specify what they thought the appropriate term would be. Judges who were told that the prosecutor had asked for a sentence of 34 months suggested, on average, that an appropriate sentence would be 28.7 months. Those who were told that the prosecutor had asked for a sentence of two months suggested an average sentence of 18.78 months: the anchoring effect had made a difference of around ten months' imprisonment in this case.

Anchoring can have a substantial effect on sentencing decisions in criminal cases

Similar results have been found for personal injury lawsuits. Gretchen Chapman and Brian Bornstein (1996) asked mock jurors (research participants acting as jurors for the purpose of the study, rather than people serving on a real trial) to consider a case in which a woman claimed that her birth control pill had caused ovarian cancer. Depending on the anchoring condition that participants had been assigned to, the plaintiff's claim was for $100, $20,000, $5 million, or $1 billion. Among those participants who decided that the defendant was liable, the monetary award increased across these anchoring conditions. The practical implication, of course, is that claimants should ask for larger awards rather than more conservative ones, as that will provide the legal decision makers with a higher anchor.

You may be thinking that the use of anchors in the studies above is reasonable. After all, in real courtrooms prosecutors have information about the sentences typically given in similar cases, and plaintiffs will have assessed their losses before deciding on their demands. Perhaps, then, the professional judges and mock jurors in these studies were justified in using the prosecutor's or plaintiff's demands as a starting point from which to anchor and adjust. Perhaps. However, research by Englich and colleagues (2006) suggests that these anchoring effects were not based on calculated logic. In a series of studies, using the same fictitious but realistic case scenario as Englich and Mussweiler (2001), and again using legal professionals, Englich and colleagues made the anchors increasingly – and increasingly obviously – irrelevant. In the first study the anchors were presented in the form of a question from a (hypothetical) journalist, who asked: 'Do you think the sentence for the defendant in this case will be higher or lower than [one or three] years?' Participants who had been presented with the 'one year' anchor gave an average sentence of 25.43 months, while participants who had been presented with the 'three years' anchor gave an average sentence of 33.38 months.

The potential for the media, even unintentionally, to influence sentencing decisions is worrying enough. However, two follow-up studies are even more worrying. In one of these the judges were told that the suggested sentence had been randomly determined, and yet a higher suggested sentence (i.e. anchor) increased the sentence that they said they themselves would give. In the final study the judges randomly determined the suggested sentence themselves by rolling a pair of dice. Unbeknown to the judges, the dice were loaded so that half of them 'randomly' rolled a low sentence and half a high sentence. Even knowing that the anchor had been determined by a dice roll, judges gave a longer sentence in the high anchor condition compared with the low anchor condition (and a no anchor control condition).

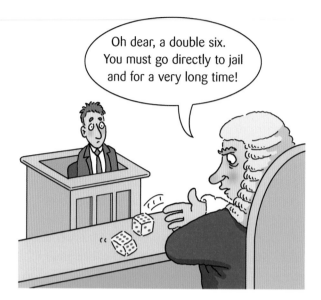

Even random anchors can affect important real-world decisions such as sentences for criminal offences

This section of the chapter has shown how three common heuristics, representativeness, availability and anchoring, can have a powerful effect on people's judgements and lead to errors in a variety of contexts, including ones involving very serious real-world consequences. Section 4 considers one of the other most common biases: the hindsight bias.

4   Hindsight bias

Hindsight bias is known colloquially as being wise after the event, sometimes expressed in the phrase 'Hindsight is always 20/20'. Outcomes that are known to have occurred seem to have always been more likely, perhaps even inevitable, when judged in retrospect, whereas outcomes that did not occur seem to have always been less likely when judged in retrospect – almost as if they *could never* have occurred. For example, thinking about it now, long after the events, it may seem inevitable that the Allies were always going to win the Second World War or that the Americans were never going to win the Vietnam war. However, at the time the events were occurring neither of those outcomes would have seemed inevitable to most people.

Hindsight bias can also affect people's retrospective judgement of what they thought would happen before the events. In the first study of the phenomenon, Baruch Fischhoff and Ruth Beyth (published in 1975, but the study began a few years earlier) asked Israeli students to make predictions about US President Richard Nixon's historically momentous visits to China and the Soviet Union in 1972. The students rated the likelihood of various events that might occur during this tour, such as the USA establishing a diplomatic mission in Peking or setting up a joint space programme with the Soviet Union. Following the tour, students were asked to recall the predictions they had made earlier. When doing so, most of them inflated their estimated probabilities for events that had occurred and reduced them for events that had not occurred. Hindsight bias made them think that they had been more accurate in their predictions than they really had been. This effect was particularly strong when the gap between the initial prediction and the recall task was three months or more.

Hindsight bias has also been observed in people's recall of events in their own lives (Fischhoff et al., 2012). Just after the 9/11 terror attacks in 2001, a sample of the US public was asked to estimate the likelihood of their being hurt in the coming year or of engaging in various behaviours to reduce the risk of coming to harm. A year later they were asked to indicate whether they had actually been hurt or engaged in those harm-reducing behaviours, and to recall or estimate their original predictions. The people who had experienced those outcomes (e.g. travelling less, screening mail) tended to misremember their original likelihood estimates as being higher than they were.

Hindsight bias
The tendency to overestimate the prior probability of events that happened, underestimate the prior probability of events that did not happen, and misremember one's own predictions about those events.

However, the majority of participants had not experienced those outcomes and they tended to misremember their original estimates as being lower than they were. Again, people generally misremembered themselves as being more right than they actually were.

Hindsight bias has troubling implications for the way people as individuals, and society as a whole, respond to negative events in everyday life. Consider a convicted offender who commits a serious offence while on parole, a doctor who fails to diagnose a malignant tumour that kills a patient, or a vehicle manufacturer that fails to identify a deadly design flaw. Each situation leads to a person or an organisation being subject to close scrutiny, often facing suspicion that they had the knowledge and the means to prevent the fatal outcome occurring. If investigators fall prey to the hindsight bias, they will judge the event that occurred to be more probable – and therefore predictable – than it really was. For example, they may feel that the parole board should have been able to predict that a particular offender was likely to be a high risk. Blame, and even legal liability, may therefore be assigned accordingly. Similarly, the people involved may feel that they 'should have seen it coming' and blame themselves, when in fact the event was unforeseeable.

4.1   Causes of hindsight bias

There is clear evidence that hindsight bias is a powerful effect, but how much do psychologists know about what causes it? Neal Roese and Kathleen Vohs (2012) reviewed three processes that may contribute to hindsight bias. One, very simple, factor is that people may fail to accurately recall their earlier response to a question and therefore rely more on what they now know to be the correct answer. A second factor is based on the reconstructive nature of human memory. New information activates existing related information in memory, makes it more accessible, and is incorporated with it. These changes to memory may influence the way people regard the predictability of events. For example, in one study of hindsight bias and reconstructive memory, Linda Carli (1999) presented participants with information about a hypothetical date between a man and a woman. One group of participants were told that this encounter had later led to rape. A week later, this group were more likely to misrecall the details of the earlier date in ways that were consistent with rape stereotypes. Carli suggests that hindsight bias may be one factor underpinning victim blaming, as victims may be expected to have been able to predict (and therefore prevent) what was going to happen, even though before the event occurred it was not actually predictable (see also Carli and Leonard, 1989).

A third factor that may contribute to hindsight bias is the human propensity for sense-making, which you learned about in Chapter 10. This goes beyond mere memory updating and involves 'explanation that achieves meaning in terms of the outcome's broader consequences for the sensemaker' (Roese and Vohs, 2012, p. 414). Mark Pezzo (2003) suggests that sense-making activity occurs in response to *initial surprise* at an outcome. If the sense-making process is successful then *resultant surprise* is reduced and hindsight bias occurs: it makes sense after the event, so it seems that it would have been predictable before the event. However, if the sense-making process fails then a high level of resultant surprise ensues and is associated with 'reverse hindsight bias', whereby the true outcome is seen as less predictable (see, for example, Ofir and Mazursky, 1997). In colloquial terms, an event causing high resultant surprise will give the observer the feeling that 'I could never have seen that coming'.

The ideas about heuristics and biases of the type discussed in Sections 3 and 4 of this chapter have been highly influential since Kahneman, Tversky and colleagues began developing them in the 1970s. However, they are not the only mental short cuts that psychologists have proposed. Section 5 briefly outlines another approach to heuristics, based largely on the work of Gerd Gigerenzer and colleagues.

5   Alternative ideas about heuristics

Although they have been, and continue to be, highly influential, the concepts of heuristics and biases developed by Kahneman and colleagues have occasionally been criticised by other psychologists. For example, the representativeness and availability heuristics have been criticised by Gigerenzer as being largely descriptions of the phenomena they try to explain, rather than really being explanations. Gigerenzer himself has proposed a different set of heuristics, known as **fast and frugal heuristics** because they operate quickly and on the basis of very little information (e.g. Gigerenzer et al., 1991; Gigerenzer and Goldstein, 1996).

Fast and frugal heuristics
Cognitive short cuts based on using a small amount of known information to make a judgement about something unknown.

While Kahneman and colleagues' heuristics are also 'fast' and 'frugal', Gigerenzer's heuristics are based on the idea that people are sensitive to statistical regularities in their environments, and can exploit their knowledge of these regularities in order to make fairly accurate judgements based on minimal information. For example, thinking back to Activity 11.6, if you have an idea that the life expectancy of the average man is around 70 years then you might estimate that J. S. Bach and Lewis Carroll died in their late sixties or early seventies. You have one piece of information about a statistical regularity (average life expectancy) and can use that to make a judgement about something unknown (albeit a judgement that, in Activity 11.6, was probably affected by the anchors you were given). In this example, setting aside the influence of the anchors, the fast and frugal heuristic would have been reasonably close to the correct answer of 65 years of age for both Bach and Carroll.

5.1   Fast and frugal heuristics

One of Gigerenzer's simplest examples to demonstrate the fast and frugal approach is the city size task, which you can try in Activity 11.7.

Activity 11.7   The city size task

Without looking up any information about them, in each of the following pairs of towns and cities which one has the larger population?

1   Manchester, UK, or Colchester, UK?

2   Auckland, New Zealand, or Wellington, New Zealand?

3   Thikri, India, or Milton Keynes, UK?

Comment

The answer to question 1 is Manchester, with a population at the time of writing of just over half a million in the city itself, more than four times the population of Colchester at around 120,000, and over 2.5 million in the Greater Manchester area. The answer to question 2 is Auckland, with a population of just under 1.5 million compared with Wellington's approximately 400,000. The answer to question 3 is Milton Keynes, with a population of nearly 230,000 to Thikri's 20,000.

How did you do? The explanations below of how fast and frugal heuristics operate in this sort of judgement may explain where you went right or wrong.

Gigerenzer and Daniel Goldstein (1996) suggest that the first step in reaching a judgement about the population question is often to apply the recognition principle: if you recognised one name in a pair but not the other then you might have assumed that the one you recognised has the larger population. Of course, if you recognised neither name in a pair then this would not help. In addition, if you recognised both names in a pair then your judgement could not be based on this particular principle. Instead, you would have to take other factors into account. Gigerenzer explains that towns and cities have various attributes, or cues, that are associated with their population size. For example, larger cities are more likely to have a football team in their country's top football league, have a station on an inter-city rail line, have an airport, be the national capital, and be home to a university. In Germany, which Gigerenzer uses in several of his studies, there are other cues too, such as whether the city was once an exposition site, whether the city is a state capital, whether the city was in the former East Germany, whether the licence plate abbreviation is one letter long, and whether the city is in the industrial belt.

Gigerenzer and colleagues suggest that people often solve problems like those in Activity 11.7 by making judgements based on a **take the best heuristic**. This assumes that the various cues, such as being a capital, having a top-flight football team, and so on, are arranged in memory according to the strength of their association with city population size. When judging which of two cities has the larger

Take the best heuristic
This involves making a judgement based on the best available piece of known information that might be a clue to the unknown information.

population, people begin by retrieving the cue that has the strongest association with population size. In many countries the national capital will have the strongest association (or cue validity, as this is called). For example, London (meaning Greater London, not the City of London) is the capital of the United Kingdom and also the largest city, so a judgement in which you compared any other UK city with London could easily be made using the capital cue. Nonetheless, there are a few countries where the capital city is not the most populous; for instance, Wellington is the capital of New Zealand but Auckland is much larger (Figure 11.5). Using the capital cue for question 2 in Activity 11.7 would have caused you to make an error.

(a)   (b)

Figure 11.5   Wellington is the capital city of New Zealand (the NZ Parliament building is shown in (a)) but more people live in Auckland (b)

However, the capital city cue is limited to comparisons where one (and only one) of the two cities under consideration is a capital. For most pairs of cities a different cue would need to be consulted. For example, neither Manchester nor Colchester is currently a capital city. However, if you know that Manchester has a football team in the Premier League (actually two, at the time of writing at least), but that Colchester does not (or you do not know), then you probably judged that Manchester has the larger population. You would have used just a single cue in order to reach a judgement, in this case a correct judgement.

Sometimes cues can compete with each other, as in question 3 in Activity 11.7. You may or may not have heard of Thikri, India, but you have almost certainly heard of Milton Keynes, home of The Open University. If so, by using familiarity as a cue you would have got the answer right. If, however, you used a different cue, for example knowing that India is the second most populous country on Earth (with over 1.25 billion people) then you might have assumed that an Indian city or town – even one you had not heard of before – might be quite large. Depending on whether you felt familiarity or country knowledge was your 'better' cue, you would have been either right or wrong.

Gigerenzer and Goldstein (1996) tested the performance of their take the best heuristic against various other approaches that rely on more information, by implementing them as strategies in a computer simulation. Using a computer simulation allowed Gigerenzer and Goldstein to assess the take the best approach in its (theoretically) ideal form, without it being affected by human error. Each strategy was applied to a large number of city population tasks, including a powerful statistical technique known as regression analysis, which uses all available information that can be represented statistically to reach a judgement. In their simulation, Gigerenzer and Goldstein found that take the best was just as accurate as regression analysis, despite using much less information to reach a response.

Demonstrating the effectiveness of a heuristic in a computer simulation is one thing, but it does not necessarily mean that people are actually using that heuristic in reality. A number of experimental studies have found evidence that people do sometimes use take the best, but have questioned how frequently or commonly they do so. For example, Ben Newell and colleagues (2003) found that only about a third of participants consistently behaved in accordance with take the best, and Arndt Bröder (2003) found evidence that take the best might not be a default strategy, but rather requires people to make a deliberate decision to implement it. Furthermore, looking specifically at the recognition heuristic, Tobias Richter and Pamela Späth (2006) and Newell and Duane Fernandez (2006) reported that participants appeared to use other forms of knowledge in conjunction with recognition, leading Newell (2011) to conclude that the very simplicity of the recognition heuristic is also 'its undoing' (p. 411).

6   Evaluating the role of heuristics in judgement

The heuristics and biases described by Kahneman, Tversky and others (e.g. Kahneman et al., 1982) are just a few of those that have been proposed in the literature on judgement, although they are widely regarded as classic – and still important – examples. However, they have not been without criticism. For example, Lola Lopes (1991) observes that Tversky and Kahneman's influential 1974 review paper in *Science* did not provide a single demonstration of heuristics leading to accurate performance, despite claiming that such heuristics are 'quite useful' (p. 1124), 'valuable estimation procedures' (p. 1128), and 'highly economical and usually effective' (p. 1131). This appears to be due to the selection of tasks that the researchers themselves intuitively expected would elicit erroneous responses. Indeed, an examination of some of the language used in this paper and by other researchers indicates a 'rhetoric of irrationality' (the title of Lopes' own paper). Gigerenzer and colleagues' fast and frugal heuristics, in contrast, have been empirically shown to be useful in making accurate judgements, not just to lead to errors.

The development of the concepts of heuristics and biases also appears to have fostered a wider focus on people's highly imperfect judgements. Before 1970, psychologists generally regarded people as quite good decision makers, and the most widely cited paper on the topic was titled 'Man as an intuitive statistician' (Peterson and Beach, 1967). However, a review of research published between 1972 and 1981 found that reports of poor performance on cognitive tasks were cited on average 27.8 times, whereas reports of good performance were cited on average just 4.7 times (Christensen-Szalanski and Beach, 1984). Clearly, there had been a shift in mood.

The heuristics and biases approach was criticised by Gigerenzer and various colleagues in a series of articles in the late 1980s and throughout the 1990s (e.g. Gigerenzer, 1991, 1993, 1994; Gigerenzer et al., 1988). Gigerenzer argues that the representativeness and availability heuristics are only descriptions of phenomena, rather than explanations, and that psychologists need to develop process models of judgement that explain *how* judgements are actually made (which he considers his own heuristics to be). Furthermore, Gigerenzer disputes the applicability of probability theory to the single-event scenarios favoured by Kahneman and Tversky – such as the 'Toyah' example in Activity 11.2 – and claims that cognitive errors may disappear when such classic problems are reframed in terms of frequencies rather than single events (e.g. Gigerenzer, 1994). An example would be asking participants to judge what proportion of people are like 'Toyah', rather than just what 'Toyah' is like.

Various responses to these arguments have been made (e.g. Kahneman and Tversky, 1996; Vranas, 2000), including a point that Tversky and Kahneman themselves (e.g. 1983) reported, namely that frequency versions of probability problems may reduce cognitive errors. However, frequency versions do not actually *eliminate* the errors. What remains clear is that human judgements are based on processes that try to make a large amount of 'sense' out of a small amount of information, and that the results are not always accurate and unproblematic.

7   Summary

In this chapter you have learned that human intuition and judgement can be deeply flawed, particularly when people are faced with random patterns and probabilities. Using the examples of Second World War German bomb hits in London, the iPad shuffle, coin tosses and lottery gambling, you learned that people can judge rare events to be common and common events to be rare, and that people will try to make sense of completely random events. You then explored some of the cognitive processes that psychologists have identified as posing particular problems, focusing on the representativeness, availability and anchoring heuristics. In addition to making poor judgements (including legal judgments in courts) because of heuristics, you also learned that people often fall prey to the hindsight bias, which can make them think that their previous judgements and predictions were more accurate than they really were.

The focus of much of the research and theory covered in this chapter has been fairly negative – it is, after all, a chapter on *errors* in making sense of the world. However, in contrast to the largely negative influences of these heuristics and biases, the work of Gigerenzer and colleagues aims to show how (largely) accurate judgements can be produced by the use of fast and frugal heuristics. After all, humans have highly developed cognitive processes for making sense of the world, and, to have evolved, these must have been useful (i.e. right) a lot of the time, not just harmful (i.e. wrong). However, just how frugal people's judgements actually are, and how accurate, continues to be the subject of much research and debate.

References

BBC News (2005) 'Number 53 brings relief to Italy', 15 February [Online]. Available at http://news.bbc.co.uk/1/hi/world/europe/4256595.stm (Accessed 20 November 2014).

Bomb Sight (n.d.) *Bomb Sight* [Online]. Available at www.bombsight.org, version 1.0 (Accessed 18 November 2014).

Bröder, A. (2003) 'Decision making with the "adaptive toolbox": influence of environmental structure, intelligence, and working memory load', *Journal of Experimental Psychology: Learning, Memory, and Cognition*, vol. 29, no. 4, pp. 611–25.

Carli, L. L. (1999) 'Cognitive reconstruction, hindsight, and reactions to victims and perpetrators', *Personality and Social Psychology Bulletin*, vol. 25, no. 8, pp. 966–79.

Carli, L. L. and Leonard, J. B. (1989) 'The effect of hindsight on victim derogation', *Journal of Social and Clinical Psychology*, vol. 8, pp. 331–43.

Chapman, G. B. and Bornstein, B. H. (1996) 'The more you ask for, the more you get: anchoring in personal injury verdicts', *Applied Cognitive Psychology*, vol. 10, pp. 519–40.

Christensen-Szalanski, J. J. J. and Beach, L. R. (1984) 'The citation bias: fad and fashion in the judgment and decision literature', *American Psychologist*, vol. 39, pp. 75–8.

Clarke, R. D. (1946) 'An application of the Poisson Distribution', *Journal of the Institute of Actuaries*, vol. 72, p. 481.

Clotfelter, C. T. and Cook, P. J. (1993) 'The gambler's fallacy in lottery play', *Management Science*, vol. 39, no. 12, pp. 1521–5.

Englich, B. and Mussweiler, T. (2001) 'Sentencing under uncertainty: anchoring effects in the courtroom', *Journal of Applied Social Psychology*, vol. 31, pp. 1535–51.

Englich, B., Mussweiler, T. and Strack, F. (2006) 'Playing dice with criminal sentences: the influence of irrelevant anchors on experts' judicial decision making', *Personality and Social Psychology Bulletin*, vol. 32, pp. 188–200.

Epley, N. and Gilovich, T. (2001) 'Putting adjustment back in the anchoring and adjustment heuristic: differential processing of self-generated and experimenter-provided anchors', *Psychological Science*, vol. 12, no. 5, pp. 391–6.

Feller, W. (1950) *An Introduction to Probability Theory and its Applications, Volume 1*, New York, Wiley.

Fischhoff, B. and Beyth, R. (1975) '"I knew it would happen": remembered probabilities of once-future things', *Organizational Behavior and Human Performance*, vol. 13, pp. 1–16.

Fischhoff, B., Gonzalez, R. M., Lerner, J. S. and Small, D. A. (2012) 'Evolving judgments of terror risks: foresight, hindsight, and emotion: a reanalysis', *Journal of Experimental Psychology: Applied*, vol. 18, no. 2, pp. e1–e16.

Gaissmaier, W. and Gigerenzer, G. (2012) '9/11, Act II: a fine-grained analysis of regional variations in traffic fatalities in the aftermath of the terrorist attacks', *Psychological Science*, vol. 23, no. 12, pp. 1449–54.

Gee, A. (2014) 'How odd is a cluster of plane crashes?', *BBC News Magazine*, 25 July [Online]. Available at http://www.bbc.co.uk/news/magazine-28481060 (Accessed 21 November 2014).

Gigerenzer, G. (1991) 'How to make cognitive illusions disappear: beyond "heuristics and biases"', *European Review of Social Psychology*, vol. 2, pp. 83–115.

Gigerenzer, G. (1993) 'The bounded rationality of probabilistic mental models', in Manktelow, K. I. and Over, D. E. (eds) *Rationality: Psychological and Philosophical Perspectives*, London, Routledge, pp. 284–313.

Gigerenzer, G. (1994) 'Why the distinction between single-event probabilities and frequencies is relevant for psychology and vice versa', in Wright, G. and Ayton, P. (eds) *Subjective Probability*, New York, Wiley, pp. 129–62.

Gigerenzer, G. (2006) 'Out of the frying pan into the fire: behavioral reactions to terrorist attacks', *Risk Analysis*, vol. 26, pp. 347–51.

Gigerenzer, G. and Goldstein, D. G. (1996) 'Reasoning the fast and frugal way: models of bounded rationality', *Psychological Review*, vol. 103, pp. 592–6.

Gigerenzer, G., Hell, W. and Blank, H. (1988) 'Presentation and content: the use of base rates as a continuous variable', *Journal of Experimental Psychology: Human Perception and Performance*, vol. 14, pp. 513–25.

Gigerenzer, G., Hoffrage, U. and Kleinbölting, H. (1991) 'Probabilistic mental models: a Brunswikian theory of confidence', *Psychological Review*, vol. 98, pp. 506–28.

Haigh, J. (2003) *Taking Chances: Winning with Probability*, 2nd edn, Oxford, Oxford University Press.

Kahneman, D., Slovic, P. and Tversky, A. (1982) *Judgment under Uncertainty: Heuristics and Biases*, Cambridge, Cambridge University Press.

Kahneman, D. and Tversky, A. (1972) 'Subjective probability: a judgment of representativeness', *Cognitive Psychology*, vol. 3, pp. 430–54.

Kahneman, D. and Tversky, A. (1973) 'On the psychology of prediction', *Psychological Review*, vol. 80, pp. 237–51.

Kahneman, D. and Tversky, A. (1996) 'On the reality of cognitive illusions', *Psychological Review*, vol. 103, no. 3, pp. 582–91.

Keren, G. and Teigen, K. H. (2004) 'Yet another look at the heuristics and biases approach', in Koehler, D. J. and Harvey, N. (eds) *Blackwell Handbook of Judgement and Decision Making*, Oxford, Blackwell, pp. 89–109.

Levy, S. (2005) 'Does your iPod play favorites?', *Newsweek*, 31 January [Online]. Available at www.newsweek.com/does-your-ipod-play-favorites-116739 (Accessed 23 November 2014).

Levy, S. (2006) *The Perfect Thing: How the iPod Shuffles Commerce, Culture, and Coolness*, New York, Simon & Schuster.

Lopes, L. L. (1991) 'The rhetoric of irrationality', *Theory and Psychology*, vol. 1, no. 1, pp. 65–82.

Newell, B. (2011) 'Recognising the recognition heuristic for what it is (and what it's not)', *Judgement and Decision Making*, vol. 6, no. 5, pp. 409–12.

Newell, B. R. and Fernandez, D. R. (2006) 'On the binary quality of recognition and the inconsequentiality of further knowledge: two critical tests of the recognition heuristic', *Journal of Behavioral Decision Making*, vol. 19, pp. 333–46.

Newell, B. R., Weston, N. J. and Shanks, D. R. (2003) 'Empirical tests of a fast-and-frugal heuristic: not everyone "takes-the-best"', *Organizational Behavior and Human Decision Processes*, vol. 91, pp. 82–96.

Ofir, C. and Mazursky, D. (1997) 'Does a surprising outcome reinforce or reverse the hindsight bias?', *Organizational Behavior and Organizational Decision Processes*, vol. 69, pp. 51–7.

Peterson, C. R. and Beach, L. R. (1967) 'Man as an intuitive statistician', *Psychological Bulletin*, vol. 68, pp. 29–46.

Pezzo, M. V. (2003) 'Surprise, defence, or making sense: what removes hindsight bias?', *Memory*, vol. 11, no. 4/5, pp. 421–41.

Richter, T. and Späth, P. (2006) 'Recognition is used as one cue among others in judgment and decision making', *Journal of Experimental Psychology: Learning, Memory, and Cognition*, vol. 31, no. 1, pp. 150–62.

Roese, N. J. and Vohs, K. D. (2012) 'Hindsight bias', *Perspectives on Psychological Science*, vol. 7, pp. 411–26.

Schwarz, N., Bless, H., Strack, F., Klumpp, G., Rittenauer-Schatka, H. and Simons, A. (1991) 'Ease of retrieval as information: another look at the availability heuristic', *Journal of Personality and Social Psychology*, vol. 45, pp. 513–23.

Terrell, D. (1994) 'A test of the gambler's fallacy: evidence from pari-mutuel games', *Journal of Risk and Uncertainty*, vol. 8, no. 3, pp. 309–17.

Tversky, A. and Kahneman, D. (1971) 'Belief in the law of small numbers', *Psychological Bulletin*, vol. 76, no. 2, pp. 105–10.

Tversky, A. and Kahneman, D. (1973) 'Availability: a heuristic for judging frequency and probability', *Cognitive Psychology*, vol. 5, pp. 207–32.

Tversky, A. and Kahneman, D. (1974) 'Judgment under uncertainty: heuristics and biases', *Science*, vol. 185, pp. 1124–30.

Tversky, A. and Kahneman, D. (1983) 'Extensional versus intuitive reasoning: the conjunction fallacy in probability judgement', *Psychological Review*, vol. 90, pp. 293–315.

Tversky, A. and Koehler, D. (1994) 'Support theory: a nonextensional representation of subjective probability', *Psychological Review*, vol. 101, pp. 547–67.

Vranas, P. B. M. (2000) 'Gigerenzer's normative critique of Kahneman and Tversky', *Cognition*, vol. 76, pp. 179–93.

Chapter 12
Conspiracy theories

Jovan Byford

Contents

1   Introduction

Many dramatic events in the world – deaths of public figures, terrorist attacks, natural disasters, plane crashes, political assassinations, military conflicts, meteorological anomalies and disease outbreaks – generate a certain amount of speculation about possible conspiracies behind them. Since the late 1990s the main medium for the transmission of conspiracy theories has been the internet, although outlandish claims of hidden agendas and secret plots receive surprisingly regular coverage on television news channels, in newspapers and magazines, on radio talk shows, and so on (Byford, 2011). Admittedly, most conspiracy theories tend to be short lived (who today remembers the conspiracy theories about the death of Michael Jackson in 2009, for example?) or of local, rather than global, consequence. Nevertheless, some – including those about the 9/11 World Trade Center attack, the assassination in 1963 of the American president John F. Kennedy, or supposed secret societies ruling the world's finances and politics – have become part of a more robust set of beliefs. These beliefs, as well as being widespread and persistent, have acquired symbolic significance and the capacity to mobilise sections of the public around the world (Heins, 2007).

Given the apparent popularity of conspiracy theories, it should come as no surprise that over the years they have attracted interest from psychologists. Conspiracy theories, as forms of explanation, pose important questions about the human mind and behaviour, some of which you have already encountered in previous chapters. How do people understand the world around them? How do they process information and interpret evidence? Why do some people respond to a dramatic event by attributing its causes to a conspiracy, and what might be the psychological dynamic behind this?

In this chapter you will learn about some of the research on the psychology of conspiracy theories. As you will discover, the central questions that have preoccupied psychologists interested in this topic are why some people are more susceptible to conspiracy theories than others, and what psychological variables differentiate believers from sceptics. Throughout this chapter you will engage critically with these questions, as well as exploring a different way of understanding the continuing appeal of conspiracy theories. This alternative approach focuses not so much on the psychological characteristics of the conspiracy theorist, but on the conspiracy theories themselves and the role they play, as social explanations, in the everyday practice of making sense of the world.

After reading this chapter you should be able to:

- explain what is meant by the term 'conspiracy theory'

- outline some studies and methods that researchers have used to identify possible psychological characteristics of believers in conspiracy theories

- discuss some of the limitations of questionnaire-based studies of conspiracy theories

- summarise the differences between studies that focus on the personality characteristics and disposition of conspiracy theorists and those that explore the conspiracy theories and their social and psychological functions.

2   What exactly are 'conspiracy theories'?

Before you begin to explore the psychology of conspiracy theories, first take a moment to think about what exactly is meant by the term 'conspiracy theory'. At first thought, the meaning of the term might seem obvious, as the word 'conspiracy' is well established in the English language. Derived from the Latin *conspirare*, meaning 'to breathe together', it signifies the joining together of two or more individuals and their acting in collusion to achieve a desired outcome (and, when used in law, a 'conspiracy' involves illegality). In the broadest sense, therefore, a conspiracy theory would be an explanation that attributes the causes of an event to a conspiracy or a plot (Basham, 2003).

However, while any explanation that suggests collusion between individuals is, in a literal sense, a 'conspiracy theory', in everyday language the term tends to be used to signify a much narrower class of phenomena. Activity 12.1 illustrates the distinction.

Activity 12.1   Identifying conspiracy theories

Consider the following statements, each of which describes a theory about a conspiracy. Which, if any, of these would you describe as a 'conspiracy theory', and why?

1   Over a number of years in the late twentieth and early twenty-first centuries, a group of financial traders in the City of London colluded in the fixing of the inter-bank lending rate (Libor).

2   Princess Diana was assassinated by rogue elements within the British establishment, and the murder was made to look like a car accident.

3   Security services in the USA and Europe conspired to secretly monitor the telephone and internet communications of their citizens.

4   No human has yet walked on the moon. The footage of the Apollo moon landings, seen by millions around the world, was faked using Hollywood-style effects.

5   The claim about the link between HIV and AIDS is a lie promoted by big pharmaceutical companies for reasons of financial self-interest.

6   Members of the al-Qaeda terrorist group conspired to carry out a series of deadly attacks on US soil on 11 September 2001.

Comment

Did you notice the difference between examples 1, 3 and 6 on the one hand, and examples 2, 4 and 5 on the other? Generally, the former tend not to be referred to as 'conspiracy theories', even though they describe a conspiracy. This is for the simple reason that they did, in fact, occur and so are widely accepted by most people as true. Financial traders have been caught and fined for secretly fixing lending rates; security services have colluded in the monitoring of communications; and the terrorists who carried out the 9/11 attacks did conspire to do so. In contrast, claims about Princess Diana being assassinated, about the link between HIV and AIDS, and about the faking of the moon landings – all of which have attracted the label 'conspiracy theory' – go against what are deemed to be the authoritative and substantiated versions of these events. Thus, in everyday language, the term 'conspiracy theory' tends to be reserved for those allegations of conspiracy that go against conventional wisdom, available evidence or scientific knowledge. Conspiracy theories in this sense also tend to view deliberate, long-standing and well-concealed plots, schemes or groups as the motive force behind events in the world.

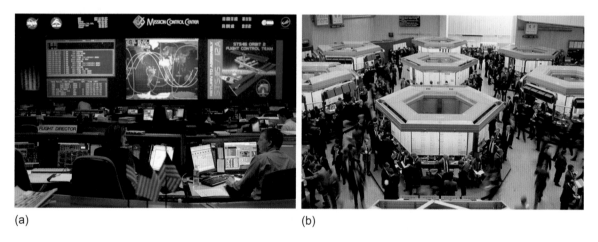

(a)   (b)

Figure 12.1   Which of these was the site of a conspiracy? (a) NASA Mission Control; (b) the trading floor of the London Stock Exchange

An important characteristic of the term 'conspiracy theory', which stems from this definition, is that it is not a neutral label used merely to describe a certain type of explanation. It is an evaluative term with significant pejorative connotations. To allude to an account as a 'conspiracy theory' implies that it is untrue, and insinuates that it is based on insufficient evidence, faulty reasoning, poor judgement, irrationality or prejudice (Coady, 2006). Michael Barkun (2006) referred to conspiracy theories as a form of 'stigmatised knowledge', alongside astrology and belief in the paranormal or in visitations by extraterrestrial life, in the sense that they consist of assumptions about the world which, while reasonably common, are nevertheless regarded as unwarranted, and are often ridiculed, by the mainstream of society.

The negative connotations carried by the label 'conspiracy theory' are important with respect to the interest that psychologists have shown in this phenomenon. In some of the classic literature on conspiracy theories, written mainly by non-psychologists, there has been a tendency to account for people's susceptibility to outlandish and often bizarre conspiracy claims by resorting to psychological vocabulary, and by questioning the reasoning ability, or even the sanity, of believers (e.g. Cohn, 1967; Hofstadter, 1967). Although psychologists who have studied conspiracy theories have, on the whole, taken a more measured approach, they have nevertheless accepted the view that there are important psychological differences between believers in conspiracy theories and non-believers, and have sought to identify what these differences are.

2.1   Why study conspiracy theories?

Over the years, conspiracy theories have attracted considerable interest from researchers working in a variety of disciplines, mainly in the social sciences. What has motivated them to explore conspiracy theories has not been just the desire to understand why people sometimes believe bizarre and unlikely things that go against the available evidence. It has also been the realisation that conspiracy theories have negative, sometimes tragic, social and political consequences.

Consider the following example. Since the 1980s the 'AIDS denialist movement' has questioned the well-established link between HIV and AIDS, attributing public concern about the spread of AIDS to a vast conspiracy involving the pharmaceutical industry and government agencies. AIDS denialists have also claimed that antiretroviral drugs used to treat HIV are more damaging than the virus itself, and therefore that patients should refuse them (Kalichman, 2009, reviews such claims in detail). In the early 2000s, the influence that denialists exercised over the then South African president Thabo Mbeki and his government caused substantial delays to the administration of medicines used in the treatment of HIV in South Africa. This contributed to the death of as many as 330,000 HIV patients (Nattrass, 2008), all because of belief in a conspiracy theory.

Also, conspiracy theories have an important political dimension. Throughout the world, stories of conspiracy feature prominently in the propaganda of oppressive regimes and are a staple ingredient of extremist politics. Authoritarian leaders from Iran to Venezuela, Belarus to Zimbabwe, have used the motif of international conspiracy as a means of reinforcing their grip on power, and as a source of excuses for economic problems and their country's marginal status in world affairs. Meanwhile, in Western democracies such as the UK, the USA and much of Europe, conspiracy theories are often held by people at the extremes of the political spectrum, both on the far left and the far right, including among radical Islamist groups. Among the latter, the myth of a Jewish or 'Zionist' conspiracy (e.g. to control the world's economy, political institutions or media) is particularly widespread, and it continues to colour the interpretation both of current events in the Middle East and of global politics (Byford, 2011).

Of course, it is not being suggested here that all conspiracy theories are necessarily dangerous. Some, such as the one about the moon landings, could be said to be quite innocuous and politically neutral. It is similarly not being suggested that everyone who believes a conspiracy theory is an extremist, or should be regarded as ideologically suspect. Having said that, the history of conspiracy theories has convincingly demonstrated what Richard Hofstadter (1964, p. 77) referred to as their 'greater affinity for bad causes than good'. For that reason, the social, cultural, political and psychological dynamics behind conspiracy theories and their continuing appeal represent important avenues for research.

3   The psychological profile of a conspiracy theorist

A common source of evidence about the popularity of conspiracy theories in the world today is opinion polls, which suggest that a substantial proportion of the population, both in the Western world and elsewhere, readily admit to believing in some form of conspiracy theory (Byford, 2011). For example, opinion polls have shown that between 20 and 40 per cent of the population in Europe and the USA believe in a conspiracy theory about the causes of the 9/11 attacks other than the actual conspiring of the hijackers (Knight, 2008; Sunstein and Vermeule, 2009). Similar results have been obtained in relation to other events, such as the assassination of US president John F. Kennedy, the death of Princess Diana, and the Apollo moon landings (Aaronovitch, 2009). In a survey conducted in the early 2000s in the USA, more than half the respondents agreed with the statement 'the US government knows more about UFOs than they are telling us', a finding that may be linked to the popularity, at the time, of the cult television series *The X-Files* (Barkun, 2006).

Is the truth out there?

What these findings clearly indicate is that some people, sometimes a sizeable percentage of the population, appear to believe in conspiracy theories that are not supported (and are often directly refuted) by the available evidence. Could these people be more susceptible to conspiracy theorising than others? This question has led psychologists to search for possible psychological factors that distinguish believers in conspiracy theories from non-believers. Marina Abalakina-Paap and colleagues (1999, p. 646) captured the essence of this strand of research when they wrote that 'history may well be a conspiracy, but apparently only certain types of people endorse this view'. The goal has been, therefore, to uncover who these 'certain types' are, and to create a 'profiling model of conspiracist individuals' (Swami et al., 2010, p. 751).

3.1   Individual differences in conspiracy beliefs

The classic stereotype of the conspiracy theorist would probably resemble Mel Gibson's character, Jerry Fletcher, in the 1997 film *Conspiracy Theory*: someone who is eccentric, obsessive and suspicious to the point of paranoia (although – spoiler alert – in the film some of Jerry's suspicions turn out to be justified). The film's characterisation is, of course, a Hollywood creation, but psychologists have studied whether there are particular personality characteristics that are typical of conspiracy theorists. For example, one variable that features prominently in the literature is authoritarianism. In their early work on the **authoritarian personality**, Theodor Adorno and colleagues (1950) postulated a link between the kind of deference to authority found in people with an authoritarian personality and belief in conspiracy theories, suggesting that authoritarian individuals are more likely to believe in conspiracy claims.

Authoritarian personality
A kind of personality typified by obedience to authority, strict adherence to rules, and hostility to anyone different from oneself.

Some psychologists have set out to test this proposed link empirically and explore whether differences in authoritarianism might account for differences in susceptibility to conspiracy theories (e.g. McHoskey, 1995; Abalakina-Paap et al., 1999; Swami et al., 2010). Psychologists have also studied whether other, more general, personality variables might also account for individual differences in conspiracy beliefs. For example, Viren Swami and colleagues (2010) and Robert Brotherton and colleagues (2013) looked at whether scores on tests of the five-factor model of personality (e.g. Costa and McRae, 1992), which conceptualises personality in terms of five broad factors named openness, conscientiousness, extraversion, agreeableness and neuroticism, were correlated with the extent of people's beliefs in conspiracy theories. Box 12.1 outlines this model of personality.

Box 12.1   Paul Costa and Robert McRae's five-factor model of personality

Costa and McRae (1992) identified five aspects of personality that they argue provide an overall description of a person's character and how they interact with the world. These five factors can be briefly described as:

openness: how open to experiences and ideas, especially new ones, a person tends to be

conscientiousness: the extent to which a person is self-disciplined, ordered and strives to honour their commitments

extraversion: how socially outgoing a person is and the extent to which they seek excitement

agreeableness: how kind, modest, compliant and trusting a person tends to be

neuroticism: how anxious, angry, depressed or impulsive a person tends to be.

There are individual differences between people on these five aspects of personality (e.g. some people are more conscientious than others), but people are assumed to be fairly consistent over time (e.g. someone who is very conscientious now will probably still be very conscientious in the future). An individual's personality will also be reflected in their behaviour: for instance, someone high in conscientiousness would make greater efforts to be on time for appointments than someone low in conscientiousness.

The personality factors identified in the five-factor model are sometimes referred to as the 'big five', and you may find this term used for them in some of the literature. However, this is not strictly accurate, and can cause confusion, as there is a different model of personality with that name (proposed by Goldberg, 1993).

How far have psychologists got in the quest for the 'psychological profile' of the conspiracy theorist? The simple answer to this question is, at the time of writing, not very far. Although some individual studies have reported statistically significant correlations between conspiracy beliefs and other psychological variables, overall the results have been somewhat mixed, allowing only tentative conclusions. For example, some studies that have looked at the link between conspiracy theories and the authoritarian personality have found a positive correlation, indicating that, just as Adorno and colleagues (1950) suggested, authoritarian individuals tend to be more likely to believe in conspiracy theories (Abalakina-Paap et al., 1999; Grzesiak-Feldman and Irzycka, 2009). However, other studies have found no correlation between the two variables (McHoskey, 1995), while one recent study found that people who are distinctly *non*-authoritarian are also susceptible to conspiracy theories (Swami et al., 2010).

Studies exploring the general personality traits of conspiracists have proven equally inconclusive. Swami and colleagues (2010), looking specifically at beliefs in conspiracy theories about the 9/11 attacks, found that only one personality trait was related to conspiracist belief: participants who scored low on agreeableness were marginally more likely to believe these theories than those scoring high on agreeableness. The authors attributed this finding to the fact that suspicion of others (typical of conspiracy theories) is one of the features of people who score low on agreeableness. However, this finding has not been replicated in subsequent studies, leading Brotherton and colleagues (2013, p. 11) to conclude that the influence of personality on conspiracy beliefs, if any, is 'small and somewhat unstable'.

Other researchers have explored the role of demographic factors. So far these studies appear to agree that educational level, gender and age are not useful factors in determining whether or not someone will believe in conspiracy theories, but a number of researchers have reported that members of minority ethnic groups tend to be more prone to conspiracy theorising than members of majority ethnic groups (Abalakina-Paap et al., 1999; Crocker et al., 1999). However, there is still much disagreement in the literature about the nature and extent of this relationship and why it might occur. For example, the apparent susceptibility to conspiracy theorising does not apply to all minority groups equally, and some conspiracy theories are specific to particular segments of the population. For example, in the USA, AIDS-related conspiracy theories are more common among members of African American communities than among other minority groups. This suggests that factors to do with the specific experiences of African Americans (including a long history of discrimination in the US health system) might be at play, rather than their minority status per se (Bird and Bogart, 2005). Also, it is unclear to what extent the relevance of minority status might reflect the fact that a sense of powerlessness and disenfranchisement – which is common among believers in conspiracy theories – tends to be more prevalent among some minority groups, especially those that have been the target of discrimination (Abalakina-Paap et al., 1999).

Taken together, these findings suggest that researchers are still far from identifying a specific set of psychological or sociocultural factors that differentiate believers in conspiracy theories from non-believers. In fact, the only consistent and robust findings yielded so far have been that those who believe in conspiracy theories tend to be disenchanted with political authority and harbour a 'feeling of alienation and disaffection from the system' (Goertzel, 1994, p. 739; see also Abalakina-Paap et al., 1999). One could argue, however, that this is a fairly obvious finding: suspicion of authority and disenchantment with 'the system' are a large part of what conspiracy theories are all about!

3.2 Conspiracy theories and faulty reasoning

As you read in Section 2, critics of conspiracy theories often portray such beliefs as the outcome of faulty reasoning or a psychological deficit which leads people to misunderstand or misinterpret the causes of world events. This has led some psychologists to investigate whether susceptibility to conspiracy theorising might stem not from personality factors, or things like authoritarianism or minority status, but from some systematic bias in reasoning that leads some people to endorse conspiracist explanations.

One avenue pursued by researchers has been to explore the role of heuristics in conspiracy beliefs. You learned in Chapter 11 that heuristics refer to basic problem-solving and reasoning strategies, (sometimes called 'rules of thumb' or mental short cuts), which are developed through experience and used in everyday life to make sense of the world. One common heuristic, identified by Daniel Kahneman and Amos Tversky (1972), is the tendency to assume that major events in the world have a major cause, while more mundane events are likely to have mundane causes. The assumption here is that there should be consistency between the magnitude of an event and its cause, and this assumption will lead people faced with a dramatic social event to seek a dramatic cause, such as a conspiracy (Keeley, 1999). This assumption is sometimes referred to as the **major event–major cause heuristic**.

Major event–major cause heuristic
The assumption that events with dramatic consequences must have dramatic causes.

Activity 12.2   Do major events necessarily have major causes?

Can you think of any major events, particularly ones which have generated popular conspiracy theories, that did *not* have major causes?

Comment

There are many examples that you could have come up with to answer this question. For example, the death of Princess Diana, felt by many people in the UK to be a major event, had an (unfortunately) everyday cause: a motor vehicle accident involving an intoxicated driver and a victim who was not wearing a seat belt. This mismatch between a major event and a mundane cause may be what led some people to speculate about something much more sinister and elaborate, such as an 'establishment' plot to kill her. In the same way, the assassination in 1963 of US President John F. Kennedy by a lone gunman (Figure 12.2) can also be seen to violate the major event–major cause heuristic, leading to much conspiracy speculation about the involvement of government agencies or the mafia. You may well have thought of several other examples, as many major events are actually the result of fairly mundane, simple causes.

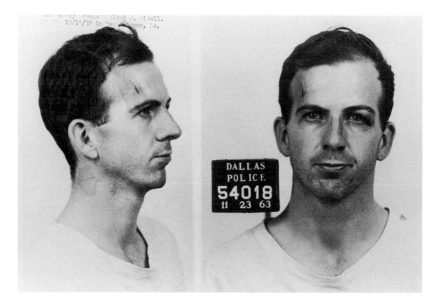

Figure 12.2   The assassination of US President John F. Kennedy gave rise to a number of conspiracy theories, even though the identity of his (lone) killer, Lee Harvey Oswald (pictured above) was known

Over the years, a number of psychological studies have examined the link between the major event–major cause heuristic and the endorsement of conspiracy-based explanations (e.g. McCauley and Jacques, 1979; Leman and Cinnirella, 2007). The experiment conducted by Patrick Leman and Marco Cinnirella (2007) is a particularly good example, and worth exploring in some detail. This experiment involved a fairly simple procedure. Sixty-four participants, all of whom were undergraduate psychology students from a UK university, were asked to read a brief vignette in the form of a newspaper report. The report described a (fictitious) assassination attempt against the president of a small, unnamed country. After reading the report, participants were presented with a series of statements about the possible causes of the event, and were asked to rate the likelihood of each statement being true (e.g. 'The gunman was part of a conspiracy to assassinate the president' and 'The gunman was a madman, acting alone'). These statements assessed the extent to which participants attributed the causes of the event described in the vignette to a conspiracy. In addition, the participants were asked to complete a questionnaire which measured their belief in conspiracy theories generally.

Although all 64 participants underwent the same procedure, they did not all read the same scenario. There were four different versions of the vignette. They were identically worded except for some crucial points of detail, namely (a) whether or not the president survived the assassination attempt, and the consequences for the country involved, and (b) whether or not the assassin's bullet hit or missed the target. The four conditions in this experiment are presented in the table below, followed by an example of two of the four vignettes.

Table 12.1 The four conditions in Leman and Cinnirella's (2007) experiment

Condition A	Condition B
President is shot and killed	President is shot at, but the bullet misses and he survives
Condition C	**Condition D**
President is hit by the bullet but survives	President is shot at, but the bullet misses. However, president dies from an unrelated cause (heart attack)

Vignette in condition A

The small nation of XXX was thrown into civil chaos last night following the assassination of President XXX. The newly-elected president, who had won 54 per cent of the votes in last month's general election, was shot as he climbed down from the stage at the end of a speech to supporters in the capital, XXX. Although medics were quickly on the scene, one bullet had penetrated the president's heart – he died almost instantly. XXX police were yesterday giving no details of their investigation. But it is widely believed that a 35-year-old man, detained shortly after the incident and suspected to be the gunman, is currently being held in custody.

Vignette in condition C

The small nation of XXX was breathing a collective sigh of relief last night following the failure of an assassination attempt on President XXX. The newly-elected president, who had won 54 per cent of the votes in last month's general election, was shot as he climbed down from the stage at the end of a speech to supporters in the capital, XXX. By pure chance, it appears a single bullet narrowly missed the president's heart. Medics reported that XXX had been released from hospital last night suffering only a minor wound to the shoulder – he will wear a sling for the next two weeks. XXX police were yesterday giving no details of their investigation. But it is widely believed that a 35-year-old man, detained shortly after the incident and suspected to be the gunman, is currently being held in custody.

(Source: Leman and Cinnirella, 2007, p. 27)

By varying the information presented in the vignettes, researchers were effectively manipulating the magnitude of the event: the scenarios where the president dies describe more dramatic consequences (the country is said to have descended into 'civil chaos') than those where he survives (where the outcome is a 'collective sigh of relief'). The authors of the study predicted that, because of the influence of the major event–major cause heuristic, the perceived magnitude of the event (the president dying versus the president surviving) would have an effect on the participants' likelihood of attributing the assassination to a conspiracy. They were also interested in whether there would be a difference between conditions B and C, that is, between the scenario where the gunman hits the president but the president survives, and the scenario where the gunman misses. Any differences between the two conditions would indicate that participants were not just drawing conclusions on the basis of the major event–major cause heuristic, but were also making a judgement about the competence of the shooter. Similarly, they were interested in any differences between conditions A and D. In condition D, the event described is dramatic (the president dies), but the death is not related to the assassination attempt (he died 'from a massive heart attack brought on, in part, by his rigorous schedule in the weeks preceding the election'). Thus, in this scenario, unlike the one in Condition A, there is no causal link between the death of the president and the assassination attempt. Take a moment before reading on to do Activity 12.3.

Activity 12.3   Thinking about the Leman and Cinnirella (2007) study

What would you predict the results of this study to be? In which of the scenarios do you think people would be most likely to endorse a conspiracy theory? Remember the influence of the major event–major cause heuristic when making your prediction.

Comment

The only significant difference in participants' responses that Leman and Cinnirella found was between the scenarios in which the president died (Conditions A and D) and those in which he survived (Conditions B and C). Participants were more likely to endorse the conspiracy-based explanation if the president died, regardless of whether he died as a result of the assassination or of a heart attack. Also, the study revealed that whether the shooter hit the president or missed his target made little impact on the participants' responses, as long as the president survived. This led the authors to conclude that, as predicted, the major event–major cause heuristic does play a role in determining the extent to which people are likely to entertain the possibility of a conspiracy. The magnitude of the event was shown to be more important than both the perceived competence of the attacker and the precise cause of death.

There was another, equally interesting, finding in the Leman and Cinnirella study. You will recall that, as well as asking them to read the vignette and answer questions about it, Leman and Cinnirella (2007) gave all participants a belief in conspiracy theories questionnaire. This was because they wanted to explore whether people who generally believed in conspiracy theories would be more susceptible to the major event–major cause heuristic, compared with sceptics. The results showed this not to be the case: people appeared to rely on the major event–major cause heuristic regardless of whether or not they generally believed in conspiracy theories. This is an important finding, because it suggests that cognitive biases such as the major event–major cause heuristic can better explain what kinds of *events* are likely to become the object of conspiracist speculation, rather than what kinds of *people* will be susceptible to it. In simple terms, any event that has highly dramatic consequences is likely to generate conspiracy theories that suggest a cause of equivalent scale, even when the real cause was an individual acting alone, as in Leman and Cinnirella's study, or the actions of a small group (e.g. the 9/11 attacks, Figure 12.3).

Biased assimilation
A tendency to uncritically accept evidence supporting a pre-existing view, while rejecting any disconfirming information.

A similar conclusion has been drawn from studies that looked at whether or not believers in conspiracy theories are more susceptible to what is known as **biased assimilation**, which is the tendency to uncritically accept evidence supporting a pre-existing view, while rejecting any disconfirming information (Lord et al., 1979; Butler et al. 1995). Biased assimilation is essentially the same concept as confirmation bias, which you learned about in Chapter 5, with the very subtle distinction that confirmation bias refers more to how people *seek out* information (seeking out information that supports their existing views or the conclusion they want to reach, avoiding information that does not), whereas biased assimilation refers more to the way people *process* whatever information they encounter (believing information that supports their existing views, disbelieving information that does not). To illustrate how subtle the distinction is, an example of confirmation bias would be choosing to read a newspaper article if you think you will agree with it and deciding not to read it if you think you will disagree with it, whereas biased assimilation would be reading a newspaper article and believing it if you agree with it and disbelieving it if you disagree with it. In practice, the distinction between the two is rarely made, as the concepts are so closely related and people generally do both together, and so the two terms are often used interchangeably.

Figure 12.3   The major cause–major event heuristic would cause people to think that an event this major could not have been carried out by a small group of lightly armed men

Biased assimilation is thought to be particularly relevant to conspiracy theories, given that conspiracy theorists are notorious for their tendency to gather and interpret evidence selectively while ignoring important information that supports other explanations (Byford, 2011). However, John McHoskey (1995) found that biased assimilation, although present among believers in conspiracy theories, is by no means limited to them. It is also present among non-believers, who are just as susceptible to systematic privileging of evidence that confirms their views.

Both of these findings suggest that conspiracy theorists might not, in fact, be as cognitively distinct as it is sometimes tempting to think. As Albert Harrison and James Moulton Thomas (1997, p. 15) put it, 'beliefs in conspiracies rest less on emotional upheaval and gross distortions of reality … than on normal, primarily rational information processing strategies that are accountable also for other beliefs'.

3.3   Looking beyond the differences between believers and sceptics

As you have read in the previous sections, identifying specific psychological factors that differentiate believers in conspiracy theories from sceptics has proved surprisingly difficult. Conspiracy theorists

109

have been shown to share with non-believers several reasoning strategies, such as biased assimilation and the major event–major cause heuristic, while the lack of a clear link between beliefs in conspiracy theories and variables such as five-factor personality traits, authoritarianism or minority status suggests that any differences between believers and non-believers may not be straightforward.

It could be argued, of course, that a clearer 'profile' of believers in conspiracy theories will emerge with time, as researchers create more sophisticated ways of studying conspiracy beliefs, or as they embark on more systematic research programmes. In psychology, one often encounters the notion that, while individual studies might offer only modest advancement in the understanding of a phenomenon, the discipline as a whole moves slowly but steadily forward. Yet there are precedents within social psychology that suggest that this is not necessarily so, and that the 'optimistic notion of cumulative progress' (Billig, 1996, p. 106) might never be realised. One example is psychological research on persuasion. Ever since the 1940s, psychologists have sought to identify factors that make a piece of communication effective in influencing the audience (e.g. Hovland et al., 1953). Over the years, hundreds of studies have been devoted to the exploration of, for example, whether messages that arouse fear are more persuasive than neutral ones, whether it is more effective to present a one-sided or a two-sided argument, whether experts are more persuasive than non-experts, and so on. However, over time, the quest for the general rules of persuasion led to a widespread sense of disappointment: for virtually every empirical finding that proposed a general principle there were myriad others that suggested some qualification, exclusion or exception (Billig, 1996). For instance, the initial finding that fear may be necessary to induce action has been found in subsequent studies to depend on a whole host of things, including the amount of fear (too much or too little fear undermines the persuasiveness of a message); the disposition of the individual who is on the receiving end of the communication (some people respond to fear-inducing messages more favourably than others); and the context in which the message is presented (Hollander, 1981). In other words, years of research and meticulous accumulation of evidence about the rules of persuasion have produced little more than a 'mass of unintegrated findings' (Billig, 2003, p. 223).

There is an important lesson in this for the psychology of conspiracy theories. One might predict that, with further research, the list of psychological factors that can be shown to be associated with conspiracy beliefs will expand, as will the number of variables that apparently mediate those associations. However, as the number of relevant factors increases, the relative importance of each factor will inevitably diminish. With time, the complexity of the psychological profile of conspiracist individuals will undoubtedly grow, but this may only make it more, not less, obscure and intangible.

3.4   Measuring belief in conspiracy theories using scales

A core factor in the different theories and studies that you have learned about so far in this chapter is that they conceptualise conspiracy theories as individual beliefs. Adherence to conspiracy-based explanations is seen as something that can be explained by reference to individual information-processing biases, attitudes or personality characteristics. This treatment of conspiracy theories as individual beliefs is reflected in the use of questionnaires or scales to measure the extent to which a person endorses conspiracy-based explanations. A typical study might involve distributing questionnaires to a sample of the population, who will vary in the extent to which they endorse conspiracy theories. The questionnaires are usually composed of different measures, or scales, similar to the ones you have previously encountered (e.g. the Rosenberg Self-Esteem Scale that you learned about in Chapter 4). In conspiracy theory research, one of the scales usually assesses the participants' belief in conspiracy theories, while others tap into whatever variables the researcher hypothesises might explain the difference in susceptibility to conspiracy-based explanations, such as the aspects of personality identified in the five-factor model that you learned about in Section 3.1. Statistical procedures are then used to assess the strength of the relationship between the belief in conspiracy theories and the other variables, all with the view of uncovering psychological factors that underpin what is often referred to as the 'conspiracy mentality' (Moscovici, 1987; Bruder et al., 2013).

A number of scales to measure people's belief in conspiracy theories have been developed, generally consisting of between 5 and 22 items asking about particular aspects of conspiracist belief. In Figures 12.4 and 12.5 you will find examples of two such scales, both of which require each individual participant to indicate their level of belief in a series of conspiracy-based statements. You will reflect on these scales in Activity 12.4.

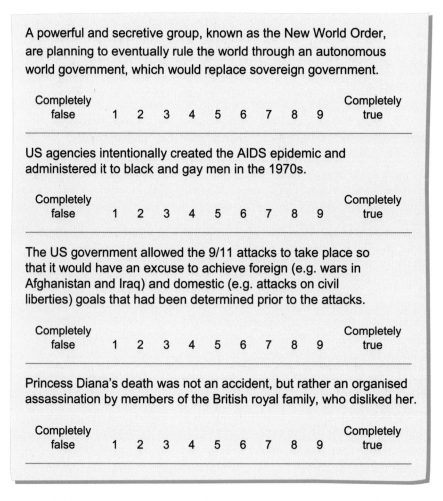

Figure 12.4   Four of the 15 items from the Belief in Conspiracy Theories Inventory developed by Swami et al. (2010)

	Definitely not true	Probably not true	Not sure/ cannot decide	Probably true	Definitely true
The government is involved in the murder of innocent citizens and/or well-known public figures, and keeps this a secret.	☐	☐	☐	☐	☐
A lot of important information is deliberately concealed from the public out of self-interest.	☐	☐	☐	☐	☐
The spread of certain viruses and/or diseases is the result of the deliberate, concealed efforts of some organisation.	☐	☐	☐	☐	☐
Certain significant events have been the result of the activity of a small group who secretly manipulate world events.	☐	☐	☐	☐	☐

Figure 12.5   Four of the 15 items featured in the Generic Conspiracist Beliefs Scale developed by Brotherton et al. (2013)

Activity 12.4   Characteristics of conspiracy belief scales

Think carefully about the two scales presented in Figures 12.4 and 12.5. Can you identify any similarities and differences between them, particularly in the kinds of questions they ask? Are there any issues arising from the type of response they ask for? In thinking about this question, you may find it useful to reflect back on the discussion of the Rosenberg Self-Esteem Scale (RSES), which you learned about in Chapter 4.

Comment

You probably noticed an important difference between the two scales. The first, the Belief in Conspiracy Theories Inventory (BCTI, Figure 12.4) requires respondents to rate the extent to which they believe a specific well-known conspiracy theory to be true. The examples above include references to the 9/11 attacks, the death of Princess Diana and the origins of AIDS. In contrast, the Generic Conspiracist Beliefs Scale (GCBS, Figure 12.5) contains more abstract questions about the role of conspiracies in world history. These questions make no reference to specific events, persons or organisations. Nevertheless, they focus on similar issues as the BCTI: the human origins of infectious diseases, deaths of public figures, shadowy groups pulling the strings of politics, and so on. In terms of the responses, you will have noticed that they ask for an indication of the level of truth or falsehood the person thinks each statement has, rather than whether they think it is or is not true. Unlike the RSES, which you will remember forces people to choose between low and high self-esteem responses, these examples do have a midpoint on the scale. Would you consider this midpoint to be neutral, though, as a midpoint on a self-esteem scale would be?

The difference between the BCTI (Figure 12.4) and the GCBS (Figure 12.5) reflects two approaches that have developed in the literature over the years. Early scales, developed in the USA, tended to fall into the first category, and included concrete questions about specific conspiracies (e.g. McCauley and Jacques, 1979). However, researchers soon realised that this presented a problem: conspiracy theories are often culturally specific, so scales developed in the USA had to be modified before they could be used elsewhere in the world. Thus, over the years, a number of culturally specific scales have been created for use in various countries including the UK (Leman and Cinnirella, 2007; Swami et al., 2010), Poland (Grzesiak-Feldman and Ejsmont, 2008; Kofta and Sędek, 2005), France (Wagner-Egger and Bangerter, 2007) and Malaysia (Swami, 2012). Also, the fact that new conspiracy theories emerge all the time and the popularity of some of the old ones diminishes means that scales have to be updated from time to time. The problem this creates is that making comparisons between studies becomes difficult. The generic scales, like the one featured in Figure 12.5, were developed to correct this shortcoming: because they do not refer to specific conspiracies, they can be meaningfully used across cultures and across time.

However, the generic scales have their own disadvantages. The items are often *too* generic, to the point where one could easily agree with a statement without necessarily being a conspiracy theorist. Note, for example, the item 'A lot of important information is deliberately concealed from the public out of self-interest' featured in the GCBS, Figure 12.5. While many believers in conspiracy theories would rate this item as 'definitely true', so would many non-believers, simply because important information often *is* concealed from the public out of self-interest (e.g. governments covering up potential scandals or corporations keeping commercially sensitive information secret). In other words, such items do not necessarily differentiate belief in conspiracy theories from healthy (or, at least, justified) scepticism of authority and reasonable suspicion towards the actions of those with power.

Regardless of the variations between the different measures, their common outcome is a single score which quantifies the extent to which an individual endorses conspiracy theories (whether specific or general). Psychology's reliance on scales as a measure of conspiracy theories should not come as a surprise, as measures of this kind are common in research on human beliefs. They are used extensively in studies of, for example, religious, mystical or paranormal beliefs (e.g. Thalbourne, 1994), or in research on authoritarianism, stereotypes or prejudice. There is an obvious advantage to using questionnaire-based measures, above and beyond the fact that they are easy and cheap to administer to large samples. Psychological measures offer a practical solution to a problem faced by psychologists interested in social phenomena, such as conspiracy theories: how to 'tailor' a complex social issue into a format that can be measured and quantified (Graumann, 1987). In other words, scales – comprising a small number of fairly simple items – reduce conspiracy theories to their bare essence, and condense them to a single and quantifiable measure of judgement or belief.

3.5   Conspiracy theory scales: a methodological critique

The use of scales to tap into conspiracy beliefs raises important theoretical and methodological questions. For example, one thing you may have noticed in Figures 12.4 and 12.5 is that, regardless of the type of items included in a scale, the belief in conspiracies is conceptualised as a *continuous* dimension. Rather than asking participants to give a 'yes' or 'no' answer, the questions require them to rate items on a sliding scale (from 1 to 5 or 1 to 9 in the above examples), with numbers representing the probability that a conspiracy theory is true (from 'definitely not true'/'completely false' to 'definitely true'/'completely true'). Therefore, although researchers, in most cases, seek to tap into the factors that differentiate 'believers' from 'sceptics', the scales do not produce a clear dichotomy: everyone in the population is assumed to fall somewhere on the continuum between complete credulity and total scepticism.

One issue with the use of continuous scales is that it is not entirely clear what it is that they measure. They certainly do not measure the same thing as questionnaires or surveys inviting a simpler 'yes' or 'no' answer (Crocker et al., 1999). In the case of continuous scales, a very low score (someone who rates all statements as 'completely false', for example) might usefully point to a definite non-believer, just as a very high score (someone who rates all statements as 'completely true') could help to identify a hard-line believer. However, the meaning of scores in the middle range is more difficult to interpret.

For example, imagine that, in response to the item 'Princess Diana's death was not an accident, but rather an organised assassination by members of the British royal family, who disliked her', someone chooses 4 or 5 on a scale from 1 (completely false) to 9 (completely true). What does this score mean in practical terms? Is this person a believer or a non-believer? You might argue that they are undecided, but what does it mean to be undecided about a conspiracy theory? Should this respondent be treated as a 'borderline' conspiracy theorist, because they endorse the possibility that something other than a car accident caused the death of Princess Diana, or as a non-believer, because they do not *fully* endorse the conspiracist explanation of this event?

This is an issue that researchers using scales to measure conspiracy beliefs have been surprisingly reluctant to address. Nonetheless, it is an important one, because scores in the middle range – which are, in fact, much more common than scores on either extreme – can actually reflect a whole range of different kinds of engagement with conspiracy theories. For example, Jennifer Crocker and colleagues (1999) suggest that such scores might indicate familiarity with particular conspiracy theories, rather than endorsement of them. The argument here is that people are generally less likely to completely dismiss explanations with which they are familiar, even if they do not believe them to be true. Going back to the item 'Princess Diana's death was not an accident, but rather an organised assassination ...', the answer '4' on a nine-point scale might indicate that the person has encountered this theory, maybe read about it, or seen it covered in a television documentary, rather than that they somewhat 'believe' it. This is especially plausible given that even among self-proclaimed non-believers there are those who, while rejecting conspiracy-based explanations, nevertheless recognise them as a legitimate opinion for others to hold. Such a position might also translate into a moderate score (Byford, 2011).

Furthermore, psychological scales overlook the possibility that conspiracy theories sometimes manifest themselves as 'quasi-beliefs', namely beliefs that are of relatively little consequence, and might even be 'fun' to hold, but which, in most cases, do not lead to action or guide behaviour in any significant way (Sunstein and Vermeule, 2009). People who engage with conspiracy theories might do so with the kind of 'suspicion of phoniness' commonly found among those who read astrology columns (Adorno, 1994, p. 49). They may read and discuss them in a playful, tongue-in-cheek way without necessarily believing them to be true. This kind of engagement with conspiracy theories, however, cannot be unproblematically mapped on to a simple continuum between strong belief and strong scepticism, of the kind found in conspiracy belief scales.

Finally, there is another methodological shortcoming of questionnaire-based research on conspiracy theories which is worth pointing out. Most studies in this area tend to be based on samples from the general population (or, as is common in psychological research, undergraduate students), among whom there are usually very few hard-line conspiracy theorists. It might seem obvious that an enquiry into factors that differentiate believers from non-believers would be based on comparisons between a subset of the population who firmly believe in conspiracy theories (those scoring at the top end of a conspiracy theory scale) and another subset comprising the biggest sceptics (those scoring at the lower end of the scale). However, this has not been the case. Rather than seeking out hard-line conspiracy theorists and giving them questionnaires, researchers have conducted their research on what are usually moderately believing (or, arguably, moderately sceptical) samples, and then simply extrapolated the findings to believers. In other words, the supposition that everyone in the population falls somewhere between firm belief and complete non-belief in conspiracy theories has been taken to mean that any factors that differentiate between, for example, a strong and a moderate non-believer also account for the difference between a strong believer and a strong non-believer. There is a problem with this assumption, above and beyond the fact that it is precisely that: an assumption that has yet to be tested. As noted above, when it comes to conspiracy belief scales, scores that point to 'moderate belief' (or non-belief) might be accounted for by considerations other than simply the strength of the belief in, or attitude towards, conspiracy theories.

Taking all these points together, the possibility emerges that conspiracy theories may simply be too complex a phenomenon to be captured by simple questionnaires, and that an individual focus may be missing important parts of the picture. Section 4 considers an alternative way of exploring conspiracy theories, one that draws more heavily on social psychology and that goes beyond 'profiling' conspiracy theorists or seeking to account for the differences between believers and non-believers.

4   Exploring conspiracy theories differently: from individual attitude and belief to social explanation

The limitations of questionnaire-based research on conspiracy beliefs, and the somewhat disappointing results, suggest that perhaps psychologists need to explore alternative approaches to the study of conspiracy theories. Maybe the individual differences approach, with its emphasis on the psychological characteristics and reasoning ability of believers, and the measurement of individual beliefs, has tackled conspiracy theories in the wrong way. As Michael Billig pointed out almost 40 years ago:

> when looking at the social psychological dynamics of so bizarre an outlook as the conspiracy theory, it is easy to overemphasise its eccentricities at the expense of noticing what is psychologically common place. It is not necessary to assume that the conspiracy theorist has a completely different cast of mind from the average person and that it must be described from a uniquely psychological perspective. History has shown that at times large numbers of both educated and uneducated people have embraced the conspiracy outlook.
>
> (Billig, 1978, p. 314)

This suggests that psychologists need to look beyond individual explanations of conspiracist beliefs and explore the role of social and cultural factors in conspiracy theories.

4.1   Social and cultural factors in conspiracy theories

The essence of Billig's argument, quoted above, is that explaining what distinguishes believers from non-believers might be far less important than accounting for how, why and when everyday thinking becomes influenced by conspiracy theories. For example, there is plenty of evidence to suggest that conspiracy theories can suddenly flourish in societies undergoing major social upheaval (e.g. a war or an economic crisis), before receding to the margins when the crisis abates (Byford and Billig, 2001). The individual differences approach cannot account for these periodic fluctuations in conspiracy beliefs. Similarly, it cannot account for the cultural differences in the prevalence of conspiracy theories. As has already been mentioned, AIDS-related conspiracy theories tend to be more common among African Americans than among White Americans. Similarly, there are parts of the world, including many Muslim countries of the Middle East, where, for various political, cultural and historical reasons, conspiracy theories form part of mainstream political discourse, much more so than in the West. For example, Matthew Gentzkow and Jesse Shapiro (2004) found that people sampled across nine predominantly Muslim countries were less likely to believe that the 9/11 attacks were the work of Islamist terrorists, and more likely to endorse the view that Israel or the USA itself was behind the attacks, if they were primarily exposed to Arab news media than if they were exposed to Western news media or no news media at all. Such *cultural* variations in conspiracy beliefs are certainly not attributable to *individual* differences in personality or cognitive biases.

Also, the attempts to reduce conspiracy theories to items on a scale and treat them as an individual attitude or belief overlook what are perhaps the most important, and the most interesting, aspects of this phenomenon: their *content* and their inherently *social* nature. There is much more to conspiracy theories than the claim that an event in history was the outcome of collusion or a secret plot. A statement such as 'The US government allowed the 9/11 attacks to take place so that it would have an excuse to achieve foreign … and domestic … goals that had been determined prior to the attacks' (see Figure 12.4) does not begin to capture the complexity of the 9/11 conspiracy theories expounded in hundreds of thousands of pages of books, newspapers and internet posts. In other words, conspiracy theories are not merely statements of belief, but intricate, convoluted and often enthralling *stories*. As you learned in Chapter 10, stories are an important part of how people make sense of the world.

It could therefore be argued that conspiracy theories are least interesting as an individual belief or attitude, and much more interesting as *shared* stories about how the world works. After all, in everyday life people do not volunteer their opinion about a conspiracy theory through simple statements, akin to those used in psychological scales, nor do they seek to quantify their belief on a numerical scale. Instead they *talk* and *argue* about conspiracy theories, *discuss* their different features and merits, *present* arguments and counter-arguments, and *exchange* dismissals and justifications. Engagement with conspiracy theories is therefore a shared endeavour and a social activity. This is an important point, because conspiracy theories have the greatest impact on society not as attitudes that people hold in their heads, but as a shared world-view on the basis of which political projects are forged and power relations challenged and sustained.

It may already have occurred to you that thinking about conspiracy theories in this way invites a different approach to their study from that examined in Section 3 and sets up a different task for the psychologist. It shifts the attention away from the individual mind and disposition of the conspiracy theorist and instead focuses it on the conspiracy theory itself, as a dynamic set of arguments and interpretations which are flexibly drawn on, modified and debated in the course of the everyday practice of making sense of, and telling stories about, the world and events in it.

Consider the following example, which illustrates the difference between the two approaches to the psychology of conspiracy theories. Research focusing on individual differences in conspiracy beliefs implies that when faced with a dramatic event (such as 9/11), people engage in a complex interpretative process which guides them towards a conclusion about the causes of that event. This process is thought to be influenced by biases in information processing and aspects of a person's disposition, such as their personality, which leads some people to endorse conspiracy theories. However, there is also another way of looking at conspiracy theories: when faced with a dramatic event, people do not need to engage in a complex inference-making process: they have at their disposal culturally available 'reservoirs of available explanations' or 'common sense theories' about why things happen in the world (Moscovici and Hewstone, 1983, pp. 121–2), that lead them to almost instantly 'know' what happened. This can be observed clearly in the case of 9/11 conspiracy theories, as most conspiracy-based explanations of this event were not newly created, but were directly drawing on other conspiracy theories, which had been used in the past to account for similar dramatic events. For example, the idea that the US government would use an attack on US soil to justify military intervention is a motif that has been around since at least the 1940s, when conspiracy theorists claimed that President Franklin D. Roosevelt deliberately allowed the Japanese air attack on Pearl Harbor (Figure 12.6) to happen, in order to overcome domestic opposition to the USA's involvement in the Second World War. In other words, previous conspiracy theories about Pearl Harbor provided a blueprint for making sense of 9/11 as an 'inside job'. Even in the 1940s, though, those who espoused conspiracy theories about Pearl Harbor were relying on motifs that had been put forward around the time of the *First* World War, when the USA's involvement in the war in Europe was attributed to a conspiracy by big business and the country's political elite. This continuity in conspiracy theorising highlights the possibility that these explanations are not simply the product of individual information processing. Instead, they are culturally available interpretations that people can draw on, and can also share, debate and modify as they make sense of the world around them.

Figure 12.6 After the Japanese attack on Pearl Harbor in the Second World War, some conspiracists claimed that US President Roosevelt had foreknowledge of the attack and deliberately allowed it to happen

Inherent in this approach to the study of conspiracy theories is a greater recognition that human thought is the product of culture and history, not just of the individual mind. As Billig and colleagues note, psychologists who are focused on the mindset of individuals 'have been notably remiss in examining how the processes of cultural and ideological history flow through the minds of their laboratory subjects' (1988, p. 2). The point therefore is not to look for individual, cognitive psychological underpinnings of social phenomena, but to look at how aspects of psychology – patterns of thinking and behaviour – reflect established traditions of explanation and storytelling and ways of interpreting events in the world.

4.2 Conspiracy theories and rumours

An area of psychological research that has been attentive to social and cultural aspects of conspiracy theories is the research on rumour. Ever since the first psychological studies on the topic were carried out in the 1940s, stories of conspiracies, plots and subversion were identified as notable examples of rumour and hearsay (Allport and Postman, 1947; Campion-Vincent, 2005; Rödlach, 2006). This is unsurprising given that many conspiracy theories began as rumours and were later incorporated into a more formal 'theory', which in turn fuelled further rumour-mongering, initiating a cycle of mutual reinforcement. For example, in the immediate aftermath of 9/11, a rumour began to circulate on the internet that 4000 Jews employed in the World Trade Center failed to turn up for work on the day of the attacks, and other rumours claimed that no Jews were killed in the attacks, because they had foreknowledge of what was about to happen. The implication here was that the destruction of the World Trade Center was a Jewish conspiracy. Later, this motif became part of a more elaborate anti-Semitic conspiracy theory, which is still propagated in parts of the Middle East and on far-right websites in the USA and Europe. In fact, approximately 10–15 per cent of the victims of the attack on the World Trade Center were Jewish (US State Department, 2005), exactly as would be expected given that 12 per cent of the population of New York City at the time was Jewish.

Although rumours are often assumed to be of temporary interest and transmitted by word of mouth, it is today widely recognised that they can become unusually persistent, and be the object of more systematic and organised dissemination through mass media, including the internet. Conspiracy theories share many features of these 'solidified rumours' (Allport and Postman, 1947, p. 167), in that they form part of a society's cultural heritage and can be invoked to shed light on events (usually dramatic ones) to which they appear to apply.

An important feature of the research on rumour is that, unlike the individual differences approach examined in Section 3, it is concerned with conspiracy theories as stories that people tell, recognising the inherently social and interpersonal nature of both people themselves and the stories they share. The creation and transmission of rumours is seen as a collective problem-solving or sense-making process, rather than as an outcome of individual psychological processes (Bordia and DiFonzo, 2005). Also, there is greater recognition that rumours, including conspiracy theories, perform certain social and psychological functions. The question arises, then: what psychological benefits do conspiracy theories bring that motivate people to believe in them?

4.3   Motivational factors in conspiracy theories

In the literature on motivational factors that contribute to the popularity of conspiracy theories, an important place is occupied by the notion of self-esteem, which you previously encountered in Chapter 4. Specifically, it has been argued that conspiracy theories allow a group's self-esteem to be protected from potentially damaging inferences. For example, the continuing presence of conspiracy theories about minority ethnic and religious groups (such as about Jewish influence on politics, the economy, the media, and so on), might be seen as an example of the psychological dynamic of **scapegoating** (e.g. Kruglanski, 1987). Scapegoating is when, in frustrating and stressful situations (e.g. in periods of economic hardship or war) in which the true causes of some social strain are unclear or out of reach, a group displaces its aggression by placing the blame for the situation on out-groups, typically minorities (Hovland and Sears, 1940). Thus, conspiracy theories about minorities represent the rationalisation of the majority group's displaced aggression and a means of externalising feelings of hostility and avoiding self-blame (Young, 1990; Goertzel, 1994).

Scapegoating
A psychological dynamic whereby, in frustrating and stressful situations, a group displaces its aggression by blaming out-groups for the situation.

Another motivational factor that draws people to conspiracy theories is the illusion of control (Bains, 1983). Rumours of conspiracy have been shown to flourish in times of war, social crisis or economic disaster, when available canons of explanation prove inadequate for explaining what is going on (Nkpa, 1975). The driving force behind rumours of conspiracy is that they bring relief to those among whom they are circulated: they restore the sense that the world is ordered. Because conspiracy theories attribute the causes of events to someone's volition and design, they imply that events are ultimately manageable and are not contingent on random and unforeseeable events, or a complex network of uncontrollable causal factors (Bains, 1983; Keeley, 1999; Kalichman, 2009). What is more, they imply a straightforward (although not always easy) solution: all that is needed is for the conspiracy to be exposed and its architects eliminated, and good will prevail over evil. Therefore, although conspiracy theories often seem threatening, they contain within them an optimistic, albeit somewhat naive, message.

Scapegoating may serve a useful psychological function for people in stressful situations

However, probably the most important and the most obvious benefit that conspiracy theories bring to those who engage with them is the feeling of 'self-assurance and superiority towards the non-initiated' (Heins, 2007, p. 792). Because conspiracy theorists assume that those who believe the official, non-conspiratorial explanations have fallen victim to the orchestrated campaign of mass manipulation, 'adherence to a conspiracy theory allows a person to see himself or herself as perfect and infallible in comparison to others who are seen as evil and defective' (Young, 1990, p. 156). The conviction that one is in possession of an unprecedented insight into the working of the world, while everyone else is wrong, is potentially a huge generator of self-esteem. It offers compensation for 'what might otherwise be insupportable feelings of powerlessness' (Barkun, 2006, p. 35). Crucially, however, being 'in the know' has its own interpersonal, social dimension: the fact that one is in the know becomes especially important when it is recognised *by others*. As research on rumour-mongering points out, knowledge about how the world works, contained in rumours of conspiracy, operates as the 'currency of power and influence'; it brings prestige and esteem through communication with others (Bordia and DiFonzo, 2005, p. 93). This is why conspiracy theories are never just individual beliefs: they are pieces of information to be traded and exchanged, debated and contested.

The fact that conspiracy theories are shared, especially among communities of believers, means that self-esteem generated through engagement with conspiracy theories has a collective dimension. Conspiracy theorists, although a diffuse group, tend to perceive themselves, as a collective, to be resourceful and competent, and 'part of a genuinely heroic elite group who can see past the official version duplicated for the benefit of the lazy and inert mass of people by the powers that be' (Aaronovitch, 2009, p. 10).

5   Summary

The term 'conspiracy theory' (and, by extension, identifying a person as a 'conspiracy theorist') is not a neutral label, as it is exclusively applied to ideas about conspiracies which do not have a factual basis. Psychologists (and others, such as sociologists) have been interested for many years in why people would believe – often passionately – in things that are demonstrably false, such as the claim that no Jews died in the 9/11 World Trade Center attacks. Much of the research into conspiracy theories has tried to find individual explanations, such as correlations between belief in conspiracy theories and personality characteristics, or differences between conspiracy theory believers and non-believers. So far, however, there is little evidence that such correlations or differences exist: in many studies, people who believe in conspiracy theories do not seem to be very different from people who do not. Part of the explanation for this may be that research using questionnaire methods has not adequately differentiated believers from non-believers, for example by not being clear what 'moderate' belief in conspiracy theories means, and by mainly studying people with moderate or low belief in conspiracy theories. Relatively little research has yet been done on people with extremely strong beliefs in conspiracy theories.

However, another important part of the explanation is that belief in conspiracy theories draws largely on ordinary, everyday psychological processes, such as biased assimilation (a form of confirmation bias) and the major event–major cause heuristic. It is also necessary to consider social, not just individual, psychological processes. Conspiracy theories are not merely individual beliefs, quietly held, but are shared, discussed, argued and counter-argued. They are cultural products which help people to communicate and understand ideas, and try to make sense of a complex world. They can also serve a protective psychological function, both for groups who can displace blame for adverse events or circumstances by scapegoating and for individuals who can gain personal self-assurance by feeling that they are 'in the know'. This latter aspect of belief in conspiracy theories may be related to self-esteem, perhaps providing a way in which the social and individual elements of conspiracy theories can be reconciled.

References

Aaronovitch, D. (2009) *Voodoo Histories: The Role of the Conspiracy Theory in Shaping Modern History*, London, Vintage.

Abalakina-Paap, M., Stephan, W. G., Craig, T. and Gregory W. L. (1999) 'Beliefs in conspiracies', *Political Psychology*, vol. 20, no. 3, pp. 637–47.

Adorno, T. W. (1994) *The Stars Down to Earth and Other Essays on the Irrational in Culture*, London, Routledge.

Adorno, T. W., Frenkel-Brunswik, E., Levinson, D. J. and Sanford, R. N. (1950) *The Authoritarian Personality*, New York, Harper & Brothers.

Allport, G. W. and Postman, L. J. (1947) *The Psychology of Rumor*, New York, Holt, Reinhart & Winston.

Bains, G. (1983) 'Explanations and the need for control', in Hewstone, M. (ed.) *Attribution Theory: Social and Functional Extensions*, Oxford, Blackwell, pp. 126–43.

Barkun, M. (2006) *A Culture of Conspiracy: Apocalyptic Visions in Contemporary America*, Los Angeles, CA, University of California Press.

Basham, L. (2003) 'Malevolent global conspiracy', *Journal of Social Philosophy*, vol. 34, no. 1, pp. 91–103.

Billig, M. (1978) *Fascists: A Social Psychology of the National Front*, London, Academic Press.

Billig, M. (1996) *Arguing and Thinking: A Rhetorical Approach to Social Psychology*, 2nd edn, Cambridge, Cambridge University Press.

Billig, M. (2003) 'Political rhetoric', in Sears, D. O., Huddy, L. and Jervis, R. (eds) *Handbook of Political Psychology*, Oxford, Oxford University Press, pp. 222–50.

Billig, M., Condor, S., Edwards, D., Gane, M., Middleton, D. and Radley, A. R. (1988) *Ideological Dilemmas: A Social Psychology of Everyday Thinking*, London, Sage.

Bird, S. T. and Bogart, L. M. (2005) 'Conspiracy beliefs about HIV/AIDS and birth control among African Americans: implications for the prevention of HIV, other STIs and unintended pregnancy', *Journal of Social Issues*, vol. 61, no. 1, pp. 109–26.

Bordia, P. and DiFonzo, N. (2005) 'Psychological motivations in rumor spread', in Fine, G. A., Campion-Vincent, V. and Heath, C. (eds) *Rumor Mills: The Social Impact of Rumor and Legend*, New Brunswick, NJ, Transaction Publishers.

Brotherton, R., French, C. C. and Pickering, A. D. (2013) 'Measuring belief in conspiracy theories: the generic conspiracist beliefs scale', *Frontiers in Psychology*, vol. 4, art. 279, pp. 1–15 [Online]. Available at http://journal.

frontiersin.org/Journal/10.3389/fpsyg.2013.00279/full (Accessed 1 December 2014).

Bruder, M., Haffk, P., Neave, N., Nouripanah, N. and Imhoff, R. (2013) 'Measuring individual differences in generic beliefs in conspiracy theories across cultures: Conspiracy Mentality Questionnaire', *Frontiers in Psychology*, vol. 4, art. 225, pp. 1–15 [Online]. Available at http://journal.frontiersin.org/Journal/10.3389/fpsyg.2013.00225/full (Accessed 1 December 2014).

Butler, L. D., Koopman, C. and Zimbardo, P. G. (1995) 'The psychological impact of viewing the film "JFK": emotions, beliefs, and political behavioral intentions', *Political Psychology*, vol. 16, no. 2, pp. 237–57.

Byford, J. (2011) *Conspiracy Theories: A Critical Introduction*, Basingstoke, Palgrave Macmillan.

Byford, J. and Billig, M. (2001) 'The emergence of antisemitic conspiracy theories in Yugoslavia during the war with NATO', *Patterns of Prejudice*, vol. 35, no. 4, pp. 50–63.

Campion-Vincent, V. (2005) 'From evil others to evil elites: a dominant pattern in conspiracy theories today', in Fine, G. A., Campion-Vincent, V. and Heath, C. (eds) *Rumor Mills: The Social Impact of Rumor and Legend*, New Brunswick, NJ, Transaction Publishers.

Coady, D. (2006) 'An introduction to the philosophical debates about conspiracy theories', in Coady, D. (ed.) *Conspiracy Theories: The Philosophical Debate*, Aldershot, Ashgate, pp. 1–11.

Cohn, N. (1967) *Warrant for Genocide: The Myth of the Jewish World Conspiracy and the Protocols of the Elders of Zion*, London, Secker & Warburg.

Costa, P. T. and McRae, R. R. (1992) *NEO-PI Professional Manual*, Odessa, FL, Psychological Assessment Resources.

Crocker, J., Luhtanen, R., Broadnax, S. and Blaine, B. E. (1999) 'Belief in U.S. government conspiracies against Blacks among Black and White college students: powerlessness or system blame?', *Personality and Social Psychology Bulletin*, vol. 25, no. 8, pp. 941–53.

Gentzkow, M. A. and Shapiro, J. M. (2004) 'Media, education and anti-Americanism in the Muslim world', *Journal of Economic Perspectives*, vol. 18, no. 3, pp. 117–33.

Goertzel, T. (1994) 'Belief in conspiracy theories', *Political Psychology*, vol. 15, no. 4, pp. 731–42.

Goldberg, L. R. (1993) 'The structure of phenotypic personality traits', *American Psychologist*, vol. 48, pp. 26–34.

Graumann, C. F. (1987) 'Conspiracy: history and social psychology – a synopsis', in Graumann, C. F. and Moscovici, S. (eds) *Changing Conceptions of Conspiracy*, New York, Springer-Verlag, pp. 245–52.

Grzesiak-Feldman, M. and Ejsmont, A. (2008) 'Paranoia and conspiracy thinking of Jews, Arabs, Germans, and Russians in a Polish sample', *Psychological Reports*, vol. 102, no. 3, pp. 884–6.

Grzesiak-Feldman, M. and Irzycka, M. (2009) 'Right-wing authoritarianism and conspiracy thinking in a Polish sample', *Psychological Reports*, vol. 105, no. 2, pp. 389–93.

Harrison, A. A. and Thomas, J. M. (1997) 'The Kennedy assassination, unidentified flying objects, and other conspiracies: psychological and organizational factors in the perception of "cover-up"', *Systems Research and Behavioural Science*, vol. 14, no. 2, pp. 113–28.

Heins, V. (2007) 'Critical theory and the traps of conspiracy thinking', *Philosophy and Social Criticism*, vol. 33, no. 7, pp. 787–801.

Hofstadter, R. (1964) 'The paranoid style in American politics', *Harpers*, November, pp. 77–86.

Hofstadter, R. (1967) *Paranoid Style in American Politics and Other Essays*, New York, Vintage Books.

Hollander, E. P. (1981) *Principles and Methods of Social Psychology*, Oxford, Oxford University Press.

Hovland, C. I., Janis, I. L. and Kelley, H. H. (1953) *Communication and Persuasion*, New Haven, CT, Yale University Press.

Hovland, C. I. and Sears, R. (1940) 'Minor studies in aggression, VI: correlation of lynching with economic indices', *Journal of Psychology*, vol. 9, pp. 301–10.

Kahneman, D. and Tversky, A. (1972) 'Subjective probability: a judgment of representativeness', *Cognitive Psychology*, vol. 3, pp. 430–9.

Kalichman, S. C. (2009) *Denying AIDS: Conspiracy Theories, Pseudoscience, and Human Tragedy*, New York, Springer-Verlag.

Keeley, B. L. (1999) 'Of conspiracy theories', *Journal of Philosophy*, vol. 96, no. 3, pp. 109–26.

Knight, P. (2008) 'Outrageous conspiracy theories: popular and official responses to 9/11 in Germany and the United States', *New German Critique*, vol. 35, no. 1, pp. 165–93.

Kofta, M. and Sędek, G. (2005) 'Conspiracy stereotypes of Jews during systemic transformation in Poland', *International Journal of Sociology*, vol. 35, no. 1, pp. 40–64.

Kruglanski, A. W. (1987) 'Blame-placing schemata and attributional research', in Graumann, C. F. and Moscovici, S. (eds) *Changing Conceptions of Conspiracy*, New York, Springer-Verlag, pp. 219–30.

Leman, P. J. and Cinnirella, M. (2007) 'A major event has a major cause: evidence for the role of heuristics in reasoning about conspiracy theories', *Social Psychology Review*, vol. 9, no. 2, pp. 18–28.

Lord, C. G., Ross, L. and Lepper, M. R. (1979) 'Biased assimilation and attitude polarization: the effects of prior theories on subsequently considered evidence', *Journal of Personality and Social Psychology*, vol. 37, no. 11, pp. 2098–109.

McCauley, C. and Jacques, S. (1979) 'The popularity of conspiracy theories of presidential assassination: a Bayesian analysis, *Journal of Personality and Social Psychology*, vol. 37, no. 5, pp. 637–44.

McHoskey, J. W. (1995) 'Case closed? On the John F. Kennedy assassination: biased assimilation of evidence and attitude polarization', *Basic and Applied Social Psychology*, vol. 17, no. 3, pp. 395–409.

Moscovici, S. (1987) 'The conspiracy mentality', in Graumann, C. F. and Moscovici, S. (eds) *Changing Conceptions of Conspiracy*, New York, Springer-Verlag,.

Moscovici, S. and Hewstone, M. (1983) 'Social representations and social explanations: from the "naïve" to the "amateur" scientist', in Hewstone, M. (ed.) *Attribution Theory: Social and Functional Extensions*, Oxford, Blackwell, pp. 98–125.

Nattrass, N. (2008) 'Estimating the lost benefits of antiretroviral drug use in South Africa', *African Affairs*, vol. 107, no. 427, pp. 157–76.

Nkpa, N. K. U. (1975) 'Rumor mongering in war time', *Journal of Social Psychology*, vol. 96, no. 1, pp. 27–35.

Rödlach, A. (2006) *Witches, Westerners and HIV: AIDS and Cultures of Blame in Africa*, Walnut Creek, CA, Left Coast Press.

Sunstein, C. R. and Vermeule, A. (2009) 'Conspiracy theories: causes and cures', *Journal of Political Philosophy*, vol. 17, no. 2, pp. 202–27.

Swami, V. (2012) 'Social psychological origins of conspiracy theories: the case of the Jewish conspiracy theory in Malaysia', *Frontiers in Psychology*, vol. 3, art. 280 [Online]. Available at http://ncbi.nlm.nih.gov/pmc/articles/PMC3412387/ (Accessed 1 December 2014).

Swami, V., Chamorro-Premuzic, T. and Furnham, A. (2010) 'Unanswered questions: a preliminary investigation of personality and individual difference predictors of 9/11 conspiracist beliefs', *Applied Cognitive Psychology*, vol. 24, no. 6, pp. 749–61.

Thalbourne, M. A. (1994) 'Belief in the paranormal and its relationship to schizophrenia-relevant measures: a confirmatory study', *British Journal of Clinical Psychology*, vol. 33, no. 1, pp. 78–80.

US State Department (2005) *The 4,000 Jews Rumor* [Online]. Available at http://web.archive.org/web/20070211085836/http://usinfo.state.gov/media/Archive/2005/Jan/14-260933.html (Accessed 1 December 2014).

Wagner-Egger, P. and Bangerter, A. (2007) 'La vérité est ailleurs: corrélats de l'adhésion aux théories du complot', *Revue Internationale de Psychologie Sociale*, vol. 20, no. 4, pp. 31–61.

Young, T. J. (1990) 'Cult violence and the identity movement', *Cultic Studies Journal*, vol. 7, no. 2, pp. 150–9.

Block 5: Living psychological issues

Chapter 13

The psychology of extreme circumstances

Nadia Marie Wager

Contents

1   Introduction

This part of the book is all about the ways in which people's experiences affect how they understand things, and how experiences impact on people's understandings. In this chapter you will focus on 'extreme circumstances', particularly considering the ways in which individuals might be affected by experiencing these kinds of situations, and the different ways in which they might be supported in coping with the effects.

You will begin by considering in Section 2 what events and/or experiences might be thought of as 'extreme circumstances'. You will then be introduced to different typologies (or categories) of extreme circumstances, which will help you to consider the different factors that might influence (a) whether an individual labels their experience as 'traumatic'; (b) the likely impact of exposure to the event or circumstance; and (c) 'appropriate' ways of, and resources necessary for, coping.

Then, in Section 3, you will be introduced to the negative impacts of exposure to a variety of extreme circumstances. You will contemplate different diagnoses that are associated with aversive reactions to extreme circumstances and the different impacts that the various extreme circumstances might entail. These include impacts that might extend beyond the individual to their social networks and community. This should help you to understand the range of needs someone might have following their extreme experience.

In Section 4 you will be encouraged to explore recovery from trauma and to contrast recovery with the concept of resilience. You will consider how some people not only prove to be resilient in the face of trauma or demonstrate a natural inclination for recovery, but in fact appear to gain something positive from their exposure to extreme circumstances. The rationale for this is that it is important not to think, after reading the first part of the chapter, that all people who have undergone a potentially traumatic experience are necessarily traumatised, or that the impact of the event on them will be persistent.

The final section of the chapter is called 'Perils, pitfalls and positive effects of psychological interventions'. Here you will be encouraged to think about the fact that there may be more than one 'best' intervention for different forms of trauma and to contemplate whether an intervention is always required.

Before you embark on working through this chapter there are a few words of warning to consider. Because of the nature of the chapter, the content will inevitably touch on some sensitive, taboo and possibly triggering topics. This includes mass school shootings, bereavement, child sexual abuse and war. It is therefore important to be mindful that some of these things either may be beyond the realm of your own experience and thus shocking to contemplate, or may serve as reminders of some of your own experiences. Please be gentle with yourself when progressing through the chapter. Perhaps this is not the best bedtime reading material and it might be wise to balance reading it with a positive activity afterwards – even if that is only a cup of tea and a chat with friends.

After reading this chapter you should be able to:

- define the meaning of the terms 'extreme circumstances' and 'psychological trauma' and identify the range of events or experiences that might be included in these definitions

- explain the potential consequences of trauma on the individual, the family and the wider society, and discuss factors (culture, gender, age, and so on) that are likely to moderate the impact of particular traumatic events or experiences

- describe models and theories of coping with extreme circumstances and recovery from associated trauma

- explore issues related to providing psychological intervention to those who have experienced extreme circumstances.

2 Defining extreme circumstances

For the purposes of this chapter extreme circumstances will be defined as extraordinary situations that extend beyond an individual's normal everyday experiences. Such circumstances are likely to tax and challenge an individual's existing repertoire of coping strategies and possibly demand resources that exceed their existing reserves. Consequently, they could have a detrimental impact on the individual's psychological well-being and development, as well as their physical integrity.

While the phrase 'extreme circumstances' does not specify a particular direction in which the 'extreme' might manifest, empirical research and theorising on this topic has tended to focus predominately on negative experiences, which are frequently referred to as traumas. This is despite the fact that it may be possible to feel overwhelmed by a positive experience and that a positive experience may ultimately serve as a catalyst for a series of less favourable experiences.

Bruce P. Dohrenwend (2010) argues that the reason for the neglect of positive experiences in this area is that only negative events are associated with psychological disturbance and disorders. Historically, psychology tended to focus on problematic aspects of human experience, such as mental health problems or anti-social behaviour, until the recent positive psychology movement which you will read about in Chapter 15. It may also be the case that negative extreme circumstances are more common than positive ones; for example, there are many more victims of crime than there are lottery winners.

The word 'extraordinary' in the definition of 'extreme circumstances' might lead you to believe that being confronted with extreme circumstances is a rare and unlikely human experience. However, a few years ago I conducted a community web survey exploring people's experiences of 'significant' events. I was actually studying sexual victimisation, but wanted to create several comparison groups, such as those who had experienced physical violence or natural disasters, and a control group of people who had not experienced something which might be considered to be a traumatic event (Wager, 2013).

Although I collected almost 500 responses, I found very few people who did not report experiencing at least one significant or traumatic event in their lives. Interestingly, the mean age of my sample was 30, so even by early adulthood many people were reporting having been confronted by an extreme experience.

Similarly, a meta-analysis by Emily J. Ozer and colleagues (2003) found that the majority of people were exposed to at least one extreme circumstance, involving threat to life or physical integrity, at some point in their life. Thus extreme experiences may not be as rare as people might like to think. (Remember from Chapter 1 that a meta-analysis is a study that brings together all the research that can be found on a topic and conducts statistical analysis across all the data.)

It could be that among the general population the experience of extreme circumstances is fairly commonplace, but for each individual the experience of a particular extreme circumstance is quite rare. For example, a number of people are injured in road accidents every day, but any one individual is unlikely to experience such an injury during their lifetime. Since extreme circumstances differ quite significantly in terms of their nature, severity and the likely impact on the life of the individual, this might add to the perceived rarity of such experiences.

An additional factor that might increase the perceived rarity is the taboo nature of some extreme circumstances (e.g. sexual assault). Since people do not typically talk openly about the fact that they have been sexually assaulted, in everyday life it is hard to estimate the proportion of the population who have this experience in common and the likely guess tends to be an underestimate (Ullman, 2010).

Now do Activity 13.1 to broadly consider the concept of extreme circumstances.

Activity 13.1   Experiences that might be considered extreme circumstances

Generate a list of experiences or events that you think might have been considered for inclusion in the definition of 'extreme circumstances' in this chapter and that have the potential to leave individuals feeling traumatised.

Once you have completed your list, turn to the end of the chapter and compare your list with the one produced for the purposes of this chapter. Do any of the entries surprise you? Would you disagree that some of them could be considered to be extreme circumstances and thus have the potential to be traumatising? Did you include any circumstances that were missed out?

Comment

It is difficult to say if it is possible to objectively determine whether a particular event or circumstance should be labelled as extreme or potentially traumatic. In some cases objectivity is likely to be possible (e.g. surviving a genocide in which the individual has lost their whole family and community). However, in the context of comparatively more mundane extreme circumstances, the way in which the event or circumstance is experienced is likely to have quite a strong subjective element.

This is reminiscent of Richard S. Lazarus and Judith Blackfield Cohen's (1977) classic psychological research on stress and coping. They contend that stress (and trauma is a form of 'extreme' stress) is likely to arise only when the individual appraises the circumstances as threatening and insurmountable. Another individual might be faced with exactly the same situation, yet see it as a challenge which they will strive to beat or overcome.

What factors might impact on the individual's appraisal of the circumstances? Such factors might be internal or external to the individual. Internal factors include the individual's personality, their life goals, established coping dispositions, previous life experiences, and so on. External factors include things such as the perceived availability of social support, social attitudes regarding the event or circumstances and the social context in which the event occurs.

2.1   Typologies of extreme experiences

It is evident that the range of experiences and events that could be considered to be extreme and potentially traumatising is vast, and thus their consequences, and coping strategies and resources necessary to deal with them, are likely to differ quite dramatically. It is therefore helpful to simplify this diversity so that it becomes easier to predict the level of distress, the likely impact and the types of resources necessary to aid coping. The construction of broad categories (or 'typologies') of events or circumstances thus becomes worthwhile. Each category exhibits a coherent set of characteristics.

Based on his extensive research in the field of extreme stress situations, Dohrenwend (2010) constructed a typology of high-risk major stressful events. In this he contends that stressful events can be characterised in terms of four specific characteristics and six general characteristics.

Dohrenwend's four specific characteristics form a hierarchy on the basis of the severity of the stressor and the intensity of the likely impact on the individual. The top of the list is the most extreme specific characteristic, while the bottom of the list is concerned with what in comparison might be considered more mundane stressors. You can see the four specific characteristics with examples of the types of circumstances in Box 13.1 and Figure 13.1.

Box 13.1   Dohrenwend's four specific characteristics of stressful events

1   A hazardous situation that poses a persistent life threat: armed conflict, warfare, natural disaster (e.g. the Indian Ocean earthquake and tsunami in 2004) and human-made disasters (e.g. the Chernobyl disaster at a nuclear power plant in April 1986).

2   A hazardous situation that poses a persistent **threat to physical integrity**: being a victim of domestic violence, child physical abuse or neglect, or being held captive or as a slave.

3   A hazardous situation that poses a persistent inability to satisfy basic needs such as food and shelter: prolonged poverty and homelessness.

4   Situations in everyday life in **peacetime communities**: bereavement, divorce, separation, life-changing medical diagnoses, redundancy, and so on.

Threat to physical integrity
Anything that interferes with a person's self-determination over their own body, such as being physically or sexually assaulted, or prevented from moving freely around the world.

Peacetime communities
Any nation or group that is not in a state of war. Wartime experiences are generally considered to be a specific kind of extreme circumstance, since people may well be fearing for their life on a daily basis.

Importantly, Dohrenwend highlights that it is highly probable that if someone is experiencing a stressor at the top of the hierarchy they will almost certainly be experiencing stressors at each of the lower levels. So, in the case of those who survived in the immediate aftermath of the tsunami of 2004, it is inevitable that some survivors continued to be subjected to conditions or sustained injuries that prolonged the threat to their physical integrity; they would have lost their homes, belongings and access to food, as well as experiencing bereavement, loss of livelihood, and so on. This demonstrates how one particular extreme circumstance can have multiple, ongoing and spreading effects in various life domains for the individual and also their communities.

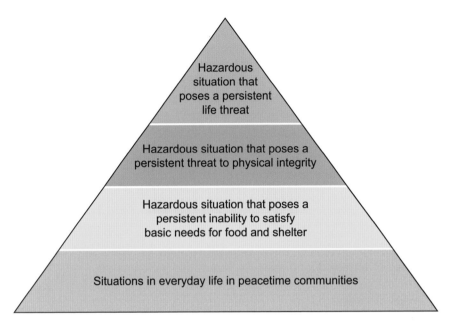

Figure 13.1   Dohrenwend's hierarchy of specific characteristics of stressful events

In addition, Dohrenwend (2010) identifies six general characteristics which can be used to categorise extreme circumstances. These are summarised in Box 13.2.

Box 13.2   Dohrenwend's six general characteristics of stressful events

1 Source

This is the origin or cause of the event. Here Dohrenwend focuses on whether the cause is internal or external to the individual. He utilises Constance Hammen's (1991) concept of 'stress-generative behaviour', which suggests that some individuals have a predisposition towards generating stressful circumstances through their own behaviours. He indicates that this might be a consequence of having a personality type which propels the individual towards sensation seeking. This may lead them to being unfaithful to their partner, for example, thereby increasing the chances of marital conflict and divorce, or to driving recklessly and having a car accident, and so on.

2 Valence

This is the emotional tone of the circumstances, which may be either positive or negative. Positive events typically involve some sort of gain, whereas negative events characteristically include a loss of some kind. Dohrenwend contends that positive circumstances are more likely to arise as a consequence of the behaviour of the individual themselves rather than external circumstances. The reverse, he says, is true for negative events for the majority of people who don't engage in stress-generative behaviour. You will consider the implications of internal and external control over circumstances further in Chapter 15.

3 Unpredictability and uncontrollability

Predictability offers the opportunity to take pre-emptive and preventive action which, in some circumstances, can give a sense of controllability, which can in turn serve to reduce the intensity of the stressor. However, in circumstances such as repeated child abuse or torture during captivity, the abuse incidents are predictable but not controllable, and thus are associated with high levels of stress.

4 Magnitude

This is the degree of change required by the individual in order for them to be able to resume their normal activities.

5 Centrality

This is the extent to which the circumstances impact on the individual's life goals, plans or concerns.

6 The propensity of the circumstance to exhaust the individual physically

Where the demand for physical exertion is high or there is considerable sleep deprivation, the exhaustion that results can negatively impact the individual's ability both to cope with the stressor and to resume normal activities.

Dohrenwend suggests that this typology might be useful in identifying people who are most likely to suffer from a psychological disorder in the aftermath of exposure to the extreme circumstance. Related to this, it could be useful in the selection of appropriate treatments or interventions. You can appraise the typology in Activity 13.2.

Activity 13.2   Reflecting on Dohrenwend's theories

Did you have any criticisms of Dohrenwend's hierarchy of stress? Do you feel that Dohrenwend's typology covers all the different aspects that might differentiate between different types of circumstances?

Comment

Thinking critically about the hierarchy model, you might be able to think of some examples where experiencing something at the top of the hierarchy would not mean experiencing the lower-level stressors. For example, somebody on death row in a country with capital punishment experiences a persistent threat to life and personal integrity, but also has food and shelter and perhaps experiences fewer everyday life stressors such as redundancy.

Personally, I also believe there were a few things missing from his six categories. Based on the other psychological literature in this field, I would have included the additional categories in Box 13.3.

Box 13.3   Possible additional categories

1 Social context

Is the event something that has only affected this particular individual, or is it something that they experienced along with others? If they experienced it alongside others, were they well acquainted with each other (e.g. from their own family and community) or people who happened to be in the same location at the same time (e.g. in a serious train crash)?

Where a whole community is affected, this is referred to as 'collective trauma' (e.g. Holman and Silver, 2011), whereas the latter is considered to be 'mass trauma' (Basoglu and Salcioglu, 2011). The reason this could be included is because it has significant implications for the resources for coping. When an individual's whole community is similarly affected, all material and psychological resources are likely to become depleted, thus coping becomes more onerous. However, where other people have been similarly affected, but they are not part of the individual's support network, they may be able to offer a source of peer support (Hoffman and Kruczek, 2011). For example, if a whole family has been in a house fire they may struggle to offer material and psychological resources to each other because they have all lost possessions and been injured, whereas if there is a fire in a public building the strangers involved will have unaffected networks of people to support them as well as potentially being able to offer each other the support of having been through the same situation.

2 Injustice versus fate

Consider human error or carelessness versus malicious intent versus a natural disaster or benign lucky circumstance such as winning the lottery. This has been included as there is a considerable difference between someone's needs when they have been harmed by another person (either intentionally or unintentionally) compared with when they have been physically hurt in a natural disaster or an accident. Those who have been harmed by another individual will often have a profound sense of injustice which needs to be rebalanced (Herman, 2005). This is a need which is not typical in the aftermath of other types of extreme circumstances.

By now you have an understanding of the diversity of circumstances that might be experienced as traumatic. The discussion of typologies should have given you some insight into the range of different ways in which 'traumatic events or circumstances' differ from one another. This should help you to understand why responses to extreme circumstances are likely to differ depending on the context.

Next you will move on to explore some of the psychological consequences of experiencing extreme circumstances. Section 3 draws on research and theory from trauma psychology. This is typically, but not exclusively, the domain of counselling and clinical psychologists. Section 4 considers the relatively new field of positive psychology (something you will return to in Chapter 15).

3   The impact of extreme circumstances

Trauma psychology tends to focus on the negative impact that extreme circumstances have on an individual's emotional and psychological well-being. It often includes a range of psychiatric diagnoses (e.g. post-traumatic stress disorder (PTSD) and borderline personality disorder (BPD)), and examines the link between victimisation and offence perpetration. In contrast, positive psychology looks at some of the more positive outcomes that occur in the aftermath of extreme events. For example, this includes post-traumatic growth (PTG) (Tedeschi and Calhoun, 1995), altruism born out of suffering (Staub and Vollhardt, 2008), **resilience** (Bonanno, 2008), and hope. Many people who have experienced extreme circumstances do not just recover and return to some pre-trauma level of functioning. Rather, some feel that their life has taken a completely new and unforeseen trajectory or path, and that they have become better people because of their experience (Tedeschi and Calhoun, 1995).

Resilience
The capacity to recover quickly, or to be less affected by adverse circumstances.

In this part of the chapter you will examine factors that influence the degree of distress which arises as a consequence of the extreme circumstances and the resources needed for **adaptive coping**. Such an understanding might help in the formulation of response strategies that can be used in the aftermath of an extreme circumstance (Box 13.4).

Adaptive coping
Strategies that generally positively help people to cope with adverse circumstances, such as anticipating them and preparing for them, accessing social support, and maintaining general health and well-being.

Box 13.4   Example of formulating a response strategy

Some years ago, I was asked to give a presentation at a conference which focused on planning a response to mass school shootings. My role was to deliver a presentation on the key issues in the aftermath of such an incident that would need to be considered and built into a pre-emptive strategy document. All schools are required to have a strategy in place for such an incident, despite them being extremely rare events globally, and particularly rare in countries such as the UK where few people own firearms.

One of the presenters at the conference was one of the first responders to the Dunblane massacre in 1996 (Figure 13.2), in which 17 people lost their lives (16 primary schoolchildren and their teacher) and a further 16 received non-fatal gunshot injuries. The incident took place in their school gymnasium. Within a month of the shooting, the gymnasium was demolished in order to remove the reminder of the tragic event. However, many of the bereaved parents were very distressed by this and it appeared to hamper their grief process as they felt they needed to be able to go to the place where their children had taken their last breath. What I learned from this is that the needs of those who have experienced extreme circumstances may be beyond common-sense understanding and they therefore require more systematic study.

I saw gunman kill my friends

The Independent, 13 March 1996

Sixteen children killed in Dunblane massacre

The Guardian, 14 March 1996

1996: Massacre in Dunblane school gym

BBC website, 13 March 1996

Figure 13.2 News media headlines following the Dunblane massacre

While there are many potential impacts on individuals who have experienced trauma, you will concentrate here on some of the most common, particularly focusing on PTSD.

3.1 PTSD

The American Psychiatric Association's *Diagnostic and Statistical Manual* version 5 (*DSM 5*), released in 2013, stipulates the necessary criteria for making a PTSD diagnosis. There are eight diagnostic criteria (A to H) which have to be evident before a diagnosis is made (Box 13.5).

Box 13.5 *DSM 5* criteria for PTSD diagnosis

Criterion A is the nature of the triggering event itself. This states that the disorder had to be preceded by an event which threatened the possibility of death or serious injury. Examples given include military combat, civilian disasters (fire, earthquake, etc.), internment in prisoner-of-war camps, concentration camps or refugee camps, rape or assault, near-fatal accidents (car crashes), hijacking, kidnapping or torture.

Also included in criterion A are situations where the individual was directly exposed to the threat themselves; where they (in person) witnessed it happening to someone else; and where they were indirectly exposed. This latter category includes situations where they learned that a close relative or friend suffered one of the above traumas or where they have experienced repeated or extreme indirect exposure to aversive details of the event(s), usually as part of their professional duties (e.g. first responders to humanitarian disasters, body part collection and identification, child protection work, counselling survivors of trauma).

Criterion B relates to what are known as intrusion symptoms. These create the persistent re-experiencing of the original trauma and can include intrusive memories, frightening and/or recurrent nightmares, dissociative reactions (a loss of conscious awareness), intense and prolonged distress following reminders of the trauma, and physiological hyperarousal. The individual only needs to have one of these symptoms for it to count towards a diagnosis.

Criterion C refers to the tendency to intentionally avoid reminders of the trauma, which might be either internally generated (thoughts or feelings) or external reminders (people, places, situations, etc.).

Criterion D refers to the negative alterations in both mood and cognition that either emerge after the traumatic event or significantly worsen after this exposure. To meet the criteria for a PTSD diagnosis the individual must experience two of the following: dissociative amnesia (inability to remember all or parts of the traumatic event); persistent negative beliefs about themselves and their world; persistent distorted self or other blame; significant reduction in interest in activities which were previously enjoyed; feeling detached from others; and/or a persistent inability to feel positive emotions.

Criterion E refers to changes in arousal and reactivity, which include: **hypervigilance**; self-destructive or reckless behaviour;

Hypervigilance
An enhanced state of sensory sensitivity accompanied by an exaggerated frequency of behaviours which aim to detect environmental threats. It is accompanied by a state of increased anxiety which can lead to exhaustion. For example, somebody who has been in a house fire might constantly scan their environment for signs of fire, the smell of smoke, and so on.

Functional impairment
The inability to maintain normal social, educational or occupational roles and responsibilities.

irritable or aggressive behaviour; an exaggerated startle reflex; difficulty in maintaining concentration; sleep disturbance. A diagnosis of PTSD requires that the individual manifests two of these.

Criteria F to H state that the symptoms have to be present for more than one month, that they result in **functional impairment** and that this disturbance cannot be attributed to any other form of illness (e.g. hyperactive thyroid), substance misuse, or the side effect of prescribed medication.

Thus, from the way in which PTSD is diagnosed it is likely that different people will display quite different combinations of symptoms. Unlike physiological illnesses, which often have quite clearly defined markers and a commonality in the way in which they manifest, the same cannot be true for psychological disorders such as PTSD. This means that diagnosis often takes longer for psychological disorders such as PTSD than for physical illnesses. It might also mean that individual treatment needs to differ as a consequence of the presenting symptoms.

Exposure to circumstances such as those listed under Criterion A does not inevitably lead to PTSD. For example, a study conducted in the USA by Ozer and colleagues (2003) found that only between 5 and 10 per cent of individuals who had been exposed to traumatic stress progressed to develop PTSD. However, it appears that some types of stressors are associated with slightly higher incidence rates than others. Investigate this in Activity 13.3.

Activity 13.3   Extreme circumstances and PTSD

Reflecting back on the list of extreme circumstances you generated in Activity 13.1, which of those events or circumstances do you feel would be most likely to result in PTSD? Why do you think those events or circumstances in particular might be more likely to result in PTSD than some of the others? Remember to look back at the events listed in Criterion A of the *DSM 5* criteria for diagnosis.

Comment

According to *DSM 5*, it appears that acts of violence or other life-threatening situations, rather than losses (e.g. redundancy, divorce, bereavement, etc.), are more likely to result in PTSD. Some people may not fully meet the diagnostic criteria for PTSD after experiencing a traumatic event, although they might still experience a range of symptoms. For example, in a study of Manhattan residents a month after the terrorist attack on the Twin Towers in 2001, while 7.5 per cent of the residents met the diagnostic criteria for PTSD, a far larger proportion (17.4 per cent) demonstrated high levels of symptoms of PTSD, but did not quite meet the full criteria (Galea et al., 2003). This group is referred to as having 'subsyndromal' PTSD. Importantly, this subsyndromal group may be at risk of developing PTSD sometime in the future. When this happens it is referred to as 'delayed PTSD'. The term 'delayed' does not mean that there was originally an absence of symptoms, rather that symptoms are reactivated or have gradually increased over time (Frueh, 2009). Delays may be anything between six months and a number of years.

George A. Bonanno (2008) suggests that between 5 and 10 per cent of trauma-exposed individuals might be at risk of developing delayed PTSD. However, Bernice Andrews and colleagues' (2007) review revealed that delayed-onset PTSD is more than twice as likely in military personnel than in the civilian population. Why does delayed PTSD occur? It has been suggested by Andrews and colleagues (2007) that the reoccurrence or increase in symptoms arises as a consequence of being exposed to a new stressor, albeit one that was possibly more 'mundane' than the original. It might be that this new stressor just completely drains the individual's coping reserves – rather like the saying 'the straw that broke the camel's back'.

3.2   Long-term impact of childhood trauma

Childhood trauma, particularly that which arises in the guise of abuse and neglect within the family, has been associated with wide-ranging and sometimes persistent symptoms and disorders. According to the World Health Organization: 'Child abuse or maltreatment constitutes all forms of physical and/or emotional ill-treatment, sexual abuse, neglect or negligent treatment or commercial or other exploitation, resulting in actual or potential harm to the child's health, survival, development or dignity in the context of a relationship of responsibility, trust or power' (WHO, 1999, p. 15). Child sexual abuse (CSA) involves exposing a child to sexual activity or behaviour. Paulo

S. Pinheiro (2006) reported that globally, 160 million girls and 73 million boys had been sexually abused.

With regards to the effects of CSA in childhood, Kate Walsh and colleagues (2010) suggest that between 10 and 25 per cent of known victims of CSA report no psychological difficulties during childhood. However, some may demonstrate a delayed effect which manifests in adolescence or adulthood as they begin to engage in their own consensual sexual relationships. Walsh and colleagues report that the possible effects that might manifest in late childhood or early adolescence include an impaired sense of self, social withdrawal (unusual because most adolescents become more drawn to their peer group), PTSD – which sometimes gets wrongly diagnosed as attention deficit disorder (with or without hyperactivity), poor performance in school, and the development of anxiety disorders or phobias.

For some CSA survivors, the effects become more deleterious as they progress towards adulthood. A large range of conditions, behaviours and attitudes in adulthood has been associated with a history of childhood victimisation, including depression and anxiety (Kaplow et al., 2005), self-harm (Gladstone et al., 2004), suicidal ideation and attempted suicide, psychosis, hostility (Young et al., 2007), fear and avoidance of dentists (Leeners et al., 2007), relationship problems (Liang et al., 2006), sexual difficulties (Sarwer and Durlak, 1996), domestic violence (Whitfield et al., 2003), substance misuse (Freyd et al., 2005), the intergenerational transmission of violence (becoming a perpetrator of child abuse or domestic violence) (Widom, 1989), developing eating disorders (Smolak and Murnen, 2002), experiencing a downward social spiral (moving towards a life of poverty and deprivation) despite relative educational success (Russell, 1986), homelessness (Rotheram-Borus et al., 1996), serving a custodial sentence (Social Exclusion Unit, 2002), and becoming a psychiatric inpatient (Spataro et al., 2004).

Psychopathology
Experiencing psychological disorders such as depression, anxiety or psychosis.

It is very clear from research evidence that adult **psychopathology** often has its origins in childhood adversity, particularly in various forms of child abuse (Terr, 1991). However, while sexually abused children may display a variety of enduring problems and difficulties in life (Carr, 2009), it is suggested that up to 50 per cent of survivors of CSA do not exhibit the most severe long-term psychiatric disorders (Finkelhor et al., 1988).

Furthermore, many survivors claim to experience PTG in the aftermath of their victimisation (Shakespeare-Finch and de Dassel, 2009), which you will learn more about in Section 4. A number of factors have been found to offer abused children some protection from the worst possible effects, including educational engagement and/or attainment, and having one supportive caregiver or positive adult role model (these might be a friend's parents, teachers, neighbours, grandparents, older siblings, etc.). It may be that these factors make children more resilient and thus less affected by the abuse, and/or that they may help the child or young person to find adaptive ways of coping in the aftermath of the abuse (Shakespeare-Finch and de Dassel, 2009).

In contrast, other factors have been found to increase the risk of having an adverse and/or a prolonged response to child abuse. These include issues such as: intra-familial abuse (where the victim and perpetrator are from the same family), early onset of abuse (the abuse started at a young age), multiple perpetrators (either during the same incident or from successive abusive incidents), the severity (the degree of force used and the nature of the sexual acts), the duration of the abuse (the average duration is about four years), and a negative response to a childhood disclosure (survivors who disclose are often disbelieved or blamed by people they tell) (Shakespeare-Finch and de Dassel, 2009).

Interestingly, there is some evidence to suggest that the factor that best predicts whether someone who has experienced CSA will develop more persistent, quality of life-limiting problems in the aftermath of abuse is the response they receive to a disclosure (Jonzon and Lindblad, 2005). To date, strangely, there is no evidence of a protective effect of receiving a positive response, but there is substantial evidence of the deleterious effect of a negative response (Ruggiero et al., 2004). Thus, from the current state of knowledge it would appear that those who never disclosed may fare just as well as those who received a positive response.

However, it might be premature to draw this conclusion, as very few studies have clearly articulated what a positive response to a disclosure would look like. Certainly, one positive response would be that the person who receives the disclosure takes protective action to prevent further harm to the child and provides the child with warm emotional support (and that would require that they both believe and not blame the child) (Wager, 2013).

I hope you can see from this discussion that while the effects of CSA can be debilitating and distressing, most survivors will go on to lead healthy, happy and productive lives. However, as you can see in Activity 13.4, the negative effects are often emphasised in writing on this topic.

Activity 13.4   Talking about trauma and the implications of the words used

Consider the passage below.

> Like childhood rheumatic fever, which causes a number of conditions in adulthood ranging from mitral stenosis to subacute bacterial endocarditis to massive heart failure, childhood psychic trauma leads to a number of mental changes that eventually account for some adult character problems, certain kinds of psychotic thinking, considerable violence, much dissociation, extremes of passivity, self-mutilative episodes, and a variety of anxiety disturbances.
>
> (Terr, 1991, p. 11)

What does this passage suggest about people who have experienced abuse or other forms of extreme circumstances in their childhoods? What effect does using the disease comparison have on your sense of the strength of the relationship between childhood abuse and the development of adult psychopathology? What implications might this view have for adults when they disclose to others about their childhood extreme experiences or when others hear details of someone else's past experiences?

Comment

Despite the positive experiences of many survivors, in the public mind survivors of childhood trauma such as CSA are often seen as excessively vulnerable and almost certainly as having psychiatric problems, which often serves to make some of their claims seem unbelievable, exacerbating the problem that they face (Reavey and Warner, 2003). The comparison with disease here implies that negative effects are inevitable, and this certainly has implications for how people are likely to view survivors and to engage with them.

You will return to some of these issues in Section 4. For now, the chapter will turn to one final example of an extreme circumstance: surviving an ethnic war.

3.3   Surviving an ethnic war

So far you have largely focused on different forms of individual trauma. Here the chapter will briefly introduce the impacts of collective traumas, that is, extreme circumstances that directly affect whole communities or populations. The example you are going to focus on here is the ethnic war in Sri Lanka that ended in 2009.

While this war, which lasted 16 years, had considerable effects on the individuals involved, it also had a profound effect on the functioning of the whole of Sri Lankan society. According to Daya Somasundaram (2003) the development of the country took a backward turn as social structures and institutions were destroyed or rendered dysfunctional. For example, the war had a significant impact on the effective functioning of families, which are the primary agents of socialisation.

The Tamil community (Figure 13.3), which comprises around 15 per cent of the population in Sri Lanka, is a collectivist society, and thus characterised by very cohesive (tightly knit) extended family units, which respond to threats as a single unit rather than as individual members. The civil war between the Tamils and the Sinhalese majority left many families displaced (forced to leave their homes and towns) or separated from other family members through detentions, migration, death and disappearances. While displacement would be bad for any community, it was particularly traumatic for the Tamils since their tradition means that their own identity is defined by their village of origin, and thus the loss of their community also impacted on their sense of self (you may find it useful to refer back to Chapters 4 and 6 to refresh your memory about the involvement of community in people's identities).

Figure 13.3 Image from Tamil community

Importantly, for the Tamil people the strategies they used to cope during the war – strategies that at the time were adaptive – have been found to be maladaptive in coping post-war. The strategies that once had survival value which later became maladaptive included remaining silent and uninvolved with others, trying always to blend into the crowd, and having high levels of suspicion and mistrust of others. As you can imagine, these strategies would not be conducive to rebuilding cohesive communities.

4   Recovery, resilience and post-traumatic growth

From what the chapter has covered so far, it is clear that by no means all people who face extreme circumstances are adversely affected by the events. Such resistance to, or ability to bounce back from, trauma therefore also needs to be considered by those researching or working clinically with potentially traumatised individuals.

4.1   Recovery and resilience

Applied psychologists and other practitioners should be aware of two concepts which have considerable implications for whether they might intervene with someone in the aftermath of trauma, and the ways in which they might do so. These two concepts are **recovery** and **resilience**.

According to Bonanno (2008), when an individual 'recovers' from a trauma they are likely to display a trajectory of psychological functioning. In the immediate aftermath there is a significant decline in well-being and a rise in symptoms of pathology which may last from several months to a number of years. Subsequently, there is a gradual improvement in functioning and a reduction in pathology until the individual achieves a level of functioning and well-being equivalent to that which they evidenced prior to the trauma.

In contrast, resilience refers to the ability to retain fairly normal levels of healthy functioning in the face of an isolated potentially traumatic event. Resilient individuals are believed to exhibit a trajectory through the event and its aftermath that tends to be relatively stable, although they may experience minor disruptions to functioning in the first few weeks following exposure to the potential stressor. These disruptions might include symptoms such as disrupted sleep or experiencing intrusive thoughts. Importantly, resilient individuals appear to be able to maintain the ability to experience positive emotions and the inclination to engage in generative behaviours (i.e. those that demonstrate concern for the advancement and development of future generations) even amid the extreme circumstances (Bonanno et al., 2001).

Recovery
'Getting over' a traumatic incident, having been initially affected by it.

Resilience
A quality enabling a person to deal with an extreme circumstance with relatively little disruption to their life.

When trauma first became a subject of research, signs of resilience in those exposed to trauma were considered to be both a rarity and pathological. For example, the absence of prolonged grief in response to the death of a loved one was, in the past, attributed to a disordered personality (Osterweis et al., 1984), and was believed to result in longer-term maladaptation (Middleton et al., 1993), or the possible risk of a delayed reaction. However, there is a lack of psychological evidence to support any of these assumptions (Bonanno, 2008).

The theoretical rationale for the notion that 'absent grief' is pathological is based on John Bowlby's (1960) attachment theory. This suggests that children develop certain attachment styles in childhood which impact on their adult relationships. Bowlby's theories were supported by Mary D. Salter Ainsworth's research (Ainsworth and Bell, 1970). This found that children who would be classified as securely attached according to Bowlby's theories would generally be somewhat upset when left with a stranger, and happy when their caregiver returned. Avoidant attachment was demonstrated by not seeming to care much when left alone. Ambivalently attached children might be highly distressed at being left, but ambivalent when the caregiver returned.

Figure 13.4 John Bowlby

The theory of 'absent grief' argues that, if a bereaved individual does not demonstrate a grief response suggestive of distress, they must be emotionally cold and distant, a state which has arisen as a consequence of a lack of secure attachment in childhood. However, Bonanno and colleagues' (2002) research found no support for such insecure attachment styles in those who demonstrated absent grief. They collected data from a large study on older people's mental health over time, focusing on those who had been through loss of a spouse during the period of the study. Their findings suggest that resilience could be partly explained by people's pre-bereavement cognitions and social circumstances. Thus the 'resilient bereaved' scored relatively higher than those who demonstrated the expected grief reactions on measures of acceptance of death and belief that the world is a fair place. They also reported having access to more practical support.

Importantly, it is not that the resilient individuals in this study were totally unaffected by their loss. They did report yearning for their lost loved one and they were troubled by intrusive thoughts and pangs of sadness. However, these tended to be transient and, more importantly, they were not so extreme that they interfered with their functioning in other life domains such as work or education. It might be that these individuals' continued engagement in either work or education provided them with a respite from reminders of their loss. Also, this may have provided opportunities to experience both positive emotions and purposeful meaning in their lives. Thus these findings do not lend support to the idea that an absence of grief is necessarily pathological. Rather, they indicate that these individuals have a different way of appraising their loss that does not leave them searching for meaning.

Possible attributes that are believed to increase the likelihood of resilience in the face of adversity include hardiness, self-enhancement, positive emotions and laughter, and **repressive coping** (Bonanno, 2008). Here you will briefly consider hardiness and self-enhancement.

Hardiness

Hardiness is argued to consist of three dimensions (Kobasa et al., 1982):

1   a commitment to finding meaning in life
2   a belief in the ability to exert a level of control over one's environment and events that occur

Repressive coping
A coping strategy where people minimise or dismiss the problems they experience or difficult emotions associated with them.

3   a belief that both positive and negative events permit the potential for learning and growth.

Thinking back to Lazarus and Cohen's (1977) contention that an individual's primary appraisal of a situation partly determines their reaction to that situation (in the discussion of Activity 13.1), hardy individuals have been found less likely than non-hardy individuals to appraise situations as threatening. So why are hardy individuals resilient? It appears that hardy people are more likely to engage in active (or problem-focused), as opposed to passive (or emotion-focused), coping strategies and they appear to more readily elicit support from their social network.

Self-enhancement

Anthony G. Greenwald (1980) and others have argued that mental health is not actually characterised by having realistic perceptions about one's own abilities and attributes. Indeed, mental health is associated with what might be called 'having an optimistic bias': this is what is meant by self-enhancement. People who are affected by mild to moderate depression appear to demonstrate a greater degree of realism (accuracy) when predicting their abilities. You might want to keep this in mind for Chapter 15 when you will consider correcting cognitive biases as a form of self-help. Perhaps some cognitive biases may actually be helpful!

4.2   Demonstrating growth in response to trauma

As you have seen, many people demonstrate profound resilience in the face of adversity, but the concept of resilience is minimalistic: it only focuses on relative normality in response to traumatic experiences, rather than on the exceptional selflessness and courage demonstrated by some individuals. To compensate for the lack of recognition of some traumatised individuals' capacity to move on from their experiences to a point of functioning exceeding their pre-trauma functioning, the concept of PTG emerged (Tedeschi and Calhoun, 1995; Linley and Joseph, 2004; Hobfoll et al., 2007). For example, Richard G. Tedeschi and Lawrence G. Calhoun report that 50 per cent of survivors of trauma identify their traumatic event as being the catalyst for personal adaptation and positive change. These positive changes may relate to self-perception, quality of relationships with others and/or general life philosophy.

Whether or not someone experiences PTG appears to depend less on the nature of events than on how events are appraised by the individual. Tedeschi and Calhoun say that the necessary conditions include a perceived threat to life, an existential struggle surrounding the events ('Why me?'-type questioning), and a successful attempt to create meaning out of events that appear meaningless. An increase in compassion for others and engagement in altruistic behaviours are key aspects of PTG: 'when people recognise their own vulnerability they may be better able to feel compassion and that some kind of trauma may be a kind of empathy training. Out of this ... may come the need to help ... this is likely to occur after certain time has passed' (Tedeschi et al., 1998, p. 12).

The most important point about PTG is not just that it relates to a positive change in life trajectory for the individual, but also that these individuals are often motivated to campaign for social change: to prevent similar trauma happening to others or to fight for justice for survivors. Importantly, it is possible for someone to experience both the negative and positive outcomes of extreme circumstances simultaneously. That is, they may still manifest symptoms of PTSD, but they may also have become a very dedicated and effective volunteer for an organisation which serves the needs of others who have had similar experiences, offering them new meanings and goals in their lives.

Activity 13.5   Spotting post-traumatic growth in others

Think for a moment about whether you can name anyone – either a well-known person or someone from your own social group – who you think demonstrates PTG. Can you list their attributes or actions that you feel are indicators of growth?

Comment

The kind of people who might have come to mind include Sara Payne and Doreen Lawrence. Sara Payne MBE is the mother of Sarah Payne, who was murdered in 2000. Since her daughter's murder, she has consistently campaigned on child protection issues. Doreen Lawrence is the mother of Stephen Lawrence, who was murdered in a racist attack in 1993. Now Baroness Lawrence of Clarendon OBE, she has consistently campaigned on issues of crime, equality and diversity.

---

5   Perils, pitfalls and positive effects of psychological interventions

Bonanno (2001) makes an interesting point that has important implications for the way in which potentially traumatised individuals are signposted to support services and for the way in which interventions are developed. He says that it might be a mistake, on the part of both researchers and practitioners, to group all people who do not demonstrate PTSD in response to traumatic exposure into one homogenous group.

Bonanno suggests that an absence of PTSD might be due to a timely and effective recovery from the trauma, or that individuals may have been resilient, and thus resistant to trauma. Failing to make this distinction could cause the erroneous assumption that resilient individuals engage in the same coping processes as those who are initially traumatised by their exposure yet who go on to recover. The routes to resilience may actually differ quite significantly from adaptive coping.

5.1   Grief work and grief counselling

Mental healthcare professionals tend to endorse the need for bereaved persons to undertake what is termed 'grief work' (Stroebe and Stroebe, 1991), which involves the bringing to consciousness of all memories (both good and bad) related to the deceased. However, Robert A. Neimeyer (2000) conducted a meta-analysis on grief involving 23 studies totalling 1600 participants. He found that 38 per cent of those who received such grief-work-based counselling demonstrated deterioration in their well-being post-intervention in comparison with those in the non-intervention control group. This 38 per cent might serve as an example of the problem of **iatrogenic disorder**: the intended treatment may have caused or exacerbated a problem, rather than solving it.

Iatrogenic disorder
A disorder which is caused either directly or indirectly by a professional's intervention.

Rather than declaring that grief work should never be used again, Bonanno and colleagues (2002) suggest that such an intervention might be beneficial for those who are experiencing the highest levels of grief and distress. This contention was also supported in Neimeyer's (2000) meta-analysis, where he found that grief therapy was beneficial for those who experienced traumatic bereavement (e.g. the murder or the untimely death of a loved one), but not for those who experienced 'normal bereavement'. Only 17 per cent of those who experienced traumatic bereavement were found to be adversely affected by the therapy. Furthermore, the findings suggest that therapy might be most useful once it is recognised that grieving is not occurring according to the 'normal course', and for younger clients.

Neimeyer (2000) concluded with the suggestion that 'grief therapy is appropriately offered to mourners experiencing protracted, traumatic, or complicated grief reactions. Conversely, existing evidence from scientifically credible controlled outcome trials suggests that grief therapy for normal bereavement is difficult to justify' (p. 546). However, in 2008 he reported that he was reluctant to draw definitive guidelines as other studies were less conclusive (Currier et al., 2008) and more research was therefore necessary in this area.

This is reminiscent of a principle in the forensic psychology literature which refers to the rehabilitation of offenders. D. A. Andrews and James Bonta (1994) similarly conducted a meta-analysis, but in this instance it was to determine 'what works' in offender rehabilitation. One of the outcomes of their study was the development of the 'Risk, needs, responsivity' model of effective interventions (Figure 13.5). In the context of this chapter the principle of risk is of interest. They suggest that any intervention should be proportionate to the level of risk demonstrated by the individual awaiting intervention. In their case this is risk of recidivism (reoffending), whereas here the concern would be with the risk of protracted and debilitating grief. They argue that those who are at low risk might be best left without treatment, whereas high-risk individuals should be offered the intervention. Importantly, they suggest that subjecting a low-risk individual to the intervention will possibly exacerbate their level of risk. Thus in the context of 'normal' grief, it might be better to let the bereaved person use their own natural resources for coping, be this to maintain their resilience or to facilitate their recovery.

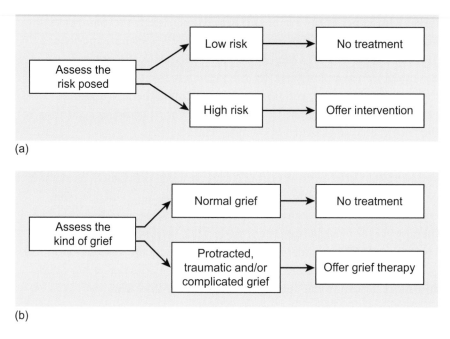

(a)

(b)

Figure 13.5   (a) Risk, needs, responsivity model; (b) the model applied to grief therapy

Neimeyer (2000) offers three speculative explanations for the limited efficacy of grief-work-based counselling, summarised in Box 13.6.

Box 13.6   Neimeyer's explanations for the limited efficacy of grief-work-based counselling

1   The relatively unfavourable findings might be an artefact of the wrong choice of outcome measure by the researchers. Neimeyer posits that there might be too much emphasis on psychiatric and physical problems rather than issues concerning attachment to the deceased. It may be that a goal of grief therapy should be to enable the transition between having a concrete relationship with the deceased to having a symbolic relationship with them; this journey might form a more suitable outcome measure. A concrete relationship means the relationship that the person had with the deceased while they were alive, while a symbolic relationship means the relationship they have with their memory of the person, imagining what they might say, and so forth.

2   Even the published reports of controlled studies assessing the efficacy of grief counselling rarely describe the conceptual models on which the therapeutic techniques are based. This

---

> finding might suggest that the techniques themselves lack a theoretical rationale.
>
> 3 Where conceptual models have been declared, the theories they come from tend to be outdated ones rather than ones that are supported by empirical evidence.

In his conclusion, Neimeyer (2000) proposes an alternative target for grief counselling, which is assisting clients with meaning making. This refers to people's capacity to find a meaning in whatever happens to them in life. Religious beliefs often involve a sense that everything is meaningful, but non-religious people can also find meaning, for example in using difficult times to develop resilience or compassion for others.

Viktor Frankl (Figure 13.6), in discussing his experiences in the Nazi concentration camp at Auschwitz, describes the process and motivation for meaning making in this way:

> We must never forget that we may also find meaning in life even when confronted with a hopeless situation, when facing a fate that cannot be changed. For what then matters is to bear witness to the uniquely human potential at its best, which is to transform a personal tragedy into a triumph, to turn one's predicament into human achievement. When we are no longer able to change a situation ... we are challenged to change ourselves.
>
> (Frankl, 1969, p. 135)

The majority of people who experience complicated or traumatic bereavement undertake a search for meaning making in relation to their loss (Currier et al., 2006). Others readily identify a meaning from the outset, and yet others do not seek meaningful reasons for their loss.

The findings from a study of parents who had lost their child to sudden infant death (Davis et al., 2000) demonstrated that the parents who fared worst were those who embarked on a search for meaning but were unable to find satisfactory answers. However, those who did not embark on this journey fared similarly to those who found meaning in the loss.

Figure 13.6   Viktor Frankl

From a clinical point of view this is important. It suggests that if the bereaved parties have not spontaneously begun to search for meaning it would be best if they are not guided down this route. However, where the client has initiated this process and has not succeeded in discovering answers after some reasonable time of searching, it might be helpful for a practitioner to assist in the process.

This discussion should have highlighted to you that not all individuals are in need of an intervention, and that to impose an intervention on resilient individuals may in fact be detrimental to their longer-term well-being. This is particularly important in relation to critical incident debriefing (CID), a stress management strategy employed by some organisations that deal with extreme circumstances, and which may be used for all exposed employees rather than in a targeted manner.

5.2   PTSD and critical incident debriefing

CID is a specific technique developed by Jeffrey Mitchell (1983) to assist individuals to process their reactions following exposure to traumatic incidents. It is intended to reduce the likelihood of developing clinical and prolonged levels of PTSD. Debriefing is often used with the emergency services and with first responders to humanitarian disasters following deployment on a particularly harrowing incident. It was originally developed as a brief group intervention which could be offered to all those who had been exposed to an incident. Debriefing allows those exposed to the incident to process the event and reflect on the impact it has had on them. One of the techniques used in CID is defusing, which allows the individual to express or vent their emotions and thoughts associated with the crisis event.

Some researchers have argued that, to be effective, the principle of proximity must be employed in delivering the intervention. That is, it should be conducted on or near the site of the event and as soon as possible after exposure, ideally within the first 24–72 hours (Mitchell, 1986). However, there is growing criticism of such a blanket or universal application of CID to all those who were exposed to the trauma, on the basis that it may imply that all people will experience traumatic responses, and thus potentially inhibit the expression of natural resilience (Mayou et al., 2000).

Brett T. Litz and colleagues (2006) therefore proposed that, rather than universally offering CID, it might be preferable to implement a brief screening of all those exposed to identify who is at risk of developing PTSD and thus has potential to benefit from the intervention. They suggested that factors which might increase the risk of PTSD could include prior exposure to, or experience of, trauma, low levels of social support, and manifest physiological hyperarousal (e.g. high heart rate or blood pressure).

5.3   Interventions with survivors of child sexual abuse

It is currently unclear whether post-traumatic responses to CSA are positively influenced by professional intervention or whether more informal support systems are better placed to help the individual move on with their life (that is, if the individual has not already demonstrated resilience).

Many treatments have been developed to provide essential care and support for survivors. The most common interventions are based on **cognitive behavioural therapy (CBT)** approaches as they have been shown to demonstrate the most positive effects. However, how effective the intervention is partly depends on factors outside the intervention itself. For example, Charles Wenar and Patricia K. Kerig (2006) argue that when the whole family is involved in an intervention for children who have been sexually abused, far more positive effects

Cognitive behavioural therapy (CBT)
A range of psychology-based therapeutic approaches which aims at changing clients' behaviours and/or cognitions in order to alleviate their problems.

are observed than when the intervention is delivered to the child on their own. When the abuse has been perpetrated by a family member, only the non-offending parties would be included in the therapy.

Even though many established treatments for sexually abused children exist, there is little evidence to support the efficacy of these treatments (Finkelhor and Berliner, 1995). Furthermore, currently in the UK, only children who demonstrate symptoms following CSA are generally offered therapeutic services, particularly by Child and Adolescent Mental Health teams. As you read in Section 3.2, this is despite the fact that **asymptomatic** children may come to manifest debilitating symptoms at later critical life periods (e.g. the onset of adolescence or the establishment of a consensual sexual relationship) (Gomes-Schwartz et al., 1990).

Asymptomatic
Not demonstrating symptoms.

It is estimated that only around one in 800 cases of CSA reach the attention of child protection services (Nurse, 2006), and are thus able to access services. This, combined with the lack of intervention for asymptomatic children, means that only a very small minority of victims of CSA are likely to be offered any form of intervention during childhood. Consequently, when considering processes involved in facilitating adaptive coping, it is unlikely that therapeutic interventions are the only helpful factor.

5.4   Interventions for former child soldiers

In Section 3.3 you read about the impact of ethnic war on the Tamil people in Sri Lanka. It was highlighted how the fact that they were a collectivist society meant that displacement from their home town had an even more profound effect than it would on Westerners, who tend to come from individualistic traditions. Collectivist societies put more emphasis on groups and communities than on the individual, whereas individualistic ones do the opposite (e.g. talk in terms of 'I' rather than 'we') (see Chapter 6). You will now continue with culture as a theme, but this time in terms of the implications it has for interventions. The key point here is that it may not always be appropriate to transport Western forms of psychotherapy to different countries and cultural groups.

Filipa Neto Marques (2001) discusses the rehabilitation and reintegration of former child soldiers in Mozambique. Western psychotherapy was found to be unsuccessful in this context. The reasons she suggests to account for the failure include the fact that the children were completely removed from their community and cultural environment during the intervention, but this made little sense since they came from a collectivist society. Additionally, Western psychotherapy encourages clients to talk about their painful memories as a way of healing, but this conflicts with cultural norms which discourage talking about the past or looking back. Rather, in many cultures in Mozambique people are expected to start afresh after certain ritual procedures. Finally, ancestral spirits and other spiritual forces are often deemed important in causing and healing psychological distress, but these notions are absent from Western therapies.

More culturally embedded rituals performed for former child soldiers in Mozambique aim at dealing with what happened during the war. They acknowledge the atrocities they committed and a subsequent break from that past is then permitted through a ritual performance. There are different types of rituals for those who have participated in the war but did not kill and those who actually killed other people. Symbolically breaking with the past is achieved through rituals such as washing their body in the river so that the dirt of the war will go away, burning of their hut and the clothes they brought from the war, and herbal remedies to cleanse the body internally (inhaling and drinking) and externally (bathing and rubbing). Can you imagine a Western psychologist recommending any of these interventions?

6   Summary

In this chapter you have considered the meaning of 'extreme circumstances', the range of experiences that this might cover, and the possible ways of delineating different types of circumstances and the effects they might have. Focusing on trauma, you have considered how this is currently defined in the major psychiatric manual (*DSM 5*), as well as the potential impact of trauma on individuals, families and societies, and the implications of this for psychological interventions with people who have experienced traumatic events. You have also spent some time exploring the growth experiences that many people undergo following extreme circumstances, and the implications of resilience and potential for growth on the kind of interventions employed.

You have covered a number of issues that are important for socially responsible and ethical practice in any psychological role where you might be working with individuals who have experienced extreme circumstances. These include avoiding regarding all those who have experienced a potentially traumatic experience as psychopathological, and recognising that some people successfully move on with their lives, others are resilient, and some will grow from the experience. Additionally, you have touched on the importance of culture for both understanding the impact of extreme circumstances and developing appropriate and effective interventions.

References

Ainsworth, M. D. S. and Bell, S. M. (1970) 'Attachment, exploration, and separation: illustrated by the behavior of one-year-olds in a strange situation', *Child Development*, vol. 41, pp. 49–67.

American Psychiatric Association (2013) *Diagnostic and Statistical Manual of Mental Disorders, DSM-5*, Arlington, VA, APA.

Andrews, B., Brewin, C. R., Philpott, R. and Stewart, L. (2007) 'Delayed-onset post-traumatic stress disorder: a systematic review of the evidence', *American Journal of Psychiatry*, vol. 164, pp. 1319–26.

Andrews, D. A. and Bonta, J. (1994) *The Psychology of Criminal Conduct*, Cincinnati, OH, Anderson.

Basoglu, M. and Salcioglu, E. (2011) *A Mental Healthcare Model for Mass Trauma Survivors: Control-Focused Behavioral Treatment of Earthquake, War and Torture Trauma*, New York, Cambridge University Press.

Bonanno, G. A. (2001) 'Emotion self-regulation', in Mayne, T. J. and Bonanno G. A. (eds) *Emotions: Current Issues and Future Directions*, New York, Guilford Press, pp. 251–85.

Bonanno, G. A. (2008) 'Loss, trauma, and human resilience: have we underestimated the human capacity to thrive after extremely aversive events?', *Psychological Trauma: Theory, Research, Practice and Policy*, vol. 5, no. 1, pp. 101–13.

Bonanno, G. A., Pope, A. and O'Neill, K. (2001) 'Loss and human resilience', *Applied and Preventative Psychology*, vol. 10, pp. 193–206.

Bonanno, G. A., Wortman, C. B., Lehman, D. R., Tweed, R. G., Haring, M., Sonnega, J., Carr, D. and Nesse, R. M. (2002) 'Resilience to loss and chronic grief: a prospective study from pre-loss to 18 months post-loss', *Journal of Personality and Social Psychology*, vol. 83, no. 5, pp. 1150–64.

Bowlby, J. (1960) *Attachment and Loss, Vol. 3: Loss: Sadness and Depression*, New York: Basic Books.

Carr, A. (2009) *What Works With Children, Adolescents and Adults? A Review of Research on the Effectiveness of Psychotherapy*, London, Routledge.

Currier, J., Holland, J., Coleman, R. and Neimeyer, R. A. (2006) 'Bereavement following violent death: an assault on life and meaning', in Stevenson, R. and Cox, G. (eds) *Violence*, Amityville, NY, Baywood.

Currier, J. M., Neimeyer, R. A. and Berman, J. S. (2008) 'The effectiveness of psychotherapeutic interventions for bereaved persons: a comprehensive quantitative review', *Psychological Bulletin*, vol. 134, no. 5, pp. 648–61.

Davis, C. G., Wortman, C. B., Lehman, D. R. and Silver, R. C. (2000) 'Searching for meaning in loss: are clinical assumptions correct?', *Death Studies*, vol. 24, no. 6, pp. 497–540.

Dohrenwend, B. P. (2010) 'Towards a typology of high-risk major stressful events and situations in posttraumatic stress disorder and related psychopathology', *Psychological Injury and the Law*, vol. 3, no. 2, pp. 89–99.

Finkelhor, D. and Berliner, L. (1995) 'Research on the treatment of sexually abused children: a review and recommendations', *Journal of the American Academy of Child and Adolescent Psychiatry*, vol. 34, no. 11, pp. 1408–23.

Finkelhor, D., Hotaling, G. T. and Yllo, K. (1988) *Stopping Family Violence: Research Priorities for the Coming Decade*, Newbury Park, CA, Sage Publications.

Frankl, V. (1969) *The Will to Meaning: Foundations and Applications of Logotherapy*, New York, World Publishing.

Freyd, J. J., Klest, B. and Allard, C. B. (2005) 'Betrayal trauma: relationship to physical health, psychological distress, and a written disclosure intervention', *Journal of Trauma and Dissociation*, vol. 6, no. 3, pp. 83–104.

Frueh, B. C. (2009) 'Delayed-onset post-traumatic stress disorder among war veterans in primary care clinics', *British Journal of Psychiatry*, vol. 194, no. 6, pp. 515–20.

Galea, S., Vlahov, D., Resnick, H., Ahern, J., Suzzer, E., Gold, J., Bucuvalas, M. and Kilpatrick, D. (2003) 'Trends of probable post-traumatic stress disorder in New York City after the September 11 terrorist attacks', *American Journal of Epidemiology*, vol. 158, no. 6, pp. 514–24.

Gladstone, G. L., Parker, G. B., Mitchell, P. B., Malhi, G. S., Wilhelm, K. and Austin, M.-P. (2004) 'Implications of childhood trauma for depressed women: an analysis of pathways from childhood sexual abuse to deliberate self-harm and revictimization', *American Journal of Psychiatry*, vol. 161, pp. 1417–25.

Gomes-Schwartz, B., Horowitz, J. M. and Cardarelli, A. P. (1990) *Child Sexual Abuse: The Initial Effects*, Newbury Park, CA, Sage.

Greenwald, A. G. (1980) 'The totalitarian ego: fabrication and revision of personal history', *American Psychologist*, vol. 35, pp. 603–18.

Hammen, C. (1991) 'Generation of stress in the course of unipolar depression', *Journal of Abnormal Psychology*, vol. 100, pp. 555–61.

Herman, J. L. (2005) 'Justice from a victim's perspective', *Violence Against Women*, vol. 11, no. 5, pp. 571–602.

Hobfoll, S. E., Hall, B. J., Canetti-Nisim, D., Galea, S., Johnson, R. J. and Palmieri, P. (2007) 'Refining our understanding of traumatic growth in the face of terrorism: moving from meaning cognitions to doing what is meaningful', *Applied Psychology: An International Journal*, vol. 56, pp. 345–66.

Hoffman, M. A. and Kruczek, T. (2011) 'A bioecological model of mass trauma: individual, community, and societal effects', *The Counseling Psychologist*, vol. 39, no. 8, pp. 1087–127.

Holman, E. A. and Silver, R. C. (2011) 'Health status and health care utilization following collective trauma: a 3-year national study of the 9/11 terrorist attacks in the United States', *Social Science and Medicine*, vol. 73, no. 4, pp. 483–90.

Jonzon, E. and Lindblad, F. (2005) 'Adult female victims of child sexual abuse: multi-type maltreatment and disclosure characteristics related to subjective health', *Journal of Interpersonal Violence*, vol. 20, no. 6, pp. 651–66.

Kaplow, J., Dodge, K., Amaya-Jackson, L. and Saxe, G. (2005) 'Pathways to PTSD, part II: sexually abused children', *American Journal of Psychiatry*, vol. 162, no. 7, pp. 1305–10.

Kobasa, S. C., Maddi, S. R. and Kahn, S. (1982) 'Hardiness and health: a prospective study', *Journal of Personality and Social Psychology*, vol. 42, pp. 168–77.

Lazarus, R. S. and Cohen, J. B. (1977) 'Environmental stress', in Attman, I. and Wohlwill, J. F. (eds) *Human Behavior and Environment: Current Theory and Research*, New York, Plenum Press.

Leeners, B., Stiller, R., Block, E., Gorres, G., Bruno, I. and Rath, W. (2007) 'Consequences of child sexual abuse experiences on dental care', *Journal of Psychosomatic Research*, vol. 62, no. 5, pp. 581–8.

Liang, B., Williams, L. M. and Siegel, J. A. (2006) 'Relational outcomes of childhood sexual trauma in female survivors: a longitudinal study', *Journal of Interpersonal Violence*, vol. 21, no. 1, pp. 42–57.

Linley, P. A. and Joseph, S. (2004) 'Applied positive psychology: a new perspective for professional practice', in Linley, P. A. and Joseph, S. (eds) *Positive Psychology in Practice*, Hoboken, NJ, Wiley, pp. 3–12.

Litz, B. T., Gray, M. J., Bryant, R. A. and Adler, A. B. (2006) 'Early interventions for trauma: current status and future directions', *Clinical Psychology: Science and Practice*, vol. 9, no. 2, pp. 112–34.

Marques, F. N. (2001) 'Rehabilitation and reintegration of the former child soldiers in Mozambique', *Best Paper Series, Symposium on the Global Issues in Public Administration*, Maxwell School of Citizenship and Public Affairs [Online]. Available at www.essex.ac.uk/armedcon/story_id/filipa's%20paper. pdf (Accessed 19 December 2014).

Mayou, R., Ehlers, A. and Hobbs, M. (2000) 'Psychological debriefing for road traffic accident victims: three year follow-up of a randomised controlled trial', *British Journal of Psychiatry*, vol. 176, pp. 589–93.

Middleton, W., Moylan, A., Raphael, B., Burnett, P. and Martinek, N. (1993) 'An international perspective on bereavement related concepts', *Australian and New Zealand Journal of Psychiatry*, vol. 27, pp. 457–63.

Mitchell, J. T. (1983) 'When disaster strikes… the critical incident stress debriefing process', *Journal of Emergency Medical Services*, vol. 8, pp. 36–9.

Neimeyer, R. A. (2000) 'Searching for meaning of meaning: grief therapy and the process of reconstruction', *Death Studies*, vol. 24, pp. 541–58.

Nurse, J. (2006) 'Abuse: the hidden reality', *Workshop on Patterns of Violence and Abuse: Impact on Health and Well-Being*, Thames Valley Partnership, 23 May [Online]. Available at www.thamesvalleypartnership.org.uk/wp-content/uploads/jo-nurse-23-may-06.ppt (Accessed 19 December 2014).

Osterweis, M., Solomon, F. and Green, F. (1984) *Bereavement: Reactions, Consequences, and Care*, Washington, DC, National Academy Press.

Ozer, E. J., Best, S. R., Lipsey, T. L. and Weiss, D. S. (2003) 'Predictors of posttraumatic stress disorder and symptoms in adults: a meta-analysis', *Psychological Bulletin*, vol. 129, no. 1, pp. 52–73.

Pinheiro, P. S. (2006) *World Report on Violence Against Children*, Geneva, United Nations.

Reavey, P. and Warner, S. (eds) (2003) *New Feminist Stories of Child Sexual Abuse: Sexual Scripts and Dangerous Dialogue*, London, Routledge.

Rotheram-Borus, M. J., Mahler, K. A., Koopman, C. and Langabeer, K. (1996) 'Sexual abuse history and associated multiple risk behaviour in adolescent runaways', *American Journal of Orthopsychiatry*, vol. 66, pp. 390–400.

Ruggiero, K. J., Smith, D. W., Hanson, R. F., Resnick, H. S., Saunders, B. E., Kilpatrick, D. G. and Best, C. L. (2004) 'Is disclosure of childhood rape associated with mental health outcome? Results from the National Women's Study', *Child Maltreatment*, vol. 9, no. 1, pp. 62–77.

Russell, D. E. (1986) *The Secret Trauma: Incest in the Lives of Girls and Women*, New York, Basic Books.

Sarwer, D. B. and Durlak, J. A. D. (1996) 'Childhood sexual abuse as a predictor of female sexual dysfunction: a study of couples seeking sex therapy', *Child Abuse and Neglect*, vol. 20, no. 10, pp. 963–72.

Shakespeare-Finch, J. E. and de Dassel, T. (2009) 'The impact of child sexual abuse on victims/survivors: exploring posttraumatic outcomes as a function of childhood sexual abuse', *Journal of Child Sexual Abuse*, vol. 18, no. 6, pp. 623–40.

Smolak, L. and Murnen, S. K. (2002) 'A meta-analytic examination of the relationship between child sexual abuse and eating disorders', *International Journal of Eating Disorders*, vol. 31, no. 2, pp. 136–50.

Social Exclusion Unit, (2002) *Reducing Re-offending by Ex-prisoners*, London, Social Exclusion Unit, Office of the Deputy Prime Minister .

Somasundaram, D. (2003) 'Collective trauma in Sri Lanka', *Intervention: International Journal of Mental Health, Psychosocial Work and Counselling in Areas of Armed Conflict*, vol. 1, pp. 4–13.

Spataro, J., Mullen, P. E., Burgess, P. M., Wells, D. L. and Moss, S. A. (2004) 'Impact of child sexual abuse on mental health: prospective study in males and females', *British Journal of Psychiatry*, vol. 184, pp. 416–21.

Staub, E. and Vollhardt, J. (2008) 'Altruism born out of suffering: the roots of caring and helping after victimisation and other trauma', *American Journal of Orthopsychiatry*, vol. 78, no. 3, pp. 267–80.

Stroebe, M. S. and Stroebe, W. (1991) 'Does "grief work" work?', *Journal of Consulting and Clinical Psychology*, vol. 59, pp. 479–82.

Tedeschi, R. G. and Calhoun, L. G. (1995) *Trauma and Transformation: Growing in the Aftermath of Suffering*, Thousand Oaks, CA, Sage.

Tedeschi, R. G., Park, C. L. and Calhoun, L. G. (eds) (1998) *Posttraumatic Growth: Positive Changes in the Aftermath of Crisis*, New York, Routledge.

Terr, L. C. (1991) 'Childhood traumas: an outline and overview', *American Journal of Psychiatry*, vol. 148, no. 1, pp. 10–20.

Ullman, S. E. (2010) *Talking About Sexual Assault: Society's Response to Survivors*, Washington, DC, American Psychological Association.

Wager, N. (2013) 'Sexual revictimisation: double betrayal and the risk associated with dissociative amnesia', *Journal of Child Sexual Abuse*, vol. 22, no. 7, pp. 878–99.

Walsh, K., Fortier, M. A. and DiLillo, D. (2010) 'Adult coping with childhood sexual abuse: a theoretical and empirical review', *Aggression and Violent Behaviour*, vol. 15, pp. 1–13.

Wenar, C. and Kerig, P. K. (2006) *Developmental Psychopathology: From Infancy Through Adolescence*, 5th edn, New York, McGraw-Hill.

Whitfield, C. L., Anda, R. F., Dube, S. R. and Felitti, V. J. (2003) 'Violent childhood experiences and the risk of intimate partner violence in adults: assessment in a large health maintenance organisation', *Journal of Interpersonal Violence*, vol. 18, no. 2, pp. 166–85.

Widom, C. S. (1989) 'The cycle of violence', *Science*, vol. 244, pp. 160–6.

World Health Organization (1999) *Report of the Consultation on Child Abuse Prevention*, Geneva, WHO.

Young, M. S., Harford, K. L., Kinder, B. and Savell, J. K. (2007) 'The relationships between child sexual abuse and adult mental health among undergraduates', *Journal of Interpersonal Violence*, vol. 22, no. 10, pp. 1315–31.

Answer to Activity 13.1

This is a list of potential extreme circumstances produced for the purposes of this chapter from reviewing the literature in this area to see which are commonly mentioned.

Bereavement

Car accident

Childbirth

Unplanned pregnancy

Being conscious throughout a major surgical operation but being unable to tell the surgical team that one is not fully anaesthetised

Redundancy

Divorce or separation from a long-term partner

Imprisonment

Divorce or separation of parents

Being given a life-changing medical diagnosis

Serious illness or disability of a family member

Acquiring a disability (e.g. going blind, losing a limb)

Child abuse

Discovery of an intimate partner's lack of faithfulness

Being a victim of a single-incident crime (e.g. robbery, burglary, violent assault, sexual assault)

Being the victim of repeated criminal acts (e.g. domestic violence, hate crime)

Being held hostage or kidnapped

Being held in servitude (slavery)

Witnessing violence against or the murder of another

Witnessing the accidental death or serious injury of another

Experiencing a natural disaster (e.g. hurricane, tsunami, earthquake)

Experiencing a human-made disaster (e.g. plane or train crash, sinking boat)

Surviving genocide, war, armed conflict

Unintentionally seriously harming or causing the death of another person

Having seen active service in the military

Being a former child soldier

Winning the lottery

Chapter 14
Sex and sexuality

Helen Bowes-Catton

Contents

1 Introduction

As you have already learned, this part of the book is concerned with the relationship between people's understandings of the world and their experience of it. Chapter 13 considered how people's understandings of the world both shape, and are shaped by, their experiences of extreme circumstances. In a similar way, this chapter looks at how personal, cultural and psychological understandings shape people's lived experiences of sex and sexuality, and how the usefulness of psychological approaches to sex might helpfully be examined through the lens of those experiences.

As you might expect, this chapter contains frank discussions of sexuality and sexual practices. As with Chapter 13, some of the activities involve reflecting on your own understandings and experiences and, for some readers, this may involve revisiting distressing events and emotions. With this kind of content, it is important to bear in mind that all the activities in the chapter are purely voluntary and for your own use. You may well wish to discuss some of your responses to this chapter with friends or peers, but please bear the sensitivity of this topic in mind.

After reading this chapter you should be able to:

- describe some of the main psychological and sexological theories of sex and sexuality

- consider the role of these theories in shaping popular cultural understandings

- explain the usefulness, or otherwise, of conventional understandings of sex and sexuality

- reflect on the ways in which understanding the diversity of sexual identities and sexual practices might help psychologists to find new ways of making sense of sex.

2   Examining conventional understandings of sex and sexuality

It is first worth thinking, by completing Activity 14.1, about what is meant by sex. It may seem obvious to begin with but, as you will discover throughout this chapter, it is not.

Activity 14.1   Defining sex

Spend a few minutes thinking through the questions below. The aim of this activity is to give you the opportunity to articulate your existing ideas about sex, so that you can reflect on these in relation to the ideas presented in this chapter. Keep your responses to hand: they will be useful later on.

- What is 'sex'? If someone tells you they have 'had sex', what does that mean to you? What counts as 'sex'?

- What is sex for?

- What is 'normal' sex?

2.1   Defining sex

Sexology
The scientific study of sex, which began in the nineteenth century. Sexology today includes theories and research from psychology but also from medicine, biology, sociology, cultural studies and other disciplines.

I teach part time at a sixth-form college. Recently the students and I were discussing the rather dry topic of social policies on family life, and in particular the increased prevalence of households headed by same-sex couples. A student suddenly asked, 'What do lesbians do in bed, anyway? It's not as if they can actually have sex!'

I referred the student to a sex education website and moved on with the lesson, but the question stayed with me, because it was so revealing about the student's views on what counts as 'sex'. The student's working definition of 'sex' was, I assume, one that many people share: that 'sex' involves penetration with a penis and that, in 'normal' sex, the penis is penetrating a vagina. This type of sex is usually described in contemporary **sexology** literature as 'penis-in-vagina' sex, or PIV sex for short. For the student asking the question, then, the term 'lesbian sex' was an oxymoron. In her view, it simply was not possible for two women to 'have sex', because neither of them had a penis.

This **phallocentric**, **heteronormative** definition of sex is widely accepted in Western societies. For example, in an analysis of sex advice media, Meg John Barker and colleagues (2016) found that 'having sex' overwhelmingly referred to PIV sex between a man and a woman. Other sexual practices, such as oral sex and masturbation, are often referred to as 'sex acts' or 'foreplay' rather than as 'sex'. It is worth noting, too, that things described as 'sex' tend to involve the genitals: most people would probably agree that while kissing can be sexual, it is not 'sex'.

The sociologist Gayle Rubin (1984) argues that in Western societies people tend to take a hierarchical view of sex, with some kinds of sexual relationship seen as 'proper' or 'normal' and others seen as 'kinky' or 'weird', or perhaps even 'unnatural' or 'perverted'. Rubin visualises this hierarchy as a pyramid. Those sexual relationships which are regarded as the most acceptable in the wider culture – like that between a heterosexual married couple – are placed at the top of the hierarchy, while those lower down the pyramid are seen as less acceptable.

It is important to note here that in this section, I am talking about how *society in general* sees particular kinds of sexual relationships and practices as superior to others. I am not suggesting that any particular kind of sex or relationship *actually is* more normal or natural than any other!

Rubin goes on to argue that not only sexual relationships, but also individual sexual acts, can be divided into those that are seen as examples of 'good, normal, natural' or even 'blessed' expressions of sexuality, and those that are seen as 'bad, abnormal, unnatural' or even 'damned'. She illustrates this idea with a diagram showing two concentric circles: the inner ring is a 'charmed circle' of acceptable practices, while the outer one is the 'outer limits' of sexuality: see Figure 14.1. (Note that 'vanilla' in the diagram is a term used for non-kinky sexual practices, as in vanilla ice-cream compared with ice-cream of other flavours. This is a somewhat derogatory term so is not one that will be used in the rest of this chapter.)

What this all means, then, is that one of the key ideas that shapes people's thinking about sex is that some sex is 'natural', 'normal', 'proper' sex, and other sex is not. The further away a particular sexual practice is from the cultural ideal of heterosexual PIV sex, the more likely it is to be seen as unnatural, abnormal, or even dangerous. For

Phallocentric
Penis-centred.

Heteronormative
Based on the assumption that only a particular form of heterosexuality, and associated masculine and feminine gender roles, are natural and normal.

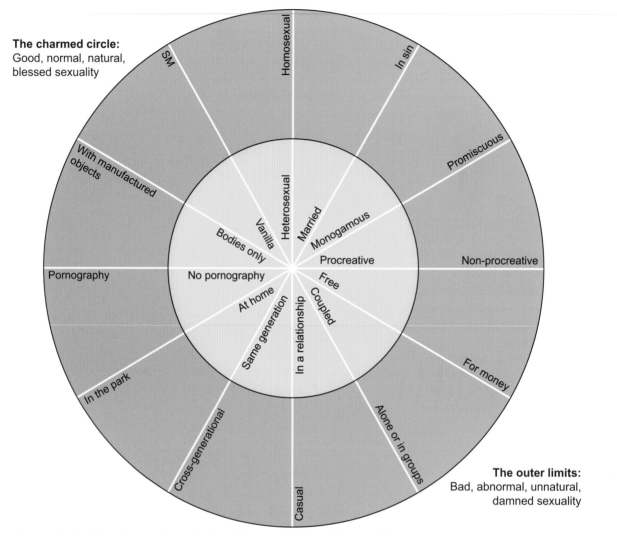

Figure 14.1   The 'charmed circle' of sex (Source: Rubin, 1984, p. 152)

example, while habitual masturbation is no longer believed to cause physical and mental illness, as it once was, enjoyment of solo sex is still regarded with suspicion, especially when associated with pornography (Barker et al., 2016). Also, even today, getting sexual pleasure from humiliation or pain is often viewed as unhealthy and abnormal (Kleinplatz and Moser, 2007). Empirical research lends credence to Rubin's theory, as the existence and negative effects of social prejudices towards those who are sexually 'different' have been well documented (Richards and Barker, 2013).

As you have already seen, some ways of being sexual are viewed as more acceptable than others. It is generally socially acceptable to admit to feeling sexual about other adults of a similar age to oneself. People are *not* 'supposed' to feel sexual about people whose age is very different from their own, or about objects, animals or plants. Read Box 14.1 to explore this subject further.

Box 14.1   Some common sexological terms

Fetish: an unusual sexual interest, usually involving an inanimate object (such as a shoe) or a particular situation (such as being naked in public).

Paraphilia: an unorthodox sexual interest or fetish (e.g. being aroused by feet – podophilia). Once regarded as inherently dysfunctional or even indicative of mental illness; however, the latest edition of the *Diagnostic and Statistical Manual* (*DSM 5*) (American Psychiatric Association, 2013; see Chapter 13) no longer considers such interests to be harmful unless they constitute a paraphilic disorder.

Paraphilic disorder: a paraphilia which causes mental distress to the person and/or makes them a threat to the well-being of another person. Someone who likes having sex in their car, for example, might be considered to have a fetish, but if they are mentally distressed by this, or can enjoy sex only while driving the car, it would be considered a paraphilic disorder.

Sexual dysfunction: an aspect of sex which is unhealthy or not operating properly.

Why is heterosexual, PIV intercourse so central to prevalent understandings of sex? Of course, one of the reasons why this kind of sex is often seen as 'proper' sex is that people often think of sex as being 'for' procreation. After all, the survival of humanity depends on reproduction! In this context, PIV sex, which has generally been the most reliable way of getting a pregnancy underway, seems 'natural' and therefore 'normal'. So, as is apparent in Rubin's sexual hierarchies (and perhaps in your own responses to Activity 14.1), types of sexual activity that are non-procreative are often seen as less natural, perhaps even 'unnatural', and are less culturally accepted or ideal.

Of course, sex is not just about procreation. Indeed, people throughout history have gone to great lengths to find ways to be sexual while avoiding unwanted pregnancies. Ancient Roman women used half-lemons as spermicidal pessaries, while Egyptian women used crocodile dung or acacia gum, and it is thought by some scholars that even humanity's prehistoric ancestors had some knowledge of herbal contraception (Taylor, 1997). Clearly, the cultural dominance of heterosexual PIV sex cannot be explained just in terms of the need to procreate to keep the species going. It is therefore also necessary to identify the social factors that contribute to this kind of sex being seen as the most 'real' kind of sex.

2.2   Judeo-Christian understandings of sex

One social factor that needs considering is religion. For much of human history, religion was humanity's main source of explanations about the nature of the world. In the Western world, where Christianity has been the dominant faith for nearly two millennia, this has led to the development of a particular set of understandings about sex. Historically, Christianity has often made a distinction between the body and the spirit, seeing the body and its appetites as a source of temptation and distraction.

Figure 14.2   *The Temptation* by William Strang shows Eve tempting Adam with the fruit of the Tree of Knowledge

Lust – that is, physical desire – has often been viewed as one of the evils brought into the world by the *Fall* (Figure 14.2). In Judeo-Christian mythology, Eve, the first woman, was responsible for bringing about the *Fall* by using her sexuality to tempt Adam, the first man, to eat the 'forbidden fruit' of the Tree of Knowledge (Carr, 2003).

In Judeo-Christian cultures, then, sex has often been seen as a necessary evil. While sex was obviously a prerequisite for the continuation of humanity, it was nevertheless a distraction from what was really worthwhile in life – achieving salvation – and therefore it was regarded as something that should be strictly rationed, and only engaged in for procreative purposes, or at least within marriage.

2.3   Scientific theories of sex

In the last few hundred years, science has at least partially taken over religion's role of explaining the world. Science has come to be seen as the only reliable way of producing knowledge, because it provides rational, logical explanations for natural phenomena, which can be tested repeatedly in order to establish a clear cause-and-effect relationship. One scientific theory of particular relevance to both popular and psychological understandings of sexuality is, of course, the naturalist Darwin's (1859, 1871) theory of natural selection, particularly his work on sexual selection.

As you read in Chapter 2, Box 2.1, Darwin's evolutionary theory states that change among living species happens when variations occur which help individuals with the new characteristic to survive and reproduce. Imagine, for example, a mouse I will call Bob. Bob was born with a shorter tail than his parents or siblings. If this adaptation is evolutionarily advantageous (e.g. making him slightly faster and thus harder for an owl to catch), Bob will survive and reproduce more successfully than his peers. The short-tailed characteristic will then be passed down through the genes of successive generations, until finally all mice of that type have the new, shorter tail. This theory, often referred to as 'the survival of the fittest', explains why there are so many different species of animals and plants.

What the theory of survival of the fittest does not explain is why many species of animal evolve traits that are not directly linked to their survival. For example, male birds such as the peacock and mallard often exhibit spectacular plumage that is not found in their relatively drab female counterparts. Darwin explains this variation in terms of sexual competition among males for mates.

If a male has a particular variation that does not give him an evolutionary advantage, but does make him more attractive to females, then he will be able to mate many times, and be successful in passing his genes on. Let's imagine that one of Bob's many short-tailed descendants, Bernard, just happens to be orange. Being orange might not give him a direct survival advantage, but female mice might find Orange Bernard sexier than his mousy-brown peers. As the local heart-throb, Sexy Orange Bernard would get plenty of opportunities to mate and pass on his genes, and so, over many generations, there would be a lot more orange short-tailed mice.

Sexual selection in action – Sexy Orange Bernard

For Darwin, then, sexual attraction was the key driver of evolution. Darwin's theories form an important part of the basis of biopsychological approaches to understanding sex and sexuality, which you will consider in Section 3.1. For now, though, you can see that the importance of procreative sex is stressed in both evolutionary and religious explanations of the world. As you will learn later on, both these explanations shaped the ideas of the first sexologists, and have continued to inform many psychological studies of sex to this day.

2.4 Defining sexuality

I used to live on a main road that was about a mile long. About a third of the length of the road was taken up by a rather grim-looking abandoned factory. The plant was so enormous that, if you stood opposite it, you could not see both ends of it at once. Being so huge, you would think that it would be very visible but, oddly, it was *because* the factory was so big that people did not really notice it. As you looked across the street at it, the factory took up so much of your field of vision that it did not seem like a discrete object, and it became, in an odd way, invisible. From a mile across town, however, you could see the whole site well, and in fact it was not until I saw the factory from this distance that I realised how enormous it actually was.

I tell this story because, when you read what I am about to say about conventional understandings of sexuality, you might wonder why I am bothering to say things that are *so* obvious. In reality, though, as my story shows, sometimes things are so obvious that people have never even thought about them, and a great deal can be gained from stepping back to examine the 'obvious' from a distance. Activity 14.2 should help you to step back from what's 'obvious' about sexuality, and begin to examine your ideas from a psychological perspective.

Activity 14.2   Defining sexuality

Spend a few minutes thinking through the questions below. Keep your answers together with your answers to the questions from Activity 14.1.

- What do you understand by the term 'sexuality'?

- How many sexualities are there?

- Do you think of yourself as someone who has a particular sexuality, or **sexual identity**? If so, what terms would you use to describe it?

- How important to your own sense of self is your sexuality? Is it a key part of your own personal identity?

Comment

Sexuality is a term used to describe an individual's sexual preference, or capacity for sexual feelings. When people talk about sexuality, they are usually drawing on a number of culturally shared understandings. For

Sexual identity
The way in which a person identifies themselves according to their sexuality, for example as gay, bisexual, heterosexual or asexual.

example, people tend to see sexuality as one fixed, fundamental characteristic of the self. They also tend to see it as relational: having to do with other people. I will elaborate on these two ideas below, and you can think about how they relate to your answers to this activity as you read on.

First, people today tend to think of sexuality, like gender, as a key aspect of a person's identity: one of the major components that make them who they are (Weeks, 2014). For example, when a colleague I have assumed is heterosexual casually mentions her girlfriend, I might feel that my sense of who she is, and how well I know her, has shifted. On the other hand, though, if she mentions that she cannot stand peas, or prefers winter to summer, that may seem like an interesting detail, rather than a big revelation about the kind of person she is. Similarly, if you have ever been in the position where someone has been mistaken about your gender or sexuality, you might know how unsettling that can feel: many people experience such mistakes as having been misunderstood on a really fundamental level.

Perhaps this sense of sexuality as fundamental to who people are is due to the fact that people also conceptualise sexuality as an integral, natural part of themselves, something that they were either born with, or acquired very early in psychological development (Fausto-Sterling, 2012). This view of sexuality as inherent and instinctive means people also tend to see it as fixed: unlikely to change. For example, if a man in his forties comes out as gay, it is common to attribute this to him having 'really' been gay all along, and hiding or denying his true desires: 'living a lie' (Weeks, 2002).

Second, when you consider all the possible ways in which a person's sexuality could be described, it is interesting that people generally describe it not in terms of the person themselves, but in terms of *other people*: the gender of the people they are attracted to.

Since Western cultures recognise only two genders, men and women, this means that only two or three sexualities are possible. A person can be attracted to their own gender, the 'opposite' gender, or perhaps both (although the existence or otherwise of bisexuality seems to be a perennial topic of debate; see Angelides, 2001).

As well as seeing sexuality as fixed and fundamental, people also tend to see their sexual relationships as their most important relationships. When someone asks them who they are 'seeing', or if there is someone 'special' in their lives, they're really asking if they are romantically or sexually involved with anyone. There is an assumption that there will be just one 'special' person, and that this relationship will be more important than any other. If they are not 'seeing' anyone, this is often seen as a bit of a shame, or even as a sign that they are not 'normal' in some way (DePaulo, 2006).

In this section of the chapter you have learned that Western understandings of sex tend to be hierarchical, with PIV sex viewed as the most acceptable kind of sex, and that sexuality is regarded as a fixed, fundamental part of a person's identity, defined in terms of the gender of the people they are attracted to. These common-sense ideas are grounded in thousands of years of Judeo-Christian culture, and in scientific theories of evolution.

Being able to see 'the strange in the familiar, and the familiar in the strange' (Hammersley and Atkinson, 1995, p. 112) is a key skill for all social scientists, including psychologists. As you have learned, it is both interesting and worthwhile to 'stand back from' common assumptions about sex and sexuality, and to see them with fresh eyes. The next section is concerned with investigating how psychology has contributed to the development of these understandings, some of which have only quite recently become commonplace. Later in the chapter, you will consider these understandings more critically, thinking about how useful they are, and how it might be necessary for both psychologists and society to move beyond them.

3   Psychology's role in producing conventional understandings of sex and sexuality

Psychology, more than any other social science, has modelled itself on the methods of the natural sciences, especially those of biology. Traditionally, psychological thought has seen biology as the main driver of human behaviour, and culture as a secondary influence, and this is still the case in much of mainstream psychology (Stainton-Rogers and Stainton-Rogers, 2001).

Accordingly, the first psychologists to study sex were primarily interested in the biological bases of human sexual behaviour and experience. It was obvious to these thinkers that sex was 'about' procreation, and that desire for the 'opposite sex' was a fundamental part of what it meant to be a man or woman. PIV sex needed no explanation, then, but these early sexologists *were* deeply interested in explaining the reasons why people might engage in 'deviant' (non-procreative) sexual behaviour.

3.1   Early biopsychological understandings of sex

Early sexologists theorised that, since sex was assumed to be rooted in biology, people who had same-sex desires must be biologically different from other people. A woman who desired other women must somehow be biologically masculine, while a man who desired men was himself, on some level, feminine (Terry, 1999; Oosterhuis, 2000; Angelides, 2001). If a person desired both men and women, it indicated that they must themselves have both masculine and feminine characteristics. This was sometimes termed 'psychic hermaphroditism' (Storr, 1999; Oosterhuis, 2000).

Aetiology
The cause(s) of a condition.

These researchers therefore looked for biological differences in sexual 'deviants' that would explain the **aetiology** of their variant behaviour, developing a range of explanations and categorisations for them. One of the first sexologists, the theologian and legal scholar Karl Heinrich Ulrichs (1898), for example, saw homosexuality as the result of a hiccup in the development of the human embryo, which led to a congenital 'third sex' of 'inverts': male souls in female bodies, and vice versa (Bristow, 2010). Ulrichs's theories were developed further by other early sexologists such as Richard Freiherr von Krafft-Ebing (1886), Magnus Hirschfeld (1922) and Henry Havelock Ellis (1933). What all these early theories had in common, however, was that they theorised non-heterosexual sexualities as having their roots in biological abnormalities. Think about this in Activity 14.3.

Activity 14.3 Reflecting on early theories of sexuality

How closely do these early theories of sexual variation resemble modern ideas about sexuality? What similarities and differences do you notice? For example, think about the links made between gender and sexuality, and the ideas around abnormality.

Comment

As you will see in the coming sections of the chapter, the idea of non-heterosexual sexualities as abnormalities lingered within psychology and psychiatry until at least the 1980s. Conventional ideas about sex do bear some resemblance to early sexological theories. For example, as outlined in Section 2, one key contemporary idea about sexuality is that it is innate and unchangeable, perhaps even written into people's DNA. Another key idea is that there is a link between sexuality and gender identity: gay men are often assumed to be effeminate or 'camp', while lesbians are stereotyped as masculine or 'butch', despite the diversity of gender expressions of people of all sexualities (Fausto-Sterling, 2012).

3.2 Psychoanalytic approaches

The work of Sigmund Freud and his followers led to a shift in understandings of sexuality (see Chapter 9, Section 3.1, Box 9.1 for an outline of Freud's overall psychoanalytic theory). Rather than explaining differences in sexual desires in biological terms, Freudians saw them as the result of psychological development, as Box 14.2 shows.

Figure 14.3   Sigmund Freud

Box 14.2   Psychosexual development

Freud defined five stages of psychosexual development. He argued
that at each stage of development, a child's libido is focused on a
different erogenous zone of the body (Freud, 1962 [1905]). He saw
variations in sexuality as the result of an individual's psychosexual
development having been impeded by faulty parenting or early
trauma, such that the individual had become 'stuck' at a particular
stage of development (Stainton-Rogers and Stainton-
Rogers, 2001).

Table 14.1 The five stages of psychosexual development

Age (years)	Stage	Normal development	Consequences of abnormal development
0–1	Oral	The child is fixated on its mouth as a source of pleasure, since it feeds at the mother's breast. It explores the world through its mouth.	An orally fixated adult may display behaviours such as smoking, sucking the ends of pens or chewing gum constantly. They may be naïve and immature. Sexually, they are likely to enjoy kissing and oral sex.
1–3	Anal	The child is preoccupied with its anus. As the child learns to control its bowel and bladder, it learns the value of self-control and delayed gratification.	Overly strict or overly permissive potty training in infancy may result in anal fixation in adulthood. Sexually, such adults might be coprophilic (sexually aroused by excrement) or enjoy other forms of anal play. Anally fixated adults may be compulsive, perfectionist and stubborn ('anally retentive') or disorganised, messy and rebellious ('anally expulsive').
3–6	Phallic	Children become interested in their genitals and begin to masturbate. They notice sex differences. Unconsciously, they wish to sexually possess their opposite-sex parent and are jealous of their same-sex parent. Girls experience penis envy (the Electra complex) while boys fear the loss of their penis (castration anxiety/the Oedipus complex). The conflict is resolved when the child learns to identify with their same-sex parent instead of seeing them as a rival.	Failure to resolve the Oedipus/ Electra complex leads to a phallic personality. Such an individual is reckless and arrogant, and finds it difficult to maintain relationships. They may be homosexual as a result of their confused feelings towards their same-sex parent. Freud argued that most women never fully resolve their Electra complex, and remain to some extent fixated at the phallic stage. An inability to achieve orgasm through PIV sex is a sign that a woman's sexuality is immature and still focused on the clitoris.

Age (years)	Stage	Normal development	Consequences of abnormal development
6 until puberty	Latency	As a result of successfully repressing their libido at the end of the phallic stage, the child now goes through a period of latency, and does not experience sexual desire.	Problems in adulthood may be caused by traumas experienced at this stage, but they are usually related to the individual's social development rather than to sexual issues.
Puberty onwards	Genital	Sexual desire re-emerges at puberty and is focused on the genitals. Women now achieve orgasm vaginally instead of clitorally. Sexual activity is partnered rather than solitary.	

Neurosis

A mild psychological maladjustment or distress.

As you will no doubt have noticed, Freud's theory of psychosexual development is very phallocentric and focused on PIV sex, with other forms of sexual expression being seen as evidence of **neurosis**.

Freud's phallocentrism is of course unsurprising given the patriarchal social and sexual mores of nineteenth-century Europe where he lived and worked. Many of Freud's intellectual descendants, including his contemporaries such as Carl Jung, have sought to develop approaches to understanding psychosexual development that theorise women as women, rather than as incomplete men, as Freud seems to do. For example, Luce Irigaray takes issue with the fact that Freud attributes women's whole sexuality to penis envy (Irigaray, 1985), while Karen Horney argues that what women envy is not the penis, but male power (Horney, 1967).

Of course, in the half-century or so since Horney's work, there is considerable evidence that gender roles have become more symmetrical, with women now being much more likely to work outside the home, and men being more involved with domestic work and childcare. Nevertheless, this research consistently demonstrates that, in male–female couples, it is the woman who retains most of the responsibility for housework and childcare, with men continuing to see themselves as breadwinners (Sani, 2014). One example of this is the low take-up rate of paternity leave among new fathers (TUC, 2013).

Despite the criticisms, it is difficult to overstate the importance of Freud's theories of psychosexual development in influencing psychological and popular understandings of sex and sexuality. The work of Freud and his followers contributed to what might be termed a *psychologisation* of sex, so that sexual desires and **sexual practices** came to be seen as the outcome of psychological development during childhood, rather than biology. It is notable, too, that in contrast to early biopsychological approaches to the study of sex, Freudian theory does attempt to explain how people become heterosexual, rather than simply taking heterosexuality as a given, and focusing only on 'deviant' sexualities.

Sexual practices
The activities that a person engages in sexually.

3.3 Studies of sexual behaviour

By the 1940s, these early scientific approaches to sex had become embedded in popular culture, and people were used to thinking of themselves and others as either sexually 'normal' or 'abnormal'. 'Normal' people, as you have already learned, were those who displayed gender-conforming appearances and behaviour and successfully navigated the conflicts of psychosexual development to arrive at an adult sexuality that was focused on heterosexual PIV sex within marriage.

In the mid twentieth century, however, work by a second wave of US-based researchers took quite a different approach to the study of sexual experience. Rather than trying to explain the *origins* of 'deviant' sexuality, this new generation of sexologists sought to explore sexual *behaviour* to find out what people actually *did* in (or out of) bed. The results shocked the USA, and called into question common-sense understandings of sex and sexuality.

The most notable of the 'second-wave' sexologists was the biologist Alfred Kinsey. Together with a team of researchers, Kinsey set out to understand human sexual behaviour, interviewing over 11,000 Americans, and publishing two landmark publications – 'Sexual behavior in the human male' (1948) and *Sexual Behavior in the Human Female* (1953) – popularly known as the Kinsey Reports. Rather than asking his participants to describe themselves as heterosexual or homosexual, Kinsey rated them on a scale, as shown in Figure 14.4. Findings from the reports are summarised in Box 14.3, and you will consider them in Activity 14.4.

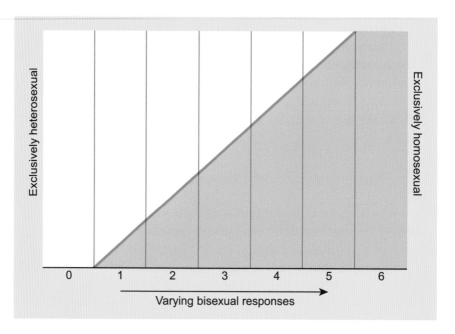

Figure 14.4   The Kinsey Scale

Box 14.3   The Kinsey Reports

The headline findings of the Kinsey Reports were as follows:

Prevalence of homosexual and bisexual experience

Of the 5300 men interviewed, only 4% were exclusively homosexual throughout their lives. However, only around half were exclusively heterosexual. 46% of men had had both heterosexual and homosexual experiences, and 37% had had at least one homosexual experience to the point of orgasm. Of the 5940 women interviewed, around 4% were exclusively homosexual. Around 10% had had a more than incidental homosexual experience. 13% of women had had at least one homosexual experience to the point of orgasm.

Prevalence of non-PIV practices and pre-marital sex

- 92% of men and 62% of women reported that they had masturbated

- 70% of couples engaged in oral sex

- 11% of men had had at least some experience of anal sex within marriage

- 12% of women and 22% of men reported being aroused by an erotic story with sadomasochistic themes

- Around 75% of men and 50% of women had had pre-marital sex.

Activity 14.4   Evaluating Kinsey

Do you find any of Kinsey's results surprising? How do they challenge sexological and psychoanalytic understandings of sexuality?

Comment

As you will have noticed from Box 14.3 and Figure 14.4, Kinsey and colleagues' data completely undermined the idea that sexual expression among 'normal' people was confined to heterosexual PIV sex, and that anyone who behaved differently was either biologically abnormal or psychologically immature. Not only was same-sex activity much more common than had previously been thought, but also sexual activities that were at the time considered taboo or unusual (such as oral and anal sex) were in fact commonplace.

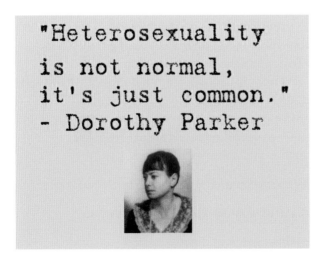

Figure 14.5   Quotation from American poet, Dorothy Parker (1893–1967)

Kinsey's work was far from perfect. Kinsey's contemporary W. AllenWallis (1949), for example, strongly criticised his quota-based sampling methods, arguing that Kinsey's sample, which overrepresented young, white, middle-class, college-educated people, was not representative of the population of the USA. Furthermore, Kinsey's research would today be considered unethical: Kinsey has faced censure for interviewing at least one person about their experiences of sexual activity with children, without reporting them to the police.

Nevertheless, the impact of the Kinsey Reports on understandings of human sexual behaviour has been enormous. By focusing on behaviour itself rather than theorising about its causes, Kinsey demonstrated the diversity of human sexuality. Kinsey's studies were the first major contribution to LGBT (Lesbian, Gay, Bisexual and Trans)-affirmative sexology which, as you will see, paved the way for other ground-breaking work.

Following Kinsey and his colleagues, William Masters and Virginia Johnson are best known for their pioneering laboratory studies of the physiology of human sexual response (Masters and Johnson, 1966). Their study featured 382 women and 312 men, mostly married couples, who took part in more than 10,000 'cycles of sexual response' under laboratory conditions. These included intercourse, masturbation and what was termed 'artificial coition': masturbation using a dildo-like device that simulated PIV sex while filming it from the inside (Stainton-Rogers and Stainton-Rogers, 2001).

Like Kinsey's, Masters and Johnson's work was characterised by its sex-positive approach: their writing took an affirmative stance towards sex as a source of pleasure and intimacy, rather than seeing it as a base instinct that needed to be controlled, as earlier writers had done. Masters and Johnson's research dispelled a large number of myths and suppositions about sex, and is the source of much current understanding of the physiology of sex. A key outcome of Masters and Johnson's work was their four-stage model of sexual response. Box 14.4 gives details of this and other key findings.

Box 14.4   Masters and Johnson's key findings

- Human sexual response has four stages:

  1 Excitement: erectile tissues in both men and women (such as the penis and clitoris) become engorged.

  2 The plateau phase: the clitoris/testes retract as orgasm approaches.

---

3   Orgasm: a series of rhythmical muscular contractions occur in the vagina and uterus/penis and urethra. Pulse rate and blood pressure peak. There is often facial grimacing.

4   Resolution: breathing returns to normal and signs of arousal gradually subside. In men, there is a refractory period of between a few minutes and several hours before rearousal can happen. This period does not exist in women, and many can reorgasm rapidly, many times over.

- The size of a flaccid penis is not a reliable guide to its size when erect. Some penises can expand by as much as 120 per cent, from three to seven inches. However, penis size does not make much difference to a woman's enjoyment of PIV sex, because the vagina is elastic and accommodates itself to the size of the penis.

- Contrary to Freud's assertion, there is no physiological distinction between vaginal and clitoral orgasm. The sensations of orgasm are always produced by the stimulation of the same network of nerves, whether this is done vaginally or clitorally.

Like Kinsey, Masters and Johnson have been criticised for relying on an unrepresentative sample: most participants were white, middle-class, college-educated, heterosexual married couples. Furthermore, Masters and Johnson's methods would not stand up to modern ethical scrutiny. For example, although most participants were married couples, participants were assigned partners randomly for the sex acts that were observed.

Also, for all the study's scientific rigour, it has also been criticised for unquestioningly incorporating cultural assumptions about sex into the interpretation of the data. Finding that 70 per cent of women could not achieve orgasm through intercourse alone, for example, Masters and Johnson put this down to sexual dysfunction, arguing that orgasm ought to be possible through PIV sex. However, other sex researchers such as Shere Hite (1976) have pointed out that Masters and Johnson's assumption that women 'ought' to be able to reach climax through penetration was based on cultural assumptions rather than scientific evidence.

What is clear, though, is that Masters and Johnson's pioneering work greatly increased scientific understanding of the physiology of sexual response, and dispelled a number of myths about female orgasm in particular: debunking the myth of the superiority of vaginal orgasm, and confirming that many women are able to experience multiple orgasms. In psychiatry, modified versions of Masters and Johnson's model of the sexual response cycle informed the definitions of sexual dysfunctions used in the *DSM-III* onwards (Morrow, 2013).

3.4   Studies of sexual identity

From the 1980s, psychological research into sexuality underwent another conceptual shift. Changing social attitudes to sex and sexuality during the 1960s and 1970s, and the work of pioneering LGBT-affirmative psychologists such as Evelyn Hooker (1957) and June Hopkins (1969) had led to the American Psychiatric Association declassifying homosexuality as a psychiatric illness in 1973. In this new, more tolerant, environment people with minority sexualities began to organise politically, campaigning for equal rights in matters such as employment, the age of consent, child custody and adoption and fostering (Weeks, 2014).

In psychology, the rise of social constructionist theories of sexuality (which you will explore in detail in Section 4) led to a new interest in studying the ways in which ordinary people made sense of their sexual identities and experiences (Plummer, 1995). In particular, there was a blossoming of research into LGBT identities and subcultures (e.g. D'Augelli and Patterson, 2001; Bower et al., 2002).

At the same time, however, a growing body of evolutionary psychology emerged, and gained popular acclaim. Evolutionary psychology seeks to apply Darwinian evolutionary logic to the study of human psychology. Although the scope and depth of this complex and growing field goes far beyond the study of human sexuality, it is evolutionary psychological explanations of human sexual behaviour that have been most taken up by and disseminated through popular culture since the 1990s. Many people, for example, are aware of the argument that men have an evolutionary interest in spreading their genes as far as possible by fathering a large number of offspring with different women, while women, whose biological investment in each offspring is greater, have a vested interest in limiting the number of sexual partners they have, and the number of children they bear (Berry, 2007).

Critics have suggested that these theories use biology to justify sexual inequality (Rose and Rose, 2000), and that there is a lack of empirical evidence in support of them. However, evolutionary psychology is a relatively new, complex, and rapidly growing field, and so perhaps it is too early to rush to judgement (Berry, 2007). What is certain, however, is that psychological theories continue to influence conventional understandings of sex and sexuality, just as they have done throughout the last 150 years.

4   Exploring the psychology of sexual diversity

In the first two sections of this chapter you considered some common-sense understandings of sex and sexuality. First, because reproduction is regarded as the main purpose of sex, PIV sex is seen as the most 'natural' and socially approved kind of sex. Second, people tend to see sexuality as a fundamental component of a person's identity. Third, people define sexuality in terms of the gender(s) of the people a person is attracted to. In Section 3 you explored the contribution of psychology and sexology to these conventional understandings. In this section you will consider why some of these past psychological and sexological ideas might be questioned.

4.1   The social construction of sex and sexuality

The first reason that psychologists might want to question conventional understandings of sex and sexuality is that, as you learned in Section 2, these understandings change significantly over time.

You might assume that this is because, as scientific theories of sex develop, new knowledge replaces the old, in a continual march of progress. However, in this section you will see that, while they have certainly offered much of value about sexuality, the psychological and sexological explanations of sex that you have considered so far have actually played a key role in *constructing* the phenomena they discuss. You will remember this idea of *social construction* from Chapters 4, 5 and 6.

Conventional understandings of sexuality tend to assume that, for example, gay men have always existed, but they were forced to 'live a lie' by the oppressive societies they lived in, and it is only now, in more enlightened times, that it has become acceptable to live openly as a gay man. Strange as it may seem, however, the notion that people have 'a sexuality' is a comparatively recent historical development, and one that is not shared across all cultures globally. This suggests that sexuality is socially constructed: that it was invented, rather than discovered. For social constructionists it does not make sense to say that, for example, Shakespeare was 'really' bisexual, because the concept of bisexuality did not exist in Shakespearian times. It is only possible to comment on his behaviours, not to apply an identity label to him, because he would not have understood such a label.

Rather than being something that has always existed in the same form, then, sexuality is a concept with a history, and has meant different things at different times and in different places. Social constructionists would argue that people's understandings of their sexualities actually have far more to do with the era and place they live in than the people they are attracted to or the practices they enjoy.

Of course, people have always had sexual preferences, that is, being attracted to particular genders or enjoying particular sexual practices, but it was not until the nineteenth century that people started to think of these preferences as fixed characteristics that were relevant to their identities. It was 1869, for example, before there was even a word for someone who was attracted to their own sex (homosexual), and the terms 'heterosexual' and 'bisexual' were coined even later (Angelides, 2001). Before this period, people did not think of themselves as 'gay', 'straight' or 'bisexual', just as people today do not think of themselves and others in terms of 'people who like ketchup on their chips' or 'people who prefer mayonnaise'. It is not that people do not *have* these preferences, it is just that they are not relevant to who they are.

What was it that led Western European societies in the nineteenth century to begin to define sexuality as a characteristic of the individual? Previously, specific sexual practices such as **sodomy** had been condemned, but these were seen as sinful acts that anyone might undertake rather than as indicators that a person was of a particular 'type'. From the late nineteenth century, however, anyone who engaged in such practices began to be seen as a distinct, and pathological, *kind of person*. This can be seen very clearly in the work of the early sexologists you examined in Section 2. Havelock Ellis, Krafft-Ebing and their contemporaries all saw sexual deviance as rooted in biological difference, while early psychoanalysts argued that sexual neuroses were caused by abnormal psychological development.

Of course, this process of **specification** was not all due to sexologists and psychoanalysts. The work of these early theorists both arose out of, and contributed to, a much broader social context, that of the Enlightenment (the period in which scientific explanations of the world began to gain more authority than religious doctrines) and the Industrial Revolution (the move from an agrarian economy to an

Sodomy
Most commonly used to describe anal sex, but it has wider connotations and is sometimes applied to all 'deviant' sexual acts.

Specification
The description of a type or species.

industrial one). You will read more about the impact of such shifts in Chapter 15.

(a)

(b)

Figure 14.6   Foucault's two types of power: (a) sovereign power; (b) biopower

The French philosopher Michel Foucault (1976) has been a major influence on social constructionist psychology in relation to sexuality, and other areas. His key work on sexuality and power is summarised in Box 14.5.

Box 14.5 Foucault and power

Foucault argued that, in pre-industrial societies, rulers had the power of life and death over their subjects. If they displeased those in power they might face execution. Foucault terms this kind of power **sovereign power**. This was useful in pre-industrial societies, where people lived in small communities and government and justice happened at a local level.

With the rise of industry, however, the nature of power changed. There was much more potential for the ruling classes to have control over the success of the economy. The prosperity of the agrarian societies of the pre-industrial era had depended largely on the weather, a factor beyond the control of the authorities. However, in early industrial economies, where manufacturing was the main industry, the success of the economy rested on the productivity of the workforce. This changed the relationship between rulers and subjects: governments now needed more day-to-day power over the bodies of individual workers to ensure they were productive. But since many people now lived in cities rather than villages, rulers had a less direct relationship with subjects. Foucault termed this **biopolitics**, hence *biopower*: a very different kind of power from sovereign power.

In this new context, power became more diffuse: spread out through society like a network rather than being a linear relationship between ruler and subject. This also meant that power was much more pervasive, because individuals came under surveillance from multiple directions at once, as Figure 14.6 shows.

Because of this need to govern the bodies of their citizens, Foucault argued, Western societies put a great deal of cultural emphasis on *bodily discipline* and the importance of achieving normality. Individuals are closely surveilled by the authorities, and by one another. Indeed, they become accustomed to such high levels of surveillance that they undertake self-surveillance, assiduously monitoring their own bodily habits and desires to ensure conformity to social norms.

Sovereign power
The power of a state to do everything necessary to govern itself, including determining whether a subject lives or dies.

Biopolitics
Politics where there is indirect control over people's bodies. The 'bio' in this sense refers to bodies, rather than to biology as in biopsychology, for example.

It is this social context, for Foucault and his followers, that has led to the emergence of sexuality as an identity category. The body, at the centre of a web of power relations, is measured and categorised in a host of different ways, of which sexuality is one (others might include gender, mental health, disability, race, and so on). Individuals have an acute sense of the extent to which they are considered 'normal' along each strand of this web, and undertake constant self-surveillance. This results in a docile population with a strong commitment to conformity, where everyone monitors their own and each other's behaviour very closely. This benefits the economy, not only by ensuring high levels of production and thus generating profit for employers, but also by inducing high levels of anxiety in individuals about whether they are normal. This makes them an easy market for products that trade on their insecurities, to the further benefit of the economy.

The central point that Foucault was making about sexuality was that the shift away from seeing sexual deviance as something that anyone might be tempted to do, and towards understanding it as a *characteristic* of a *certain type of person*, was itself a product of this shift to biopolitics: the surveillance of the body.

From a social constructionist viewpoint, then, psychology is both informed by its social context, and deeply implicated in producing that context. The work of Krafft-Ebing, Freud and their contemporaries arose out of a particular way of thinking about sex: taking PIV sex as the norm, they sought to explain why some people deviated from this norm. However, their work also managed to **reify** this view of sex by providing evidence that some people were inherently sexually different from others.

Reify
To make something real – to 'real-ify' it. If a leading scientist supports a theory, it gains a huge amount of credibility, regardless of whether the theory is actually correct or not.

The research of Kinsey and Masters and Johnson, with its emphasis on behaviours rather than typologies, challenged dominant ways of thinking about sex by showing how diverse sexual practices actually were, although this certainly did not make those researchers immune from reifying some of these ideas too. Remember that Hite criticised Masters and Johnson for taking it as read that women 'ought to' be able to reach orgasm through PIV sex.

Similarly, LGBT-affirmative psychology was informed by its social context (the rise of the gay liberation movement and LGBT identity politics), and also helped to produce that context. The work of LGBT-affirmative psychologists was part of the evidence that persuaded the

American Psychiatric Association to remove homosexuality from the *DSM* in 1973.

Finally, the immense popularity of evolutionary psychological explanations of sexual attraction and courtship has also emerged in a particular cultural context (the gender politics of the 1990s and early 2000s), and continues to contribute to popular understandings of gendered sexual behaviours.

4.2 'But it's natural!' Questioning biological understandings of sex

As interesting as all this is, it could be argued that, at the end of the day, on a biological level sex is really about procreation, and that PIV sex is (for the most part) the mechanism through which procreation happens. For all the theorising of the social constructionists, some would argue that it is a basic biological fact that PIV intercourse really is the most natural, 'normal' form of sex.

As you have already seen, Darwin's theory of sexual selection has become the dominant explanation of sexual behaviour among animals (including humans), and this has been taken up by evolutionary psychology, and reproduced in turn in popular culture. However, in recent years several biologists, such as Joan Roughgarden (2004) and Anne Fausto-Sterling (2012), have begun to question some of the assumptions of the Darwinian evolutionary understanding, presenting evidence that sex and gender are much more diverse than most people imagine.

Evolutionarily speaking, such researchers point out that sex is a recent phenomenon. Sexual reproduction in animals started 300 million years ago (Fausto-Sterling, 2012) and it requires a great deal more time and energy than asexual reproduction, as well as the risk of not finding a mate (Mackay, 2001). Across animals and plants there is diversity in how reproduction occurs, with many reproducing asexually (without a partner), and many species changing sex during their lifetime (a particularly common occurrence in fish, to the point that fish which do not change sex are regarded as rather unusual; Hird, 2006).

Roughgarden (2004) has also proposed that the social function of sex is at least as important as its reproductive function among animals, as sex often serves to strengthen bonds and ties between animals, and within a group. Box 14.6 summarises some of the findings on sexual diversity in the animal world which lend support to such theories.

Box 14.6   Sexual diversity in the animal world

In 2006, science studies professor Myra Hird wrote a piece for *The Psychologist* magazine summarising the research in this area, based on the extensive documenting of sexual behaviour in animals by researchers such as Bruce Bagemihl (1999) and Roughgarden (2004). Here is an excerpt from that article.

Homosexual behaviour occurs in over 450 different species of animals, is found in every geographic region of the world, in every major animal group, in all age groups, and with equal frequency amongst females and males (Bagemihl, 1999; Hird, 2004). Homosexual behaviour in animals is enormously diverse, and in some species is more diverse than heterosexual behaviour (Pavelka, 1995). Lifetime pair-bonding of homosexual couples is not prevalent in mammal species, but nor is heterosexual lifetime pair-bonding. More than half of mammal and bird species engage in bisexual activities. Non-human animal homosexual behaviour varies in frequency within and between species from nonexistence (that is, it has not been observed by zoologists) to levels that meet or surpass heterosexual behaviour.

…

Nor do many animals have sex solely or primarily in order to reproduce. Although generally ignored, pleasure is an organising force in relations between non-human animals. Many female animals engage in sex when they are already pregnant, and many animals masturbate (Bagemihl, 1999). Birth control is not restricted to human animals: many non-human animals practise forms of birth control through vaginal plugs, defecation, abortion through the ingestion of certain plants, ejection of sperm and, in the case of chimpanzees, nipple stimulation (Bagemihl, 1999). Trans-species sex also occurs. Sexual behaviour between flowers and various insects is so commonplace that it is rarely recognised as trans-species sexual activity. Other examples now appear in the literature; for instance, Krizek (1992) observed and documented a sexual

> interaction between two different orders of insects – a butterfly
> and a rove beetle.
>
> (Hird, 2006, p. 31)

So it seems that sexual behaviour among animals is at least as diverse as that among humans, and that reproduction is only one of many reasons why animals – including humans – are sexual. In Section 4.3 you will turn to considering human sexual diversity, and what can be learned from it when psychologists focus on that diversity, rather than on delineating 'normal' from 'abnormal' sex.

4.3   New ways of making sense of sex? Learning from sexual diversity

As you have learned, early attempts to understand sexual diversity mostly centred on explaining why some people's sexual identities and preferences did not fit in with what was then understood as 'normal, natural' sexuality, that is, heterosexual PIV sex. Later work moved away from this emphasis on aetiology, first towards describing sexual behaviour, and then to listening to the ways in which ordinary people understood and experienced their sexualities. Much contemporary psychological research on sex aims to learn from sexual diversity, rather than to explain it.

In Section 2, you learned that sexuality tends to be defined in terms of the gender of the people to whom someone is attracted. However, as discussed in Section 3, this need not be the case. People might now be thinking of themselves as 'brunettesexual', 'nipplesexual' or 'once-a-weeksexual'. Of course, people generally define their sexualities in relation to gender because the idea of sexuality emerged in a cultural context in which a person's gender was seen as the most important characteristic in relation to sexuality.

Activity 14.5   'Outer limits' sexualities

Table 14.2 shows just some examples of sexual identities that would probably be placed on the 'outer limits' of Rubin's 'charmed circle' (Figure 14.1). Would you group any of them together (e.g. ones relating to gender of attraction, ones relating to amount of desire)? What patterns do you notice when you read through the table?

Table 14.2   Some sexual identities

Term	A person who...
Asexual	does not experience sexual attraction
Bisexual	is attracted to more than one gender
BDSMer	is interested in bondage (using restraints such as a rope or handcuffs), discipline (being punished and rewarded); and/or domination and submission (taking charge of an encounter, or allowing a partner to take charge); and/or sadism (administering pain); and/or masochism (receiving pain). BDSMers who enjoy being in positions of power may identify as top/dominant, those who enjoy the other role may identify as bottom/submissive, and those who enjoy both may identify as switch/versatile
Demisexual	only experiences sexual attraction to someone they already have an emotional connection with
Kinky	enjoys BDSM, or other sexual practices that are not considered 'usual'
Lesbian	is a woman who is attracted to other women
Gay man	is a man who is attracted to other men
Pansexual	experiences sexual attraction to people of all sexes and genders
Queer	is non-heterosexual (usually). Queer was used as a pejorative term for non-heterosexuals, but has been reclaimed by LGBT communities and is often used as an umbrella term to refer to people (usually non-heterosexuals) whose sexuality is not seen as conventional by society
Questioning	is questioning or exploring their sexuality
Same-gender loving	is attracted to members of the 'same' sex. This is a term used by some African American people in preference to 'gay', 'lesbian' or 'bisexual'
Sapiosexual	is primarily attracted to intelligence
Skoliosexual	is attracted to people of non-binary genders (who do not identify as men or women)

Comment

Many of the terms in Table 14.1 demonstrate that sexuality need not necessarily be defined in terms of the gender of the people someone is attracted to (e.g. 'sapiosexual', 'BDSMer') or in terms of other people at all (e.g. 'questioning', 'queer'). Also terms such as 'asexual' and 'demisexual' make it clear that not everyone experiences sexual desire routinely, or indeed at all (Carrigan et al., 2013). Terms such as 'questioning', 'switch' and 'bisexual' are helpful reminders that sexuality can change over time. Perhaps psychology can learn from the 'outer limits' of sex that sexuality and gender are not always linked, that sexual attraction is not universal, and that it can be fluid rather than fixed.

Recent psychological research on one sexuality – BDSM – demonstrates how research that focuses on *experience* rather than *explanation* can take place in practice. Until recently, an interest in BDSM was seen as symptomatic of psychological disturbance. The *DSM* listed sadism and masochism as sexual disorders until as late as 2013 (American Psychiatric Association, 2013). However, social constructionist and existential psychologists (see Chapter 5) have questioned the association between engaging in kinky practices and mental illness for some time, pointing out that no research on BDSM communities supports such a link. Peggy J. Kleinplatz and Charles Moser (2007) argue that the lack of objective criteria for diagnosing 'normal' sexuality made it easy for clinicians to be guided by cultural values, rather than scientific evidence, when diagnosing practitioners of BDSM and other paraphilias as sexually 'abnormal'. They argue that instead of pathologising such practices, and thus reifying social prejudices against them, clinicians should listen to the subjective accounts of their clients, who often describe their experiences of BDSM as 'growth-enhancing and life-affirming' (p. 257).

Psychologists such as Gary W. Taylor and Jane M. Ussher (2001) and Darren Langdridge and Trevor Butt (2004) have done just this, using qualitative approaches to try to understand BDSM from a practitioner's perspective. Their studies show that participants report experiencing BDSM as a source of intimacy, pleasure and transcendence, as a way of resisting socially prescribed sex and gender roles, and as a means of personal growth.

One of the key themes to emerge from such work is the centrality of consent and communication in BDSM practices. For example, Taylor and Ussher's (2001) interview study of BDSM practitioners' experiences found that consent was continually negotiated during the time that people were engaged with each other. Scenarios were planned in advance and safe words established so that either party could stop what was happening at any time.

Similarly, Langdridge and Butt's (2004) analysis of BDSM websites found that consent was a key theme. They cite the following excerpt from a fetish website as an example of how BDSM 'communities ... emphasise not the desirability, but the necessity of open communication within sadomasochistic relationships' (p. 46):

> Probably the most important concept in erotic power exchange is the concept of negotiation. Partners negotiate about their fantasies, feelings, needs, dreams, barriers and hidden desires. This is not the 'if I give this I get that' type of negotiation. The objective is to exchange your feelings, barriers and fantasies in an open and honest way. The partners try to establish where they meet, how much common ground they can cover and what are absolute 'no go' areas. In fact there is no other relationship that requires so much communication. Both partners, dominant as well as submissive, share an equal responsibility towards themselves and each other.
>
> (Quoted in Langdridge and Butt, 2004, p. 46)

This subcultural emphasis on consent and negotiation is perhaps something that many people whose sex lives are more 'conventional' could benefit from. Indeed, it is a topic which is often neglected within mainstream sex advice despite the high prevalence of sexual abuse and violence (Barker et al., 2016).

In this section you have seen how Western understandings of sex and sexuality have changed significantly over the last couple of hundred years. Social constructionist theorists such as Foucault have argued that these understandings are the product of a particular social and historical context: that of biopolitics. The discipline of psychology both emerged from, and contributed to, this context, which resulted in certain sexual behaviours and identities being accepted or idealised, while others were pathologised or criminalised.

However, in recent years, as you saw in Section 3, psychology has become much more affirming of sexual diversity, and many sexual practices and identities which were formerly seen as 'deviant' are now seen as part of the normal range of human sexual behaviour. The work of critical biologists, as well as critical psychologists, has added credence to such diversity-affirming understandings of sex and sexuality.

5   Summary

In this chapter you have seen that psychology has been deeply implicated in the development of contemporary understandings of sex and sexuality. It has ometimes fallen into the trap of reifying cultural assumptions about what counts as 'normal' sex, without sufficient evidence to back up its theories. At other times it has been at the forefront of progressive efforts to normalise sexual diversity. Indeed, as you have seen, there have been many times when the psychology of sexuality has done both of these things simultaneously!

In general terms, psychological approaches to understanding sex and sexuality have shifted over time from a biological and psychoanalytic focus on the specification, aetiology and treatment of sexual 'abnormality' to an interest in documenting sexual behaviour, and finally to a more social focus on lived experiences and subjective understandings of sex and sexuality.

References

American Psychiatric Association (2013) *Diagnostic and Statistical Manual of Mental Disorders, DSM-5*, Arlington, VA, APA.

Angelides, S. (2001) *A History of Bisexuality*, Chicago, IL, University of Chicago Press.

Bagemihl, B. (1999) *Biological Exuberance: Animal Homosexuality and Natural Diversity*, London, Macmillan.

Barker, M. J., Gill, R. and Harvey, L. (2016) *Mediated Intimacy: Sex Advice in Media Culture*, Cambridge, Polity.

Berry, D. S. (2007) 'Evolutionary perspectives on mate preferences', in Davis, S. F. and Buskist, W. (eds) *21st Century Psychology: A Reference Handbook*, London, Sage.

Bower, J., Gurevich, M. and Mathieson, C. M. (2002) '(Con)tested identities: bisexual women re-orient sexuality', in Atkins, D. (ed.) *Bisexual Women in the Twenty-First Century*, New York, Harrington Park Press.

Bristow, J. (2010) *Sexuality: The New Critical Idiom*, London, Routledge.

Carr, D. M. (2003) *The Erotic Word: Sexuality, Spirituality and the Bible*, Oxford, Oxford University Press.

Carrigan, M., Morrison, T. and Gupta, K. (2013) 'Asexuality special theme issue', *Psychology and Sexuality*, vol. 4, no. 2, pp. 111–20.

Darwin, C. (1859) *On the Origin of Species*, London, John Murray.

Darwin, C. (1871) *The Descent of Man and Selection in Relation to Sex*, New York, D. Appleton and Company.

D'Augelli, A. R. and Patterson, C. (eds) (2001) *Lesbian, Gay, and Bisexual Identities and Youth: Psychological Perspectives*, Oxford, Oxford University Press.

DePaulo, B. M. (2006) *Singled Out: How Singles are Stereotyped, Stigmatized, and Ignored, and Still Live Happily Ever After*, London, Macmillan.

Fausto-Sterling, A. (2012) *Sex/Gender: Biology in a Social World*, New York, Routledge.

Foucault, M. (1976) *The Will to Knowledge: The History of Sexuality 1*, Harmondsworth, Penguin.

Freud, S. (1962) [1905] *Three Essays on the Theory of Sexuality*, New York, Basic Books.

Hammersley, M. and Atkinson, P. (1995) *Ethnography: Principles in Practice*, London, Routledge.

Havelock Ellis, H. (1933) *Studies in the Psychology of Sex*, London, Random House.

Hird, M. (2004) *Sex, Gender and Science*, Basingstoke, Palgrave Press.

Hird, M. (2006) 'Sex diversity and evolutionary psychology', *The Psychologist*, vol. 19, no. 1, pp. 30–2.

Hirschfeld, M. (1922) *Homosexuality of Men and Women*, New York, Prometheus Books.

Hite, S. (1976) *The Hite Report on Female Sexuality*, New York, Seven Stories Press.

Hooker, E. (1957) 'The adjustment of the male overt homosexual', *Journal of Projective Techniques*, vol. 21, pp. 18–31.

Hopkins, J. (1969) 'The lesbian personality', *British Journal of Psychiatry*, vol. 115, pp. 1433–6.

Horney, K. (1967) *Feminine Psychology*, New York, Norton.

Irigaray, L. (1985) *This Sex Which Is Not One*, New York, Cornell University Press.

Kinsey, A. C., Pomeroy, W. R. and Martin, C. E. (1948) 'Sexual behavior in the human male', *American Journal of Public Health*, vol. 93, pp. 894–8.

Kinsey, A. C., Pomeroy, W. R. and Martin, C. E. (1953) *Sexual Behavior in the Human Female*, Bloomington, IN, Indiana University Press.

Kleinplatz, P. J. and Moser, C. (2007) 'Is S/M pathological?', *Lesbian and Gay Psychology Review*, vol. 6, pp. 261–7.

Krafft-Ebing, R. F. (1886) *Psychopathia Sexualis*, Stuttgart, Verlag Von Ferdinand Enke.

Krizek, G. O. (1992) 'Unusual interaction between a butterfly and a beetle: "sexual paraphilia" in insects?', *Tropical Lepidoptera*, vol. 3, no. 2, p. 118.

Langdridge, D. and Butt, T. W. (2004) 'A hermeneutic phenomenological investigation of the construction of sadomasochistic identities', *Sexualities*, vol. 7, no. 1, pp. 31–53.

Mackay, J. (2001) 'Why have sex?', *British Medical Journal*, vol. 322, p. 623.

Masters, W. H. and Johnson, V. E. (1966) *Human Sexual Response*, New York, Bantam Books.

Morrow, R. (2013) *Sex Research and Sex Therapy: A Sociological Analysis of Masters and Johnson*, London, Routledge.

Oosterhuis, H. (2000) *Stepchildren of Nature: Krafft-Ebing, Psychiatry, and the Making of Sexual Identity*, London, University of Chicago Press.

Pavelka, M. M. (1995) 'Sexual nature: what can we learn from a cross-species perspective?', in Abramson, P. and Pinkerton, S. (eds) *Sexual Nature, Sexual Culture*, Chicago, IL, University of Chicago Press.

Plummer, K. (1995). *Telling Sexual Stories: Power, Change, and Social Worlds*, Abingdon, Psychology Press.

Richards, C. and Barker, M. (2013) *Sexuality and Gender for Mental Health Professionals: A Practical Guide*, London, Sage.

Rose, H. and Rose, S. (2000) *Alas, Poor Darwin: Arguments Against Evolutionary Psychology*, New York, Harmony Books.

Roughgarden, J. (2004) *Evolution's Rainbow: Diversity, Gender, and Sexuality in Nature and People*, Oakland, CA, University of California Press.

Rubin, G. (1984) 'Thinking sex: notes for a radical theory of the politics of sexuality', in Rubin, G. (ed.) *Deviations: A Gayle Rubin Reader*, Durham, NC, Duke University Press, pp. 137–81.

Sani, G. M. D. (2014) 'Men's employment hours and time on domestic chores in European countries', *Journal of Family Issues*, vol. 35, pp. 1023–47.

Stainton-Rogers, W. and Stainton-Rogers, R. (2001) *The Psychology of Gender and Sexuality*, Buckingham, Open University Press.

Storr, M. (ed.) (1999) *Bisexuality: A Critical Reader*, London, Routledge.

Taylor, G. (1997) 'The discursive construction and regulation of dissident sexualities: the case of SM', in Ussher, J. M. (ed.) *Body Talk: The Material and Discursive Regulation of Sexuality, Madness and Reproduction*, London, Routledge, pp. 106–30.

Taylor, G. and Ussher, J. M. (2001) 'Making sense of S&M: a discourse analytic account', *Sexualities*, vol. 4, pp. 293–314.

Terry, J. (1999) *An American Obsession: Science, Medicine, and Homosexuality in Modern Society*, London, University of Chicago Press.

Trade Unions Congress (TUC) (2013) 'Just 1 in 172 fathers taking additional paternity leave' [Online]. Available at www.tuc.org.uk/workplace-issues/just-one-172-fathers-taking-additional-paternity-leave (Accessed 9 February 2014).

Ulrichs, K. H. (1898) *Studies on the Riddle of Male–Male Love*, trans. Lombardi-Nash, M. A., Buffalo, NY, Prometheus Books.

Wallis, W. A. (1949) 'Statistics of the Kinsey Report', *Journal of the American Statistical Association*, vol. 44, pp. 463–84.

Weeks, J. (2002) *Sexuality and its Discontents: Meanings, Myths, and Modern Sexualities*, London, Routledge.

Weeks, J. (2014) *Sex, Politics and Society: The Regulation of Sexuality Since 1800*, London, Routledge.

Chapter 15

Self-help: changing people's understandings to change their experience

Scott Cherry and Meg John Barker

Contents

1   Introduction

This final chapter is about the role of self-help in society. It explores how self-help has informed wider understandings of the self and what it means to be an individual, as well as considering the potential for psychologically informed kinds of self-help to improve people's lives.

In these two books you have touched several times on popular psychology and self-help. For example, in Chapter 4 you studied how self-help campaigns and books understand, and promote, self-esteem.

This part of the book has covered how people's experiences shape the ways in which they understand the world, and also how the ways in which people understand things shape their experience. For example, in Chapter 13 you saw how going through an extreme circumstance can impact people's identities, emotions and perceptions. In Chapter 14 you considered how the different ways in which people have understood sexuality over time and across cultures have shaped the ways in which they experience their sexuality.

Following on from these considerations, this last chapter explores the cultural phenomenon of self-help. Historically, most self-help has been produced by people who are not psychologists and who are not drawing on psychological theories and research. Therefore the chapter considers the extent to which psychologists – and others who are informed by psychology – might be able to produce forms of self-help which provide ways of understanding that could help with people's experiences. Additionally, this chapter examines the more insidious role that the self-help industry has had in shaping how people in Western cultures think about themselves and experience their lives.

The chapter begins by tracing the history of the concept of self-help. It then draws out the main features of self-help by considering the current context of mainstream self-help culture, with a particular focus on self-help books. While academic psychology has historically distanced itself from self-help as a form of 'popular psychology', the recent positive psychology movement is one example of where psychology has engaged with self-help. This movement researches how people can increase their levels of happiness and well-being, and has been more proactive than other forms of psychology in communicating its findings to the general public. After considering positive psychology, the chapter sets out a critical perspective on mainstream self-help practices, and introduces some critical-psychology informed types of self-help.

Through the chapter there is a widening out from a conception of the self as an autonomous individual to recognising the self's connectedness to other people and to social and cultural practices. In this way it should be a helpful reminder of the ways of understanding the self that you came across back in Chapters 4, 5 and 6. Twentieth-century self-help, and the positive psychology movement, generally thought of people as separate independent individuals, whereas more recent approaches have taken a more relational and social constructionist approach. These approaches view the individual as socially and culturally embedded, and also highlight the role of the self-help industry itself in shaping contemporary culture.

After reading this chapter you should be able to:

- describe the history of the phenomenon of self-help

- explain the main features of conventional self-help in contemporary culture

- identify the connections between self-help and psychology

- consider what critical perspectives on self-help offer for an understanding of the individual as socially and culturally embedded.

2   The history of self-help

> I went to a bookstore and asked the saleswoman, 'Where's the self-help section?' She said if she told me, it would defeat the purpose.

This quotation from comedian George Carlin captures a paradox of self-help. It is meant to be about people helping themselves, but generally speaking it involves engaging with other people in some way. Explore this in Activity 15.1.

Activity 15.1   Is there such a thing as self-help?

Take a few moments to consider the phenomenon of self-help as you currently understand it. Is it an individual activity? Is it still self-help if you turn to somebody else for assistance? What types of other people might be involved when someone engages with self-help? Do people need others in order to help themselves?

Comment

In terms of the other people who are involved in self-help, you might have considered the 'experts' who write self-help books, provide online self-help advice, or present self-help TV shows. You might also have thought of the friends and colleagues who recommend books, discuss magazine articles together, or engage in more formal self-help groups, workshops or online forums.

This apparent paradox of self-help – that it is both individual and social – is addressed throughout the chapter. For now it is important to first get a sense of the history of the phenomenon of self-help, as this has very much shaped the way in which self-help takes place today.

2.1   The history of the self

Despite its current wide popularity, self-help is a very modern phenomenon. In fact, the current understanding of self-help that people have was totally absent during much of the past.

This is largely down to the fact that conceptions of 'the self' are relatively recent, historically speaking. As you touched on back in Chapters 4 and 7, the notion of a separate individual self, particularly the kind that self-help operates with, is founded on a specifically Western tradition, originating in the late eighteenth century (Gergen, 1991; Sampson, 1993). Before this time, it would have been difficult to conceive of a self as a single, independent and autonomous unit. Rather, people would often have been regarded much more as part of wider units, perhaps in relation to their families, their trade, or other communities.

Capitalism
An economic system based primarily on private ownership of the means of production, and the creation of goods and services for profit.

Social psychologists suggest that the notion of the modern individual self has its roots in **capitalism**. During the eighteenth century, populations moved from rural life into the cities. For economic reasons people began to move around a lot more in the course of their lives, making the individual self a more relevant unit which could be carried between different communities and jobs.

During the nineteenth century, there was also an increasing understanding that laid 'central stress on unseen, even sacred forces that dwell deep within the person' (Gergen, 1991, p. 18). In Chapter 9 you learned, for example, how these ideas were popularised in the work of Sigmund Freud and his theory of the unconscious at the beginning of the twentieth century. There was increasing concern for the emergence of something within the person – a self – that required attention: something that could be worked on and developed.

It was this individual self that was then targeted by the consumer capitalism that developed through the twentieth century (Box 15.1). Advertisers sold products on the basis that they would appeal to a certain kind of individual: the housewife, for example, or the teenager, or the carefree bachelor. In so doing they really began to create certain kinds of individuals, and to reinforce the idea that people were separate selves, made up of a certain set of beliefs, values, attitudes and tastes (see Chapter 14, Figure 14.6, for a reminder of how this worked).

Box 15.1 Self-help as a US phenomenon

It is important to also note that self-help particularly emerged within a twentieth-century *American* cultural context, before becoming popular elsewhere in the Western world. There it was particularly informed by the tenets of the 'American dream': that citizens can become whatever they desire, regardless of class or wealth, if they just apply themselves. For example, the US Declaration of Independence (which dates from the eighteenth century) states that one of the 'inalienable rights' of citizens is the 'pursuit of happiness'. This is a right of all human beings, which the US government should therefore protect and encourage.

During the last few decades, the USA and other capitalist cultures have developed a social and political context which has been called **neoliberalism**. Several commentators have suggested that neoliberalism is responsible for the contemporary version of the individual self (Peters, 2001; McNamee and Miller, 2004; Amable, 2011;). Governments' neoliberal policies place the highest value on individual responsibility, so the self is very much seen as an individual unit responsible for its own well-being. However, the state remains involved as it acts alongside many other commercial and non-commercial agencies (including education, medicine and the media) to encourage individual citizens to 'freely' make the 'right' choices to ensure that they are 'self-reliant' rather than dependent on the state.

Neoliberalism
A set of values and strategies that prioritises individual rights and responsibilities over state-provided support, such as forms of welfare.

With this broad overview of the history of the self, you now have a good basis on which to consider the notion of the self in self-help. It is this that you will now turn to.

2.2   The rise of self-help culture

This section explores the emergence of self-help culture, which has taken the principle of the individual self and has developed it into a hugely significant feature of popular culture. You will focus here on self-help *books* as one of the earliest – and most enduring – forms of self-help. However, it is worth remembering throughout that self-help also takes other forms, some of which you will touch on later in the chapter.

Many academics have charted the rise of self-help through the emergence of self-help literature: manuals that advise readers how to be a 'better' person in prescribed ways. Laura Vanderkam (2012) suggests that Benjamin Franklin's (1757) *The Way to Wealth* was one of the earliest self-help texts, with Samuel Smiles's (1859) *Self-Help* being another. Both writers advocated thrift, hard work and – above all – self-education. It was suggested that the individual could triumph against adversity, even transcending poverty and low-class status, if they applied themselves.

These kinds of books rose steadily in popularity as the twentieth century unfolded. During the second half of the twentieth century, they skyrocketed as a publishing phenomenon (Whelan, 2004). It has been reported that, as of 2000, Americans spent nearly $600 million on self-help books (Paul, 2001). Dale Carnegie, author of a single self-help book, has sold over 50 million copies (O'Neil, 2003). Self-help books also became a global phenomenon. However, although there is some cultural diversity in the messages within such books, the vast majority of bestselling self-help books emerged within a Western – often US – context.

Box 15.2   Classic self-help books

In his research on the history of self-help books, Tom Butler-Bowdon (2003) lists many of the self-help books which have become bestsellers and are now regarded as 'classics':

- Dale Carnegie (1936) *How to Win Friends and Influence People*

- Norman Vincent Peale (1952) *The Power of Positive Thinking*

- Stephen Covey (1989) *The 7 Habits of Highly Successful People*

- M. Scott Peck (1978) *The Road Less Traveled*

- John Gray (1992) *Men Are From Mars, Women Are From Venus*

- Richard Carlson (1997) *Don't Sweat the Small Stuff … and it's All Small Stuff*

- Phillip McGraw (1999) *Life Strategies: Doing What Works, Doing What Matters*

Figure 15.1 shows a selection.

Figure 15.1 Self-help books

Think a bit more about these books in Activity 15.2.

Activity 15.2   What constitutes self-help?

Reflect on these self-help book titles. Can you think of other books that might be added to this list? What might constitute a 'self-help book'?

Comment

You will see from this list, and perhaps from the other books that you thought of, that self-help books generally aim to help people to improve something: their relationships, their success at work, or their stress levels, for example. They generally aim to do this through teaching some kinds of skills, for example the 'life strategies', 'habits' or ways of not 'sweating the small stuff' mentioned in the book titles.

The sales figures for self-help books indicate something critical in the history of self-help. From the 1960s, and certainly from the 1970s, self-help had developed from merely a publishing success into a social phenomenon in its own right (McGee, 2005).

The popularity of self-help books is just the tip of the iceberg. The concept of self-help has expanded across the social landscape, including self-help groups, popular talk show and makeover television formats, and women's magazines that are largely based on advice and self-help suggestions. New terms have been introduced, for example 'self-improvement' is often now substituted for self-help, although these terms are still used interchangeably. This all marks the emergence of a self-help culture.

2.3   Different forms of self-help

Empowerment
The thesis that people are responsible for their own experiences and actions and can therefore have the power to take control.

You have now seen how the concept of the individual self emerged over recent centuries and how the development of self-help culture has reflected, and reproduced, this understanding of the self, and the neoliberal sense that individuals are responsible for engaging in a project of self-improvement. In relation to the theme of this part of the book you can see how a certain way of *understanding* the self has, through self-help, impacted on how people *experience* their lives and the kinds of projects that they engage in: trying to learn habits and strategies to make them more successful, for example.

Victimisation
The thesis that people are not responsible for their own experiences and actions, but rather are victims of outside forces beyond their control.

In this section you will learn about the two main forms of self-help and the different understandings (and experiences) each of these has promoted.

Steve Salerno (2005) proposes that the main narrative of the self-help movement regularly shifts between **empowerment** and **victimisation**.

Empowerment self-help suggests that people have the control to determine their own lives. Victimisation self-help suggests that people's lives are controlled by outside forces and can take directions that are not of their choosing.

These two common types of self-help map closely on to the psychological theory of the **locus of control** (Rotter, 1966). This refers to the extent to which people believe they can have an impact on how events unfold in their lives. Those with a high level of 'internal' locus of control believe they are responsible for their own actions and their future path, and attribute praise or blame to themselves for their actions. Those with a high level of 'external' locus of control believe they are not responsible for their actions, and attribute the way their lives have unfolded to external factors such as their upbringing.

Locus of control
The extent to which people believe they are able to control events that affect them.

Empowerment self-help is firmly centred on an internal locus of control: the idea that people can change their lives as an active agent. Perhaps the most popular version of this is the self-help idea that 'positive thinking' can change people's lives. This was first popularised with Norman Vincent Peale's (1952) book *The Power of Positive Thinking*. Peale suggested that readers should engage in the 'happiness habit', which is 'developed by simply practising happy thinking'. If they should struggle with a negative thought they should 'immediately stop, eject it, and substitute a happiness thought' (p. 70). The principle here is that the way in which people think about the world determines how that world will be. If they think happy thoughts, it will be a happy world for them; if they think sad thoughts, it will be a sad world for them.

Victimisation self-help emerged in the 1960s, perhaps as a reaction to the empowerment self-help literature of the time, which left no space for people to find external reasons for their distress, or to find changing their lives to be a struggle (Salerno, 2005). Books in the victimisation genre include Thomas A. Harris's (1963) *I'm OK, You're OK*, which focused on the involvement of early childhood experiences, particularly poor parenting, in problems experienced in adulthood.

The 12-step programmes that became popular around this time were another example of victimisation self-help. These programmes, which started with Alcoholics Anonymous, took people in groups through 12 steps which aimed to help them recover from addiction. They focused on relabelling behaviours that had previously been blamed on the individual as diseases – such as alcoholism – which were regarded as beyond individual control. It was seen as important that people admitted that they were powerless over their problems and that they required help.

Melodie Beattie's (1987) popular book *Codependent No More* was part of the addiction and recovery movement. It argued that people develop a tendency towards 'codependency' – or overly dependent relationships – during early life, and that this is unhealthy. For example, she said: 'the surest way to make ourselves crazy is to get involved in other people's business, and the quickest way to become sane and happy is to tend to our own affairs' (p. 113).

It can be seen from these examples that a key feature of victimisation self-help is attributing the cause of problems to external factors (often child rearing and early experiences). Therefore this kind of self-help proposed an entirely external locus of control. However, victimisation self-help is generally just as **individualistic** as empowerment self-help because the focus is often still on achieving individual independence.

Individualistic
Focused on the individual.

Generally speaking, individualistic theories put problems down to individual causes (e.g. a disease, or a person having faulty thought processes). Individualistic solutions focus on approaches which treat the individual (e.g. drug treatments, or a person trying to change their attitude). Individualistic theories and solutions are criticised by those who believe there is a sociocultural element to most human struggles (see Chapter 5, Section 4). The codependency literature is a particularly clear example of an individualistic set of theories and solutions.

Following this turn towards victimisation self-help, there was a reversion to empowerment self-help, which suggested that people were responsible for their behaviours and experiences, and that they could determine the direction of their lives (internal locus of control). Perhaps this occurred because empowerment narratives fitted better than victimisation ones within the wider culture of the 1980s: economic booms meant that there was even more emphasis on advertising and consumption, and there was an increasing neoliberal political move towards focusing on individual responsibility rather than on providing social welfare.

A common version of empowerment self-help at this time took it to extremes with a belief in the so-called 'law of attraction'. For example, the hugely popular self-help 'guru' Anthony Robbins (2001) argued in his books that if people send the right messages out into their environment, and envision the life they desire, then they will 'attract' the success they want. It is all about having a vision and pursuing it. This idea was also put forward in Rhonda Byrne's (2006) extremely popular book *The Secret*. Byrne argued that how people feel inside 'transmits' a frequency out into the world that in turn attracts back a corresponding frequency.

This 'law' of attraction requires mystical thinking in order to believe that outside forces will reflect back the messages people put out into the world (see Block 4 for more on the problems with this kind of thinking). However, more conventional forms of empowerment self-help also reflect a similarly internal locus of control. For example, Richard Carlson's (1997) self-help book *Don't Sweat the Small Stuff … and it's All Small Stuff* draws heavily on thinking as a basis for people getting the life they want. For example:

> Because you're always doing it [thinking], it's easy to forget that it's happening, and it becomes invisible to you. … [F]orgetting that you are thinking can cause some serious problems in your life, such as unhappiness, anger, inner conflict, and stress. …
>
> Try getting angry without first having angry thoughts! … You can't do it – it's impossible. The truth is, in order to experience a feeling, you must first have a thought that produces that feeling.
>
> Unhappiness doesn't and can't exist on its own. Unhappiness is the feeling that accompanies negative thinking about your life.
>
> (pp. 227–8)

You may notice that Carlson's theories are contradicted by many psychological understandings of how emotions operate (see Block 1). Emotions are by no means always preceded by thoughts in this way. Another self-help author, Gael Lindenfield (2000), advises:

> Do you often find your behaviour is your worst enemy? Do you hear yourself regularly saying:
>
> 'I wish I didn't always …'
>
> 'If only I could stop …'
>
> 'I can't help it, I always …'
>
> 'I couldn't stop myself …'

If you do, I suggest that a battle with your self-destructive habits must be a priority.

(p. 51)

A key way in which she suggests doing this is by restating such thoughts more positively.

Consider your opinions about empowerment and victimisation in Activity 15.3.

Activity 15.3   Empowerment and victimisation

Having read about empowerment and victimisation understandings, which do you find yourself more drawn to? Do you prefer the understanding of a person as responsible for their own problems and for getting out of them (empowerment) or the understanding that external factors are to blame for problems that people experience and that part of the process of moving forward is recognising their lack of control over their lives (victimisation)? What do you think are the problems with these two approaches? Can you imagine an alternative version of self-help beyond either empowerment or victimisation?

Comment

Considering this question, you might have reflected that the understanding you prefer depends on what the problem is. For example, there is a big difference between an issue such as alcoholism and one such as lack of confidence. Perhaps some problems are more within people's control than others. Perhaps different things work for different people at different times. You might also have reflected that there are often multiple causes for experiences in life, combining some elements that are within a person's control, and some that are not.

However, as you have seen in this section, self-help has generally presented people as either individuals who are at the mercy of external forces in their development (victimisation self-help), or – more commonly – as individuals who are capable of, and responsible for, improving their lives through self-transformation (empowerment self-help). Such understandings are likely to have a major influence on how people experience their lives, whether they feel themselves to be entirely in control, or at the mercy of external forces.

In both forms of self-help the emphasis is on the individual to help or improve themselves, and there is very little consideration of the impact of the social world around the individual. This is an issue you will return to later in Section 4.

3   Positive psychology: psychologically informed self-help

You might be wondering by this point where the discipline of psychology fits in with self-help. Surely self-help is asking the very questions that psychology is best placed to answer: about why people have emotional and relationship difficulties, for example, and about the best ways of improving their thoughts, feelings and behaviours.

However, most self-help has not been written by professional psychologists. Indeed, professional psychology has largely questioned the role of self-help as an adequate form of psychological intervention in people's lives (e.g. Bergsma, 2008; Rosen et al., 2008). This is based on the observation made by many psychologists that self-help gurus are typically untrained, have few or no professional qualifications, and are unaccredited to engage in psychological work of this nature (Richardson et al., 2010).

There has also been a concern that the foundation of the psychological professions is undermined by self-help. In the 1980s clinical psychologist Gerald M. Rosen argued that self-help books posed a threat to the professional standards of psychology, as 'the quality of do-it-yourself treatment books is decreasing while their number is on the rise' (1981, p. 189). Rosen suggested that 'unlike the typical author, clinical psychologists are in a position to assess do-it-yourself treatments systematically and to educate consumers in the proper use of these programs' (1987, p. 46).

Positive psychology
The field of psychology that focuses on determining what maximises happiness and well-being, rather than dealing with the more negative aspects of human experience.

During the 1990s psychology began to produce its own, psychologically informed, form of self-help with the development of a new field of study known as **positive psychology** (e.g. Csikszentmihalyi, 1990; Peterson and Bossio, 1991; Seligman, 1991). This has become a major academic project (Ahmed, 2010; Seligman, 2011; Fredrickson, 2013).

Psychologist Martin Seligman's (1991) experiments on 'learned optimism' proved to be ground-breaking for this fledgling field. His studies, and those based on his work, suggest that people can become happy by changing the ways in which they respond to recognisably negative events. In other words, they can learn an optimistic way of responding.

Kennon M. Sheldon and Sonja Lyubomirsky's (2006) study is a good example of research in this area. Students were given a 'best possible selves' exercise. This involved them imagining – over several weeks – their best possible future self, in which they supposed they had worked hard and accomplished all their life goals. Findings suggested that those who carried out the exercise demonstrated a significant lift in mood relative to those who did not.

Seligman illustrates another of the common findings of positive psychology with the story of one of his students, a part-time waitress, who hated the heavy trays, rude customers and dismal tips that her job involved. Drawing on the positive psychology finding that it is helpful for people to apply their strengths to new areas, Seligman helped her to identify her strength as 'social intelligence'. He then recommended 'recrafting' her job, and applying her strength, making her encounters with customers the highlight of their evening. The result for this student was that waitressing became more fun, and the tips became larger (Seligman, 2011).

Although positive psychology shares with self-help culture a quest for 'the good life', it bases its advice about achieving happiness and well-being on experimental psychological research. Seligman argues that the 'positive thinking' of so much self-help is 'an armchair activity'. Positive psychology, on the other hand, 'is tied to a program of empirical and replicable scientific activity' (2002, p. 288). Seligman defines the key elements of positive psychology as: positive emotion, engagement, relationships, meaning and accomplishment – using the acronym PERMA for short. Techniques are developed to address each of these elements, and these are researched experimentally using large-scale studies to determine whether they are effective at improving scores on measures of individual happiness and well-being. Try applying this to yourself in Activity 15.4.

Activity 15.4   How happy are you?

Positive psychologists Lyubomirsky and Heidi S. Lepper (1999) have developed a method of measuring happiness called the Subjective Happiness Scale. For each of the following statements and/or questions, please identify the point on the scale that you feel is most appropriate in describing you.

As a student of psychology, do not think too deeply about the questions, or begin a process of soul searching; rather, just make a quick decision on the extent to which you agree or disagree with the statements. The focus here is not your actual score, but the processes involved in answering the questions.

1   In general, I consider myself:

Not a very happy person	1	2	3	4	5	6	7	A very happy person

2   Compared with most of my peers, I consider myself:

Less happy	1	2	3	4	5	6	7	More happy

3   Some people are generally very happy. They enjoy life regardless of what is going on, getting the most out of everything. To what extent does this characterisation describe you?

Not at all	1	2	3	4	5	6	7	A great deal

4   Some people are generally not very happy. Although they are not depressed, they never seem as happy as they might be. To what extent does this characterisation describe you?

A great deal	1	2	3	4	5	6	7	Not at all

Calculating the score:

Step 1: Total = item 1 + item 2 + item 3 + item 4 =

Step 2: Happiness score = Total (from above) divided by 4 =

Now consider whether this score is a good reflection of how happy you are as a person, and what you think of this idea of measuring happiness in general.

Comment

Producing a personal score from scales such as this is an important way in which positive psychologists believe someone can identify their happiness. As you considered with self-esteem (Chapter 4) and aggression (Chapter 5), you might, however, question the degree to which subjective experiences can be measured quantitatively.

A key aspect of positive psychology is that it puts forward the argument that happiness is achievable for everybody. Seligman's theory of learned optimism is just that – something that is learned and not something people are born with. Positive psychologists believe that people can change how they feel: sad can be transformed into happy.

Positive psychologist Lyubomirsky (2013) states this even more strongly, arguing that society has perpetuated a number of myths of happiness. She suggests that people have been deceived into thinking that the attainment of material goods – money, property, jewellery, fast cars, and so on – will result in their happiness. However, positive psychology has found that material gain beyond a certain point does not predict happiness (Easterlin, 2004).

Another set of positive psychology studies has focused on the impact of materialistic, versus other, kinds of goals. Carol Nickerson and colleagues (2003) studied the attitudes of 12,000 students at elite universities when the students were 18, and then measured their life satisfaction at age 36. Those expressing materialistic aspirations as their primary goal at undergraduate level were less satisfied with their lives two decades later. Also, Patricia Cohen and Jacob Cohen (1996) found that materialists were more likely than non-materialists to experience psychological and emotional difficulties.

Instead of material gain, positive psychologists argue, happiness derives from changes in thinking, and is an internal, psychological phenomenon. As Lyubomirsky argues, 'how you think about yourself, your world and other people is more important to your happiness than the objective circumstances of your life' (2007, p. 87). Lyubomirsky and colleagues (2011) found that many of those students who thought excessively about negative experiences impeded their performance at demanding everyday tasks such as reading and writing. Thus positive psychologists suggest techniques such as 'recrafting' what you do according to your skills (as in the waitress example above), writing letters to express gratitude to people in your life, and thinking of three things that have been positive each day before going to sleep (Seligman et al., 2006).

Reflect on this in Activity 15.5.

Activity 15.5   Thinking critically about positive psychology

In what ways do you think that positive psychology has improved (or not) on non-psychological forms of self-help? Has it removed the problems with self-help that you considered earlier in the chapter?

Comment

Like the previous examples of self-help that you have considered, the emphasis of positive psychology remains on individual change, and on the internal locus of control idea that people can improve their experience by altering how they think about things. Positive psychology is, however, much more rigorous than much self-help literature, as it tests its theories, tools and techniques with empirical research.

Marginalisation
The process of being systematically removed from, and denied participation in, the cultural and social activities of a society.

You might question whether all happiness and well-being can be put down to the ways in which people think. For example, it is widely established that those in poverty (e.g. Jenkins et al., 2008; Serr, 2006) and those who experience **marginalisation** (e.g. Fernando, 2010; Potter, 2000) suffer from greater levels of distress, lower feelings of self-worth, and more mental health problems, and this is due to their real-life circumstances and is certainly not restricted to simply how they think about things. You might also think back to the experiences of trauma discussed in Chapter 13 as an external social factor which certainly seems to impact on people's experience.

4   Critical psychological self-help

In addition to the positive psychology approach, recent years have seen some attempts by more **critical psychologists,** and those drawing on their work, to produce self-help which is rooted in such theories and research. This is often in contrast to the ideas put forward in positive psychology, as it questions the emphasis on the individual, and the idea that happiness is necessarily what people should be striving towards.

4.1   Critical approaches to self-help

The philosopher Michel Foucault (1975), who you learned about in Chapter 14, famously used the idea of the **panopticon** (Box 15.3) to describe the ways in which contemporary society works.

Critical psychologists
Psychologists who challenge other parts of the psychology discipline for their failure to recognise the sociocultural influences on individual experience and behaviour.

Panopticon
An idea by eighteenth-century social reformer Jeremy Bentham for a prison where all prisoners could be observed at any time.

Box 15.3   The panopticon

Figure 15.2 Panopticon

A panopticon (Figure 15.2) is an institutional building (typically a prison) designed so that a single guard can observe inmates, usually from a centre point. Although inmates are aware that they are being observed, they do not know when: it could be at any time. Subsequently, inmates will internalise the sense of being watched and start to monitor themselves for appropriate behaviour at all times. Foucault used this idea to characterise the ways in

---

Self-monitoring
The practice of people continually checking and evaluating their behaviour and self-presentation to ensure its acceptability to others around them and wider culture.

which people in society become so aware of the various critical gazes upon them that they end up **self-monitoring** their own actions and behaviour through fear that they might not be acceptable to others. This has developed into a self-policing culture, where everybody polices themselves through fear of punishment, ridicule and disapproval.

Foucault suggested that contemporary culture works in this way (see Chapter 14, Section 4.1 for more detail of the thinking behind his theories). People are encouraged to scrutinise and judge themselves at all times, to self-improve, to work on themselves, and to present a positive and successful self to the world. This is linked to consumerism, which is all about seeing ourselves as lacking and needing something to compensate for that lack. Advertising, and many other forms of media, create fears (e.g. you might look bad, be out of date or be a failure) and then offer products to allay those fears (e.g. beauty products and diets, the latest fashion, or recipes for success in various arenas). You might also think about the ways – more recently – in which phenomena such as social networking encourage people to present a certain kind of self, and to monitor themselves in comparison with other people's presentations (see Chapter 7, Section 4.1).

Hopefully you can see the ways in which the self-help culture that this chapter has considered fits into this wider self-monitoring society. It suggests that people are flawed in some way (not successful enough or happy enough, or struggling in their relationships) and then offers 'expertise' to help individuals to address that flaw in their selves. Foucault's ideas have been hugely influential in the development of critical psychology (Box 15.4), which you will now go on to explore.

Box 15.4   Critical psychology

Critical psychologists share a concern for the way that much of psychology has reduced human experience to the level of the individual and ignored the impact of society and wider culture. Critical psychologists Dennis R. Fox and Isaac Prilleltensky (1997) provide the following example of how a critical psychological approach may differ from a more standard psychological approach:

An individual may experience job-related stress, for example, and seek help from a clinician. What is the job of the psychologist here? How should he or she analyse this stress? Is the goal to teach the 'client' or 'patient' stress-management techniques? To investigate what it is about the client that causes an apparent inability to cope with normal job requirements? Or is it, perhaps, to examine the nature of the job setting, in an effort to alter workplace demands?

(1997, p. 12)

Thus critical psychology moves away from 'the individual' (the employee) as the problem, towards the context in which the individual is situated (the workplace).

Similar questions to those in Box 15.4 could be asked in relation to self-help on this topic (job-related stress). Is it the job of self-help authors to teach individual strategies, or – perhaps – to suggest that stress emerges in certain social contexts, and that collective action, or resistance to problematic workplace norms, might be possible ways forward?

In its recognition of the individual being firmly embedded within society, this critical perspective draws on sociological, as well as psychological, theory and practice. The work of Vivien Burr and Angie Burns (Chapter 5) and Michael Billig (Chapter 6) are examples of critical psychology.

A critical perspective was growing at the fringes of psychology as early as the 1970s, around the time, you will recall, that self-help was gaining an unprecedented following in popular culture. Critical psychologists argued that psychology's attempts at theorising, measuring and defining the individual as the sole unit of analysis had a mistaken conception of the person (e.g. Gergen, 1973, 1985; Harré, 1979). Critical psychologists place any sense of the individual in webs of relationships with other social groups, cultural practices and political struggles for power (Burman, 1990; Parker, 1992). Thus they put forward quite a different way of understanding people, which would likely result in very different ways of people experiencing and addressing the issues that confront them.

Community psychologists
Psychologists who investigate the individual in the context of social and cultural practices.

For example, **community psychologists** are a related group of psychologists who have argued that individuals should be understood in the context of community-based practices (Rappaport, 2005; Orford, 2008; Kagan et al., 2011). For instance, a strong association has been found between neighbourhood social and structural factors and individual mental health (Osypuk et al., 2012). Examples of applied work in this area include youth programmes, which have been found to promote and reinforce healthy development (Leventhal and Gunn, 2000), and parenting training, which has been found to strongly improve long-term family relations (Caldwell et al., 2010).

Such critical perspectives underscore the importance of the connection of the individual to other people, to the world, to social justice and to stewardship, that is, to the management and organisation of social, economic and political resources within which the individual is embedded. You may well see some connections between this approach and the psychology of the environment (or 'ecospychology') which you covered in Block 3, particularly Chapter 9.

Individualisation
The process of separating people by treating them as independent of one another.

While self-help culture celebrates the idea of 'an autonomous self' and the increasing **individualisation** of society, critical psychologists argue for the need to provide a more **contextual account**. Critical psychologists therefore argue that both self-help and positive psychology understandings of the self are problematic (Held, 2001, 2002). Critical psychology regards self-help culture as part of a society that operates like the panopticon, by encouraging people into increasing scrutiny of themselves and attempts at improving their experience through self-transformation.

Contextual account
How people see something in terms of the details within which that thing is situated.

You can see that critical psychology perspectives set up strong challenges to self-help culture and to positive psychology. These challenges focus on the dangers of taking a purely individualistic approach to human beings, and of ignoring the social and cultural embeddedness of human experience.

4.2   Critical approaches to positive thinking

Along with many other critical psychologists (e.g. Greco and Stenner, 2013), Barbara S. Held (2002) questions the focus of self-help and positive psychology on positive thinking, in various guises. She poses the question: 'If there indeed now exists unprecedented pressure to accentuate the positive, could it then be that the *pressure itself* to be happy contributes to at least some forms of unhappiness?' (p. 980).

Joanne V. Wood and colleagues (2009) studied the use of **positive affirmations** found in much self-help literature, and revealed some serious issues with these techniques. The researchers divided people into two groups, one group of people with low self-esteem, the other with high self-esteem. They asked both groups to undertake a writing task. On occasion, when a bell rang, participants would be asked to repeat a positive affirmation. Surprisingly, those with low self-esteem actually became *less* happy after producing the positive affirmation. Positive thinking, in this case, actually had the opposite effect. The researchers explained this by pointing out that positive affirmations conflict with the feelings of low self-esteem that those participants had to begin with: a form of cognitive dissonance (see Chapter 5). Thus they disrupt the person's sense of coherence, leading to more negative feelings.

Positive affirmations
Positive statements people repeat to themselves, such as 'I am a good person'.

In another study, psychologists Heather Barry Kappes and colleagues (2012) examined the self-help technique of visualisation. They got a group of participants to become dehydrated and then asked them to visualise drinking a glass of ice-cold water. Strangely, visualising the cold drink actually reduced participants' energy levels, making them relax, giving the impression that the thirst need had already been satisfied. They argued that this would mean, in the real world, that positive visualisation would not invoke a helpful response (getting up and fetching a drink); on the contrary, it would make it less likely.

In *Bright-Sided: How the Relentless Promotion of Positive Thinking Has Undermined America*, social critic Barbara Ehrenreich (2009) recalls when she was diagnosed with breast cancer. All of the available self-help suggested viewing the disease *positively*, to the extent of viewing it as a 'gift'. Ehrenreich questions the various ways in which such a 'survival culture' has encouraged a positive attitude, to the extent of 'forbidding' negative feelings which most people are likely to experience on receiving a cancer diagnosis, and dealing with the treatment involved. Positive thinking will likely have a particularly negative impact on the high proportion of cancer sufferers who also experience depression (Walker et al., 2014). Interestingly, one study found that participants who thought that they received benefits from having cancer actually experienced a poorer quality of life compared with those who did not perceive such benefits (Dittman, 2004). This brings into question the idea that it is always valuable to focus on the positive, or to reframe things in a positive way.

4.3 Towards a new form of self-help

Critical psychological approaches open up the potential for a different version of psychologically informed self-help: one which understands the self in a more socially embedded way, and which focuses more on wider culture and the connections between people. There are currently few people who are actively writing psychologically informed self-help from a more critical perspective. Here you will be introduced to two: Oliver Burkeman (2012) and one of the authors of this chapter, Meg John Barker (2013b), whose work you also read about in Chapter 5. Burkeman is a journalist who draws on psychological and philosophical research and theories in his self-help books, and Barker is a critical psychologist.

Burkeman (2012) has made a career out of critical observations on mainstream self-help's failure to make people happy. As with the critical perspectives you considered in the previous section, Burkeman regards the self-help quest to eliminate negativity in the pursuit of happiness as part of the problem, rather than part of the solution. He repeats Held's (2002) point that the pressure to feel happy can often make people feel quite the opposite.

As an alternative to positive thinking, Burkeman proposes a path he calls 'negative thinking'. This is not simply endorsing being miserable! Rather, it proposes a value to people not always trying to see the world positively.

Stoicism
The idea that people's experience of the world should reflect its nature. People should learn to accept failures, uncertainties and setbacks as part of life, and as part of the 'balance' of individual experience.

This alternative draws heavily on the philosophical ideas of **stoicism**. Striving for happiness, Burkeman argues, may depend on, and be driven by, negative feelings. Denying that there is a negative character to the world, and to people's experience of it, and only focusing on positivity, may produce a fear of anything that is not positive. Burkeman cites the research of psychologists Christina Moutsiana and colleagues (2013), who studied this cognitive bias. They found that people display a psychological preference towards optimism, discounting negative, unpleasant feelings or bad news, even if there is no sound basis on which to do so.

Drawing on the work of psychologist Albert Ellis (1962) (Figure 15.3), Burkeman argues that, in many cases, facing the negative sides of life is not nearly as bad as people imagine it will be. Ellis was the inventor of the approach of **rational emotive behaviour therapy (REBT)**, a form of cognitive behavioural therapy (see Chapter 13). This approach proposed that people's beliefs about the circumstances they faced were highly important in determining the consequences of those circumstances for them. According to this approach, it is often the belief that something will have negative consequences that makes it so emotionally difficult.

Rational emotive behaviour therapy (REBT)
A form of cognitive behavioural therapy (CBT) that emphasises shifting people's beliefs in order to alter the impact that adverse circumstances have on them.

Figure 15.3 Albert Ellis

Burkeman conducted an interview with Ellis shortly before the latter's death. In it, Ellis advised Burkeman to place himself in a socially embarrassing circumstance that he would normally avoid at all costs: a classic technique of REBT. Burkeman agreed. While journeying on the underground, he proceeded to loudly announce the names of the stations as the train reached them. To his amazement, with the exception of a few glances, passengers failed to take any notice. Burkeman actually felt *better* for having the courage to confront what was, in reality, something quite unremarkable and mundane. This is an intriguing technique to contrast with the positive thinking techniques of self-help and positive psychology.

Burkeman also includes the work of psychologist Gabriele Oettingen in his writing. Oettingen was one of the researchers who conducted the glass of water study that you read about in the previous section. Oettingen has conducted a number of further studies which demonstrate that people imagining something they want often makes it more difficult to achieve in reality. One study found that people who fantasised about losing weight were less likely to do so than those who did not (Oettingen and Wadden, 1991). Another found that those who fantasised about doing well on an upcoming task then had lower energy for actually engaging in that task than those who had fantasised about doing badly on it (Kappes and Oettingen, 2011). Finally, people who imagined having a productive week ended up achieving less than those who did not (Oettingen and Mayer, 2002).

Finally, Burkeman draws on the recent psychological turn towards **mindfulness**: a set of therapeutic practices, rooted in **Buddhism**, which suggest that much of human distress is rooted in people's tendency to strive to attain everything they want and to avoid – or eradicate – anything they do not want (Barker, 2013a). Psychological research in this area has found that mindful meditation practices are effective in reducing experiences of anxiety, stress, depression, and even physical pain (Kenny and Williams, 2007; Piet and Hougaard, 2011; Vøllestad et al., 2012; Zeidan et al., 2011). Such practices involve people sitting still and attempting to be aware of all their experiences, rather than endeavouring to keep hold of positive feelings, thoughts or sensations and get rid of negative ones. For example, with depression, it appears that it is often the spiral of negative thoughts that happen when somebody realises that they are sad – and their attempts to get rid of that feeling because they think that they should not be feeling that way – which exacerbates their depression (Williams et al., 2007).

So Burkeman's 'negative thinking' alternative to positive thinking involves facing up to the inevitable difficult experiences in life, rather than hoping they will not happen. It involves challenging beliefs and assumptions about what adverse circumstances will actually be like. It suggests having realistic imaginings about what will happen rather than positive fantasies. And it advocates trying to accept experiences as they are instead of endeavouring to maximise 'positive' experiences and eradicate 'negative' ones.

Burkeman concludes that his more critical version of 'self-help' is not about achievement – of goals, social standing, motivation, happiness and so forth – but rather about experiencing oneself in harmony with

Mindfulness
A range of therapies and self-help practices drawing on Buddhism which encourages people to be present with their experiences, paying gentle and curious attention to them, rather than trying to get rid of them or clinging on to them.

Buddhism
A range of philosophies that share a belief in embracing the inevitable pain and uncertainty of life, and regarding suffering as rooted in patterns of craving (people trying to get all of what they want and none of what they don't want).

nature. Again, you might notice links between this and the ecopsychological approaches discussed in Block 3. Such harmony involves learning to develop awareness of a world that is not fixed and that changes continuously. Wisdom is regarded as living within this impermanence. This is a journey, but not to a destination or an end point, 'or maybe it makes more sense to say the path is the destination?' (Burkeman, 2012, p. 212).

Try putting these approaches into practice in Activity 15.6.

Activity 15.6 Positive and negative thinking

Consider a difficult situation in your own life (ideally one from the recent past that isn't currently troubling you, so that you can consider it fairly calmly). Think about how a 'positive thinking' approach might encourage you to engage with this experience. Then think about an alternative way in which Burkeman's 'negative thinking' approach might encourage engaging with it.

Comment

You might have suggested here, for example, that 'positive thinking' could involve reframing something as a positive experience, replacing negative thoughts about it with positive ones, or otherwise taking individual responsibility for 'getting over' it. 'Negative thinking', on the other hand, might involve recognising the inevitability of some difficult situations in life, and allowing all the emotions you have about it to be experienced, including negative ones. What are your views about how useful the different approaches would be?

Hopefully you can see here that more critical approaches to self-help promote rather different ways of understanding ourselves, which also lead to quite different ways of experiencing life. You will now turn to a specifically critical psychological example of a self-help book.

Psychologist and one of the authors of this chapter, Meg John Barker (2013b), has attempted to draw on critical psychological ideas to produce a different form of relationship self-help from the common approaches put forward in popular self-help books. Relationship self-help books, such as Ellen Fein and Sherrie Schneider's (1995) *The Rules*, generally present one story about relationships as the truth, notably the idea that it is vitally important for people to form a long-term monogamous love relationship and that the main way of doing this is through embracing the common cultural rules of conventional femininity and masculinity.

Inspired by critical feminist research in psychology (e.g. Kitzinger, 1987; Burman, 1990), Barker questions the idea that there is only one way of engaging in relationships, instead considering the wide diversity of different forms of singledom (DePaulo, 2006), monogamous and non-monogamous coupledom, and other relationship forms that exist (Barker and Langdridge, 2010).

Instead of locating the problems that people experience with relationships in the individual, Barker instead locates them in the messages about love, relationships, sex and the like that people receive from the culture around them, for example from Hollywood movies, women's and men's magazines, and indeed relationship self-help books. Barker suggests that challenging these messages, and the pressures they put people under, may be a more valuable way forward than trying to create the kinds of unrealistically perfect relationships depicted in this culture. For example, as you saw in Chapter 5, ideals of meeting 'the one' perfect partner and finding a 'happy-ever-after' are associated with relationship distress, rather than with relationship well-being.

Like Burkeman, Barker suggests embracing uncertainty, in this case in relationships. Rather than becoming attached to a certain ideal or set of rules, there may be more to be gained in a fluid and flexible approach which recognises that different things work for different people, and that both relationships and people shift and change over time.

Consider your responses to critical self-help in Activity 15.7.

Activity 15.7   Critical self-help

Having read Section 4 so far, do you think that critical psychologically informed self-help is a useful idea? Can it escape the problems of conventional, or positive psychological, self-help?

It may be that it would be very difficult for self-help writing to completely escape the suggestion that people should engage in individual projects of self-transformation. Even books like Burkeman's and Barker's suggest many individual practices that people might engage with in order to think more critically or to become kinder towards themselves. Perhaps a social approach would be a more appropriate way of trying to change sociocultural norms and rules. It is to this that you will turn in Section 4.4 of this chapter.

4.4 Self-help groups

The other author of this chapter, Scott Cherry, has studied another form of self-help which is more obviously social than the kinds of books (and magazines, TV programmes and the like) that you have covered so far in this chapter: self-help groups (Cherry, 2012). Given the social embeddedness of individual experience highlighted by critical psychologists, perhaps such groups can offer something beyond what an individually read self-help book, however critical, can manage (Figure 15.4).

Figure 15.4 A self-help group

Cherry studied self-help groups that were set up around a wide variety of issues, including Parkinson's disease, cancer, visual impairment and arthritis. He noticed that self-help group members generally neither displayed noticeably negative attitudes, nor used the language of positive thinking. Rather, he recorded a good deal of chatting about holidays, television, the weather, family and pets. Lots of activities took place as well, for example Scrabble, music, bowls, darts, singing, and dancing. Such conversations and activities often involved a good deal of joking and banter between the group members.

Having interviewed the members of the self-help groups individually, Cherry knew that they had a great deal of experience of living with illness. However, this often was not spoken about in any depth during the group meetings, despite what you might expect about it being the focus of the groups.

The reason for this seemed to be that, in these self-help group meetings when members are all together, illness is removed by the very fact that it impacts on all of them, and is what bonds them together. Members can be 'normal' again: they can be included in the culture of the group, rather than being a marginalised individual within wider society due to their ill health or disability (Radley, 2009).

Cherry concluded that these self-help groups involved a highly social, connected, interrelated and communal quest for self-fulfilment and well-being, compared with that suggested in most self-help books and other literature. The prioritised experience, in the case of such groups, is not that of the individual, in terms of thoughts and self-reflections. Rather, it is the experience between people who are sharing in the production of each other's lives, deriving pleasure and joy from the pleasure and joy of others.

Furthermore, members of these groups were aware of a world that could not be controlled, where illness ensured that they could not make definite plans. They experienced good days, and they experienced bad days. In other words, in many ways such groups inherently involve a recognition of the kind of impermanence, fluidity and uncertainty discussed by Burkeman and Barker.

You have seen, in this final part of the chapter, that more critical forms of self-help offer different ways of understanding the self, which are likely to result in different experiences and different ways of addressing any difficulties that people have. For example, someone might engage in practices which involve facing the uncertainties of life rather than endeavouring to change themselves or to blame others; they might locate their struggles in cultural messages and attempt to transform those rather than themselves; and/or they might engage in groups in order to access social support, to engage in social action, and to experience themselves in ways in which their problems are, for once, in the background rather than the foreground.

5   Summary

This chapter has taken you through the historical foundations of self-help as well as examining its contemporary developments within popular culture. You have seen how the self-help industry both emerged within, and influenced, a culture of individualism where people were regarded as responsible for transforming and improving themselves. You have also learned that the kind of self-monitoring that much self-help encourages could well be detrimental rather than beneficial to people.

In relation to psychology, you have considered the attempts of both positive psychologists, and those influenced by critical psychology, to produce alternative forms of self-help. You have seen that positive psychology is far more grounded in empirical research than most self-help, but that it shares the problem of focusing on individual selves rather than people within their sociocultural context. Critical psychological approaches have challenged the notion that positive thinking is necessarily beneficial, and such approaches have led to forms of self-help which propose more acceptance of the inevitable uncertainties and pains of life, and more challenges to outer messages (rather than internal 'flaws'). Finally, you have explored the potential of more social and relational forms of self-help, such as groups, to be a space where a critical psychological kind of self-help might take place.

In addition to considering self-help from a general psychological and a critical psychological perspective, you have begun to develop your understanding of the self from previous sections, particularly Block 2 (Chapters 4, 5 and 6). Hopefully you have been left with your own ideas about what a psychologically informed version of self-help might look like in future.

References

Ahmed, S. (2010) *The Promise of Happiness*, Durham, NC, Duke University Press.

Amable, B. (2011) 'Morals and politics in the ideology of neo-liberalism', *Socio-Economic Review*, vol. 9, no. 1, pp. 3–30.

Barker, M. (2013a) *Mindful Counselling and Psychotherapy: Practising Mindfully Across Approaches and Issues*, London, Sage.

Barker, M. (2013b) *Rewriting the Rules: An Integrative Guide to Love, Sex and Relationships*, London, Routledge.

Barker, M. and Langdridge, D. (eds) (2010) *Understanding Non-Monogamies*, New York, Routledge.

Beattie, M. (1987) *Codependent No More: How to Stop Controlling Others and Start Caring For Yourself*, San Francisco, Harper & Row.

Bergsma, A. (2008) 'Do self-help books work?', *Journal of Happiness Studies*, vol. 9, no. 3, pp. 341–60.

Burkeman, O. (2012) *The Antidote: Happiness For People Who Can't Stand Positive Thinking*, London, Canongate.

Burman, E. (ed.) (1990) *Feminists and Psychological Practice*, London, Sage.

Butler-Bowdon, T. (2003) *50 Self-Help Classics: 50 Inspirational Books to Transform Your Life From Timeless Sages to Contemporary Gurus*, London, Nicholas Brealey.

Byrne, R. (2006) *The Secret*, New York, Beyond Words Publishing.

Caldwell, C. H., Rafferty, J., Reischl, T. M., De Loney, E. H. and Brooks, C. L. (2010) 'Enhancing parenting skills among non-resident African American fathers as a strategy for preventing youth risky behaviors', *American Journal of Community Psychology*, vol. 45, nos 1–2, pp. 17–35.

Carlson, R. (1997) *Don't Sweat the Small Stuff ... and it's All Small Stuff*, London: Hodder & Stoughton.

Carnegie, D. (1936) *How to Win Friends and Influence People*, New York, Simon & Schuster.

Cherry, S. (2012) *How to Stop Reading Self-Help Books: Some Simple Steps and a Dash of Critical Thinking*, self-published.

Cohen, P. and Cohen, J. (1996) *Life Values and Adolescent Mental Health*, Mahah, NJ, Erlbaum.

Covey, S. R. (1989) *The 7 Habits of Highly Successful People*, New York, Simon & Schuster.

Csikszentmihalyi, M. (1990) *Flow: The Psychology of Optimal Experience*, New York, Harper & Row.

DePaulo, B. M. (2006) *Singled Out: How Singles are Stereotyped, Stigmatized, and Ignored, and Still Live Happily Ever After*, London, Macmillan.

Dittman, M. (2004) 'Benefit-finding doesn't always improve lives for breast cancer patients', *Monitor on Psychology*, vol. 35, no. 2, p. 12.

Easterlin, R. A. (2004) 'The economics of happiness', *Daedalus*, vol. 133, no. 2, pp. 26–33.

Ehrenreich, B. (2009) *Bright-Sided: How the Relentless Promotion of Positive Thinking Has Undermined America*, New York, Metropolitan Books.

Ellis, A. (1962) *Reason and Emotion in Psychotherapy*, New York, Stuart.

Fein, E. and Schneider, S. (1995) *The Rules: Time-Tested Secrets for Capturing the Heart of Mr Right*, New York, Warner Books.

Fernando, S. (2010) *Mental Health, Race and Culture* (3rd edn), London, Palgrave.

Foucault, M. (1975) *Discipline and Punish: The Birth of the Prison*, New York, Pantheon.

Fox, D. and Prilleltensky, I. (eds) (1997) *Critical Psychology: An Introduction*, London, Sage.

Fredrickson, B. (2013) *Love 2.0: How our Supreme Emotion Affects Everything We Feel, Think, Do*, New York, Hudson Street Press.

Gergen, K. (1973) 'Social psychology as history', *Journal of Personality and Social Psychology*, vol. 26, no. 2, pp. 309–20.

Gergen, K. (1985) *The Social Construction of the Person*, New York, Springer-Verlag.

Gergen, K. (1991) *The Saturated Self: Dilemmas of Identity in Contemporary Life*, New York, Basic Books.

Gray, J. (1992) *Men Are From Mars, Women Are From Venus*, New York, Harper.

Greco, M., and Stenner, P. (2013) 'Happiness and the art of life: diagnosing the psychopolitics of wellbeing', *Health, Culture and Society*, vol. 5, no. 1, pp. 1–19.

Harré, H. R. (1979) *Social Being: A Theory for Social Psychology*, Oxford, Blackwell.

Harris, T. A. (1963) *I'm OK, You're OK: A Practical Guide to Transactional Analysis*, New York, Harper & Row.

Held, B. S. (2001) *Stop Smiling, Start Kvetching: A 5-Step Guide to Creative Complaining*, New York, St Martin's Griffin.

Held, B. S. (2002) 'The tyranny of the positive attitude in America: observation and speculation', *Journal of Clinical Psychology*, vol. 58, pp. 965–92.

Jenkins, R., Bhugra, D., Bebbington, P., Brugha, T., Farrell, M., Coid J., Fryers, T., Weich, S., Singleton, N. and Meltzer, H. (2008) 'Debt, income and mental disorder in the general population', *Psychological Medicine*, vol. 38, no. 10, pp. 1485–93.

Kagan, C., Burton, M., Duckett, P., Lawton, R. and Siddiquee, A. (2011) *Critical Community Psychology*, London, Wiley-Blackwell.

Kappes, H. B. and Oettingen, G. (2011) 'Positive fantasies about idealized futures sap energy', *Journal of Experimental Social Psychology*, vol. 47, no. 4, pp. 719–29.

Kappes, H. B., Schwörer, B. and Oettingen, G. (2012) 'Needs instigate positive fantasies of idealized futures', *European Journal of Social Psychology*, vol. 42, pp. 299–307.

Kenny, M. A. and Williams, J. M. G. (2007) 'Treatment-resistant depressed patients show a good response to mindfulness-based cognitive therapy', *Behaviour Research and Therapy*, vol. 45, no. 3, pp. 617–25.

Kitzinger, C. (1987) *The Social Construction of Lesbianism*, London, Sage.

Leventhal, T. and Gunn, J. (2000) 'The neighborhoods they live in: the effects of neighborhood residence on child and adolescent outcomes', *Psychological Bulletin*, vol. 126, no. 2, pp. 309–37.

Lindenfield, G. (200) *Self Esteem: Simple Steps to Develop SelfvWorth and Heal Emotional Wounds*, London, Element Books.

Lyubomirsky, S. (2007) *The How of Happiness: A Practical Guide to Getting the Life You Want*, London, Sphere.

Lyubomirsky, S. (2013) *The Myths of Happiness: What Should Make You Happy, But Doesn't, What Shouldn't Make You Happy, But Does*, New York, Penguin.

Lyubomirsky, S., Boehm, J. K., Kasri, F. and Zehm, K. (2011) 'The cognitive and hedonic costs of dwelling on achievement-related negative experiences: implications for enduring happiness and unhappiness', *Emotion*, vol. 11, pp. 1152–67.

Lyubomirsky, S. and Lepper, H. (1999) 'A measure of subjective happiness: preliminary reliability and construct validation', *Social Indicators Research*, vol. 46, no. 2, pp. 137–55.

McGee, M. (2005) *Self-Help, Inc.: Makeover Culture in American Life*, Oxford, Oxford University Press.

McGraw, P. (1999) *Life Strategies: Doing What Works, Doing What Matters*, London, Vermilion.

McNamee, S. J. and Miller, R. K., Jr (2004) *The Meritocracy Myth*, Lanham, MD, Rowman & Littlefield.

Moutsiana, C., Garrett, N., Clarke, R., Lotto, R., Blakemore, S. and Sharot, T. (2013) 'Human development of the ability to learn from bad news',

Proceedings of The National Academy of Sciences of The United States of America, vol. 110, no. 41, pp. 16396–401.

Nickerson, C., Schwartz, N., Diener, E. and Kahneman, D. (2003) 'Zeroing on the dark side of the American Dream: a closer look at the negative consequences of the goal for financial success', *Psychological Science*, vol. 14, pp. 531–6.

Oettingen, G. and Mayer, D. (2002) 'The motivating function of thinking about the future: expectations versus fantasies', *Journal of Personality and Social Psychology*, vol. 83, no. 5, p. 1198.

Oettingen, G. and Wadden, T. A. (1991) 'Expectation, fantasy, and weight loss: is the impact of positive thinking always positive?', *Cognitive Therapy and Research*, vol. 15, no. 2, pp. 167–75.

O'Neil, W. J. (2003) *Business Leaders and Success: 55 Top Business Leaders and How They Achieved Greatness*, London, McGraw-Hill.

Orford, J. (2008) *Community Psychology: Challenges, Controversies and Emerging Consensus*, London, Wiley-Blackwell.

Osypuk, T. L., Schmidt, N. M., Bates, L. M., Tchetgen-Tchetgen, E. J., Earls, F. J. and Glymour, M. M. (2012) 'Gender and crime victimization modify neighborhood effects on adolescent mental health', *Pediatrics*, vol. 130, no. 3, pp. 472–81.

Parker, I. (1992) *Discourse Dynamics: Critical Analysis for Social and Individual Psychology*, London and New York, Routledge.

Paul, A. M. (2001) 'Self-help: shattering the myths', *Psychology Today*, vol. 34, p. 60.

Peale, N.V. (1952) *The Power of Positive Thinking*, New York, Fawcett Crest.

Peck, M. Scott (1978) *The Road Less Traveled*, New York, Arrow.

Peters, M. A. (2001) *Poststructuralism, Marxism and Neoliberalism: Between Theory and Politics*, New York, Rowman and Littlefield.

Peterson, C. and Bossio, L. M. (1991) *Health and Optimism*, New York, Free Press.

Piet, J. and Hougaard, E. (2011) 'The effect of mindfulness-based cognitive therapy for prevention of relapse in recurrent major depressive disorder: a systematic review and meta-analysis', *Clinical Psychology Review*, vol. 31, no. 6, pp. 1032–40.

Potter, G. A. (2000) *Deeper Than Debt: Economic Globalisation and the Poor*, London, Latin America Bureau.

Radley, A. (2009) *Works of Illness: Narrative, Picturing and the Social Response to Serious Illness*, Ashby-de-la-Zouch, Inkerman Press.

Rappaport, J. (2005) 'Community psychology is (thank God) more than science', *American Journal of Community Psychology*, vol. 35, pp. 231–8.

Richardson, R., Richards, D. A. and Barkham, M. (2010) 'Self-help books for people with depression: the role of the therapeutic relationship', *Behavioural and Cognitive Psychotherapy*, vol. 38, no. 1, pp. 67–81.

Robbins, A. (2001) *Unlimited Power: The New Science of Personal Achievement*, London, Pocket Books.

Rosen, G. M. (1981) 'Guidelines for the review of do-it-yourself treatment books', *Contemporary Psychology*, vol. 26, no. 3, pp. 189–90.

Rosen, G. M. (1987) 'Self-help treatment books and the commercialization of psychotherapy', *American Psychologist*, vol. 42, no. 1, pp. 46–51.

Rosen, G. M., Glasgow, R. E. and Barrera, M., Jr (2008) 'Good intentions are not enough: reflections on past and future efforts to advance self-help', in Watkins, P. L. and Clum, G. A. (eds) *Handbook of Self-Administered Therapies*, New York, Lawrence Erlbaum.

Rotter, J. B. (1966) 'Generalized expectancies of internal versus external control of reinforcements', *Psychological Monographs*, vol. 80, p. 609.

Salerno, S. (2005) *SHAM: Self-Help and Actualization Movement*, London, Nicholas Brealey.

Sampson, E. E. (1993) *Celebrating the Other: A Dialogic Account of Human Nature*, Hemel Hempstead, Harvester Wheatsheaf.

Seligman, M. (1991) *Learned Optimism: How to Change Your Mind and Your Life*, New York, Knopf.

Seligman, M. (2002) *Authentic Happiness: Using New Positive Psychology to Realize Your Potential for Lasting Fulfilment*, New York, Free Press.

Seligman, M. (2011) *Flourish: A Visionary New Understanding of Happiness and Well-being*, New York, Free Press.

Seligman, M., Rashid, T. and Parks, A. (2006) 'Positive psychology', *American Psychologist*, vol. 61, pp. 774–88.

Serr, K. (ed.) (2006) *Thinking About Poverty*, Sydney, NSW, The Federation Press.

Sheldon, K. M. and Lyubomirsky, S. (2006) 'How to increase and sustain positive emotion: the effects of expressing gratitude and visualizing best possible selves', *Journal of Positive Psychology*, vol. 1, pp. 73–82.

Vanderkam, L. (2012) 'The paperback quest for joy: America's unique love affair with self-help books', *City Journal*, Autumn [Online]. Available at www.city-journal.org/2012/22_4_self-help-books.html (Accessed 5 January 2015).

Vøllestad, J., Nielsen, M. B. and Nielsen, G. H. (2012) 'Mindfulness-and acceptance-based interventions for anxiety disorders: a systematic review and meta-analysis', *British Journal of Clinical Psychology*, vol. 51, no. 3, pp. 239–60.

Walker, J., Holm Hansen, C., Martin, P., Symeonides, S. Ramessur, R., Murray, G. and Sharpe, M. (2014) 'Prevalence, associations, and adequacy of treatment of major depression in patients with cancer: a cross-sectional analysis of routinely collected clinical data', *The Lancet Psychiatry*, vol. 1, no. 5, pp. 343–50.

Whelan, C. D. (2004) *Self-Help Books: And the Quest For Self-Control in the United States 1950–2000*, Unpublished D. Phil thesis, University of Oxford.

Williams, M., Teasdale, J., Segal, Z. and Kabat-Zinn, J. (2007) *The Mindful Way Through Depression*, New York, Guilford Press.

Wood, J. V., Perunovic, W. Q. and Lee, J. W. (2009) 'Positive self-statements: power for some, peril for others', *Psychological Science*, vol. 20, no. 7, pp. 860–6.

Zeidan, F., Martucci, K. T., Kraft, R. A., Gordon, N. S., McHaffie, J. G. and Coghill, R. C. (2011) 'Brain mechanisms supporting the modulation of pain by mindfulness meditation', *Journal of Neuroscience*, vol. 31, no. 14, pp. 5540–8.

Conclusion

Jim Turner

Closing thoughts

Throughout Books 1 and 2 of *Living psychology* you have read about a very broad range of theories and research in psychology, contextualised within an equally broad range of real-life issues from the everyday to the extraordinary. As I bring the books to a close, I would like to highlight just a few things, which go beyond the material in the chapters, that I hope you will find thought provoking.

Psychology is everywhere

It is no exaggeration to say that psychology is everywhere in human life, and that every question about people is (at least in part) a psychological question. Having now read 15 very different chapters, covering many different aspects of human life and experience, you have probably established that psychology is an incredibly pervasive subject. The other authors and I hope that our chapters have opened your mind to the relevance of psychology to all areas of human experience, and perhaps challenged a few preconceptions that you may have had about the limits of the discipline.

Before reading these books, you may have expected to find psychology on the therapist's or counsellor's couch, or in the psychiatrist's or clinical psychologist's practice. You would, of course, have been right, as Chapters 5 and 13 showed in the contexts of close relationships and post-traumatic stress disorder, respectively. However, would you have expected to find psychology in the robotics engineer's workshop (Chapter 3) or the town planner's office (Chapter 8)? You may have expected that a concept such as self-esteem was fundamentally psychological in nature (Chapter 4), but would you have thought the same about sexuality (Chapter 14)? The self-help industry may be something you would have thought of as essentially psychological but, as Chapter 15 explained, much of it has little or no basis in real psychology. On the other hand, 'mindreading' probably seemed like a fantastical ability (that you may or may not have believed in), but after reading Chapter 1 you now know it is something that, on some level, most people do every day. The beliefs that some people have in conspiracy theories may have been something you thought of as having a psychological basis, since you were probably aware of the stereotype of the 'crazy' or 'paranoid' conspiracy theorist, but, as Chapter 12 showed, the real psychology of conspiracy theories is far more complicated (and interesting) than that.

There are also aspects of human life that you may have expected to 'belong' to different academic disciplines, but you now know are part of (or at least shared with) psychology. Debates around nationality and immigration are probably things you previously thought of as being 'politics'. However, Chapter 6 showed how nationality and immigration are fundamentally psychological issues, as are the debates around them, affecting and being affected by people's sense of identity both as individuals and as members of groups. The problem of human-generated climate change, and how to combat it, may also have seemed as though it was 'politics', along with the various physical sciences that are involved in gathering data on climate change; Chapter 9 highlighted the importance of a psychological approach to these issues.

Even away from your studies, you may have found yourself noticing 'psychology' in places where you perhaps would not have expected to find it before you began reading these books. The types of cognitive errors and heuristics covered in Chapter 11 form a very good example of this: airports, casinos and courtrooms may seem unlikely places to find psychology but, as Chapter 11 made clear, gambling behaviour, judges' sentencing decisions and fear of flying are all influenced by psychological processes. Even more prosaically, if you have a pet, or spend much time around non-human animals, then Chapter 2 may have made you think about them, and yourself, differently, particularly by highlighting what is, and is not, unique about humans. Having read Chapter 7, you have probably given some thought to what makes you 'you', and may even have thought about your body and mind in a way you had not considered before. Similarly, Chapter 10 may have made you think about the way you perceive and make sense of the world, perhaps being more conscious of how your expectations can affect what you (think you) see and hear, and the assumptions you make about the world. All of these are aspects of 'living psychology': making psychology a central part of how you live your life, particularly how you think about yourself, the world, and the people around you.

Psychology is timeless

I do, of course, mean this figuratively rather than literally, but psychology is timeless. It it is one of the youngest academic disciplines, generally tracing its birth back to Wilhelm Wundt's work in the late nineteenth century (if you are interested in learning more about Wundt, and the history of psychology, you can visit the *Investigating Psychology* 'Investigate conceptual and historical issues in Psychology' resource on OpenLearn at www.open.edu/openlearn/health-sports-psychology/psychology/investigating-psychology). However, the issues that psychology deals with are age-old. For example, much of what is covered in Chapter 2, such as experiencing emotions and developing the cognitive abilities required to solve problems, pre-dates *Homo sapiens* as a species. Similarly, the preference for natural environments that you learned about in Chapter 8 also has its roots in prehistory, as does the tendency to make errors (so long as they are relatively low cost) that is the central principle of error management theory (Chapter 10). The difficulties in intimate relationships discussed in Chapter 5 have probably existed since there have *been* intimate relationships between people; and the problems of post-traumatic stress disorder outlined in Chapter 13 may have been identified as a clinical condition only relatively recently, but they are likely to have been affecting people for at least as long as there has been organised warfare.

One of the main purposes of these books has been to give you an overview of the development of psychological ideas, so the chapters have covered some quite 'old' research in places (even, on occasion, going back to the nineteenth and early twentieth centuries). Sometimes, as you have learned, old ideas have been superseded by later ones, such as some of the early ideas about sex and sexuality covered in Chapter 14. Other ideas retain their relevance to this day. For example, evolutionary theory was originally developed in the mid nineteenth century (by naturalists – remember that psychology did not exist as a separate discipline back then). However, evolutionary theory retains its relevance to psychology today and will never become irrelevant, as humans will always have the species' evolutionary history behind them and will continue to evolve into the future. Similarly, Rosenberg's concept of self-esteem, developed half a century ago, continues to be of contemporary relevance, and indeed has taken on a new relevance for (self-)objectification in the modern age of mass communication and online interactions.

Alongside learning about the historical development of the discipline, you will also have noticed throughout these books that psychology is highly contemporary. Chapter 3 is an excellent example of this, as cutting-edge work in artificial intelligence draws heavily on psychological theories and research. Indeed, in this as in many other areas, there is a very good chance that new and interesting advances have already been made in the short period of time between the books being printed and you reading this sentence now! This is, of course, another meaning of the term 'living psychology': psychology is a discipline that continues to grow and change, both responding to and affecting the world around it.

Psychology is personal ... to everyone

Some of the things that these books have covered are universal, that is, they apply to everyone. For example, every human being has a brain that has been shaped by the evolutionary pressures through which the ancestors of the species lived. However, much of what has been covered applies differently to different people (for example, some people are believers in conspiracy theories while others are sceptical), or applies to the same person differently at different times in their lives (for example, people enter and leave intimate relationships, and those relationships change over time).

I expect that much of what you have read throughout these books will have had resonances with experiences in your own life, and will probably continue to do so in the future. Exactly which parts have been personally meaningful, or will come to be personally meaningful later on, are obviously individual to you. Each person who reads these chapters will have a different experience of them. This reflects another key aspect of psychology as a discipline: the exploration of a multitude of individual experiences and the attempt to make sense of them. It also highlights something else that the authors of these books mean by 'living psychology': it is something that everyone is doing, throughout their lives, in ways both everyday and extraordinary.

Acknowledgements

Every effort has been made to contact copyright holders. If any have been inadvertently overlooked the publishers will be pleased to make the necessary arrangements at the first opportunity.

Grateful acknowledgement is made to the following sources:

Book cover

Cover images: Neural Network image (centre): © Pseudolongino/Dreamstime.com; Man-profile-visible-brain (bottom left): © Carla F. Castagno/Dreamstime.com; Feeling Implantataion (middle left): © Yannis Ntousiopoulos/Dreamstime.com; What makes us human? image (top): © James Balog/Getty Images; Woman Meditating (middle right): © iStockphoto.com/GlobalStock.

Chapter 10

Figure 10.2(a): Bjorn Rorslett/Science Photo Library; *Figure 10.2(b)*: Bjorn Rorslett/Science Photo Library; *Figures 10.5 (a & b)*: © R Beau Lotto; *Figure 10.6 (b & d)*: Taken from http://www.richardgregory.org/papers/brainmodels/illusions-and-brain-models.pdf; *Figure 10.7*: © Jim Turner; *Figure 10.8(a)* & *Figure 10.13(a)*: © iStockphoto.com/4x6; *Figure 10.8(c)* & *Figure 10.13(c)*: © Homer Sykes Archive/Alamy.

Chapter 11

Figure 11.1: www.bombsight.org-10/03/2015; *Extract 11.1*: http://news.bbc.co.uk/1/hi/world/europe/4256595.stm/BBC News; *Figure 11.2*: © Jim Turner; *Figure 11.3*: © iStockphoto.com/Elenathewise; *Figure 11.4(a)*: Taken from http://www.jsbach.net/bass/elements/bach-hausmann.jpg; *Figure 11.4(b)*: © Sam Abell/Getty Images; *Figure 11.5(a)*: © iStockphoto.com/travellinglight; *Figure 11.5(b)*: © Doug Pearson/JAI/Corbi.

Chapter 12

Figure 12.1(a): © NASA; *Figure 12.1(b)*: © John Sturrock/Alamy; *Image* Is the truth out there?, page 99: © Joshua Roberts/AFP/Getty

Images; *Figure 12.3*: © AFP/Stringer/Getty Images; *Figure 12.6*: © REX/Sipa Press.

Chapter 13

Figure 13.3: © Sanka Vidanagama/AFP/Getty Images; *Figure 13.4*: Original source unknown; *Figure 13.6*: © Imagno/Getty Images.

Chapter 14

Figure 14.2: © Steve Vidler/Alamy; *Figure 14.5*: Original source unknown.

Chapter 15

Image page 229: © Jeff Greenberg "0 people images"/Alamy; *Figure 15.2*: Mary Evans/Peter Higginbotham Collection; *Figure 15.3*: Original source unknown; *Figure 15.4*: © David J. Green/Alamy.

Index